The Making of the 20th Century

This series of specially commissioned titles focuses attention on significant and often controversial events and themes of world history in the present century. Each book provides sufficient narrative and explanation for the newcomer to the subject while offering, for more advanced study, detailed source-references and bibliographies, together with interpretation and reassessment in the light of recent scholarship.

In the choice of subjects there is a balance between breadth in some spheres and detail in others; between the essentially political and matters economic or social. The series cannot be a comprehensive account of everything that has happened in the twentieth century, but it provides a guide to recent research and explains something of the times of extraordinary change and complexity in which we live. It is directed in the main to students of contemporary history and international relations, but includes titles which are of direct relevance to courses in economics, sociology, politics and geography.

The Making of the 20th Century

Britain and Vichy

The Dilemma of Anglo-French Relations 1940–42

R. T. Thomas

St. Martin's Press   New York

D
750
.T43
1979

© R. T. Thomas 1979

Library of Congress Cataloging in Publication Data

Thomas, R   T
   Britain and Vichy.

   (The Making of the 20th century)
   Bibliography: p.
   Includes index.
   1.   World War, 1939-1945—Diplomatic history.
2.   Great Britain—Foreign relations—France.
3.   France—Foreign relations—Great Britain.   I.   Title
D750.T43   1979   327.41'044   78-14236
ISBN 0-312-09822-7

Contents

To G. C. T.

Preface

I owe an enormous debt of gratitude to Christopher Thorne for his unfailing support and guidance and for innumerable refinements to the text; and to my wife, without whom the book could not have been written, and to whom it is dedicated. The responsibility for what appears below, however, is mine alone.

R. T. T.

Introduction

In June 1940, after a battle which had lasted only six weeks, the French government signed an Armistice agreement with Germany. If he had wished to do so, Hitler could have overrun the whole of France without difficulty, since the French Army had been routed and further resistance was out of the question. Recognising, however, that such action might provoke the French government to flee abroad and there continue the fight, he chose instead to offer terms which to a nation and government reeling from the shock of defeat seemed more generous than they had a right to expect. The French Fleet was to be demilitarised, but remained in French hands. The Colonial Empire was untouched. Most important of all, a substantial portion of French metropolitan territory was left unoccupied and a government enjoying at least some of the attributes of sovereignty was allowed to establish itself in Vichy.

The continued existence of a semi-independent French government, in particular one controlled by elements which were known to have opposed the war and some of which openly advocated a Franco-German alliance against Britain, confronted the British government with complex and intractable dilemmas. The governments of other countries overrun by Germany in 1939 and 1940 had fled to London; although relatively powerless, they remained Britain's allies, with a strong claim to be restored to their ruling positions in the event of an Allied victory. The French government, on the other hand, which had been constituted in accordance with the laws of the Republic and enjoyed the widespread and often enthusiastic support of the French people, remained in France in order to bring hostilities to an end and, later, to work towards the restoration of Franco-German relations. The Free French movement which was established in London by General de Gaulle was thus not a government in exile but only a convenient rallying-point for the small minority of Frenchmen who chose to reject defeat.

De Gaulle subsequently established his undisputed leadership of the Resistance movements both within and outside France and assumed power in 1944 as head of the Provisional French Government. The rest is history: no other French politician of the post-war era rivals him in stature and no other statesman has had so profound an influence upon the shape of modern Europe. It has been natural, therefore, for British historians tracing the course of Anglo-French relations in this century to draw an unbroken line from the Third Republic to the Fourth, and to focus their attention upon the relationship – so significant in terms of later events – between the Anglo-Saxon powers and de Gaulle, and to ignore the apparently inconclusive relations between Britain and Vichy which seemed to have no sequel after the abrupt termination of Vichy's remaining independence in November 1942. Although American policy towards Vichy aroused considerable controversy at the time and has stimulated some research since the war, historians appear to have assumed that Britain's dealings with the regime were somehow incidental to the mainstream of Anglo-French relations. This tendency has been reinforced, perhaps, by a reluctance to dwell on the Vichy episode in French history, in that it would seem to reflect little credit on France; in addition, the demonstrably clumsy nature of post-war attempts to prove the existence of 'secret treaties' between Britain and Vichy has had the paradoxical effect of concealing the very complex and multifarious links which the British government did maintain with the regime.

The present study, too, grew out of what was initially an enquiry into British policy towards de Gaulle, and it was only when the archives were examined that the extent of British preoccupation with the Vichy government was revealed. It then became apparent that in the two years after France's collapse, the Prime Minister, the War Cabinet, the Chiefs of Staff and the Foreign Office devoted much more time to the problem of Vichy than to that of de Gaulle, and that when they spoke of 'France' they understood this to mean the government of Marshal Pétain, not the Free French movement. It also became clear that, when de Gaulle's appeal for wholesale resistance to the Germans had largely failed, the prime concern of the British government was to stabilise relations with Vichy and that to do this it was willing to abandon de Gaulle or at least to force him to accept the leadership of men who had formerly given their allegiance to Vichy. Although increasingly aware of the growing power and influence of the Free French movement which it had sponsored, the British government was concerned above all to avoid needless conflict with Vichy and tailored its policy towards de Gaulle accordingly. In short, the major element in Anglo-French relations during the two years after the French collapse was essentially that of British policy towards Vichy. Only after the Allied invasion of French North Africa and the total occupation of France by German forces in November 1942 did the centre of gravity in Anglo-French relations shift towards de Gaulle, and then reluctantly.

Thus the purpose of this book is to restore as far as possible the perspectives of the time and to correct the distortions which subsequent events have imposed upon a vital period in Anglo-French relations. Recent writings have stressed the continuity between the Vichy period and preceding aspects of French history, demonstrating that the policies which that government tried to pursue in the domestic and foreign spheres were the reflection of enduring themes in French political life. This study aims in a similar way to remove the notion that the Vichy regime was a mere parenthesis, and to relate British policy towards Vichy to the course of Anglo-French relations in this century. In particular it seeks to show how the hostile reflexes which brought the two countries to the brink of open conflict in 1940 were the result of perceptions which had been shaped by a long tradition of mutual resentment and antagonism and to suggest how this tradition has in turn been reinforced by the events of 1940–4. The precipitate collapse of France and her defection from the Alliance seemed to provide the British with ample confirmation of French weakness and instability, while the French found their deepest suspicions of British callousness and treachery borne out by the naval attack at Mers-el-Kébir. These perceptions have continued to play no small part in Anglo-French relations since 1945, finding expression on the British side in renewed fears of French political domination of Europe, and on the French side in the Gaullist opposition to Britain's entry into the European Community. In the same way, the effect of America's disastrous Vichy policy upon France's post-war relations with the Anglo-Saxon powers could hardly be exaggerated.

This book also attempts to show how the debate on policy towards Vichy which went on within the British government and later, between London and Washington, came to involve some of the most serious issues posed by the war. The Vichy problem, although only occasionally the most urgent concern of the Allied governments, was nevertheless unusually perplexing and many-sided. It presented the British government with cruel dilemmas involving the use of military and economic sanctions against recent allies and subject populations; it injected a further element of instability into every strategic calculation;

it became one of the most contentious issues in Anglo-American relations and lay at the heart of Allied disagreements over post-war European and colonial policies. Above all, it forced the British government to measure its support of the principles it proclaimed against the need to compromise and appease when issues other than those of immediate survival were at stake. Upon Churchill, in particular, the devious and clandestine nature of Britain's relations with Vichy exerted a powerful fascination, and his influence upon the shaping of even the finest details of policy was both vigorous and decisive. Even in its contradictions, the policy which emerged bore, to a remarkable extent, the imprint of his extraordinary personality.

1 From Versailles to Réthondes: Anglo-French Relations, 1919–40

THE violent outburst of hostility between Britain and France which accompanied the signature of the Franco-German Armistice in 1940 was the culmination of a long tradition of antagonism between the two countries. Colonial rivalries in the late nineteenth century were particularly acute and almost led to open conflict on more than one occasion; and although the *Entente Cordiale* in 1904 formed the basis for close military co-operation during the First World War, good relations did not long survive the end of hostilities in 1919. 'Within an hour after the Armistice I had the impression that you had become once again the enemies of France,' remarked Clemenceau to Lloyd George. To which the latter replied, 'has that not always been the traditional policy of my country?'[1] In the Middle East, colonial rivalries were for a time renewed. Much more serious, however, was the lack of agreement over the peace settlement in Europe. With the destruction of Germany as a colonial and naval power, the British attained their primary objective: the security of the British Isles. They had little sympathy with France's preoccupation with the security of her eastern borders, and were more concerned with the dangers of German collapse than with the distant possibility of German resurgence. The Versailles treaty came to be seen in Britain as both unjust and unworkable, and successive British governments saw their role as that of a mediator between the European powers rather than as an active partner in maintaining Anglo-French dominance. The First World War came to be regarded as an 'abnormal' occurrence, and military preparations were undertaken with a view to the defence of imperial interests, not with the idea of gathering a massive continental army. Even after the abolition of the 'Ten Year Rule', in 1933,* the British seemed content to assume that, in the event

---

* This assumed that Britain would not be involved in a major war for a decade. First approved in 1919, it was put on a moving basis in 1928 and thus continually postponed military planning for a ten-year period.

of war with Germany, the French would hold the line with only token British support until forces were built up once more.[2]

The French were bound to take a very different view. They knew that victory had been won by the narrowest of margins against an adversary whose latent industrial strength would give him the advantage in a renewed conflict. However, France's efforts to establish a credible alliance system in the West to meet the threat of renewed German aggression were brought to nothing by America's retreat into isolationism and Britain's refusal to commit herself to an active European role. Early attempts to maintain a stranglehold on the German economy through the exaction of reparations served only to strengthen Germany's determination to dismantle the Versailles settlement, while later efforts to pursue a policy of conciliation were frustrated by the Nazi revolution, which destroyed whatever basis may have existed for a lasting peace. France's desperate attempts to enlist British support in the face of this renewed threat were to no avail, and successive British governments proved only too eager to appease the growing strength of Germany at France's expense.

These differences took their steady toll of any good will generated by wartime co-operation. In Britain, horror at the war and disillusionment with the fruits of victory brought about a profound reaction against the Anglo-French alliance and a revival in many circles of anti-French feeling. Paradoxically, it was often the same people who denounced French militarism in the 1920s who condemned French unwillingness to risk war with Italy in 1935. In John Cairns's words, 'Between the wars the British never quite knew what to make of France: she was too weak or too strong, too independent or too obviously dependent, too much a reminder of the bloody past, too much a warning, with her alliances, of possible trouble to come.'[3] The French, in their turn, blamed the British for cheating them of their security at Versailles and later thwarting the Geneva Protocol, for opposing the occupation of the Ruhr and refusing to take a firm stand over Hitler's occupation of the Rhineland, and, finally, for drawing France into the humiliation of Munich. At every turn, it seemed, the British had thwarted France's quest for security and rewarded her loyalty with callous indifference.

THE PHONEY WAR

The onset of hostilities in 1939 seemed for a time to clear the air between the two countries. An Anglo-French Supreme War Council was set up, and unified military command, which had taken three years to achieve in the First World War, was established straight away. Britain and France were nevertheless very far from achieving unity of purpose. Serious differences of view during the final stages of the Polish–German crisis, over the last-minute Italian proposals and over the timing of the ultimatum to Germany, continued after the outbreak of war with disagreements over strategy, in the Balkans, in the Baltic, over the bombing of the Ruhr and over Belgian neutrality. In addition, a constant low murmur of mutual criticism was evident throughout the uneasy early months of war. The small size of the British military contribution – initially two divisions against France's eighty-five – occasioned much sarcastic comment in French military circles, especially in view of the fact that there were a million unemployed in Britain. The opinion in France was that Britain's war effort was slack and that their ally was taking the opportunity of war to expand its export trade instead of concentrating everything on the mobilisation effort.[4] The British, in their turn, were uneasy about the French political situation and feared that Daladier's government was being undermined by the forces of appeasement from both right and left.

Most important of all was the lack of any agreement over long-term strategic and political aims. A good deal of discussion took place in early 1940 about the need to further Anglo-French unity and construct the basis for permanent co-operation after the war. In so far as this had a practical effect, it was to emphasise further the deficiencies of the Alliance. Nothing more clearly illustrates this than the lengthy discussions which preceded the issuing, in March, of a joint declaration in which each country pledged itself not to sign a separate armistice or peace without the prior consent of the other. The ostensible purpose of this declaration was twofold: to counter German propaganda, and to express the determination of the two countries to co-ordinate their policies after the war. The undertaking not to negotiate for a separate peace, it has been argued, was regarded as a formality.[5] Thus, the French premier, Paul Reynaud (who replaced Daladier on 22 March) told the Chamber of Deputies that 'in reality, the question [of a separate peace] does not arise'.[6] The fact that Reynaud's public utterances were echoed on several occasions in the privacy of the British Cabinet lends support to this view. On 7 December 1939, for example, Lord Halifax, the Foreign Secretary, told his colleagues that it was 'inconceivable that we should wish to make peace unless the French Government were prepared to do so also, while, if the French Government wanted to make peace, we should not be able to carry on the war by ourselves'.[7] Daladier, too, told Neville Chamberlain a few days later that France and Britain 'neither could nor would make peace the one without the other'.[8]

In reality, of course, British and French politicians were not so naïve. Halifax's remark, after all, ruled out the possibility of a separate peace not because it was unthinkable that France would seek terms, but because Britain would be obliged to follow suit if she did. In fact, protests that the declaration was only for propaganda purposes scarcely concealed the mounting uncertainty in London about the reliability of the French. As the South African High Commissioner pointed out: 'Generally, such declarations are made when mutual trust and loyalty are not above suspicion, and in this case too it may raise questions and have the opposite effect to what is intended.'[9] As the months passed the British government became more and more seriously troubled by the political situation in France. It was well known that many French Communists followed Moscow's line of opposition to the 'imperialist' war, and also that the extreme right was inclined to prefer the Nazis to the *Front Populaire*. A powerful group of politicians – including Bonnet, Flandin and Laval, all of whom had held office as Foreign Minister – continued to favour an accommodation with Germany. British anxieties on this score were sharpened by the weakness of Daladier's position and by the promptings of other members of the French government, notably Georges Mandel, the Minister of the Interior. Daladier's government was sound, Mandel told Sir Ronald Campbell, the British ambassador, but he 'would not put his hand in the fire for any other'.[10] These warnings had their effect. 'French opinion and morale were not so entirely reliable that we could afford to neglect a declaration which might very well strengthen the hands of some future Government at a time of difficulty,' Chamberlain told the Cabinet in March.[11] Reynaud was equally keen to mark his accession to power with a dramatic demonstration of his resolve to pursue the war with vigour.[12] Anxiety in both British and French minds over defeatist elements in French political circles had thus become a factor of major importance in bringing about the joint declaration. The prohibition upon the negotiation of a separate peace was not a formality: it arose from a very real fear that things might one day come to such a pass.

The declaration was published in Paris and London on 28 March, after a meeting of the Supreme War Council:

The Government of the French Republic and His Majesty's Government in the United Kingdom of Great Britain and Northern Ireland mutually undertake that during the present war, they will neither negotiate nor conclude an armistice or treaty of peace except by mutual agreement. They undertake not to discuss peace terms before reaching complete agreement on the conditions necessary to ensure to each of them an effective and lasting guarantee of their security.

Finally, they undertake to maintain, after the conclusion of peace, a community of action in all spheres for so long as may be necessary to safeguard their security and to effect the reconstruction, with the assistance of other nations, of an international order which will ensure the liberty of peoples, respect for law, and the maintenance of peace in Europe.[13]

THE BATTLE OF FRANCE

On 10 May 1940, the battle in the west began with the German offensive into Holland and Belgium. In accordance with the plan approved by the Supreme War Council, the Allied armies advanced to the Antwerp–Namur line. This was a disastrous mistake. The Belgian army was unable to hold up the German advance, and even the Ardennes proved to be no obstacle to the German armoured divisions. Within four days the enemy forces had crossed the Meuse at Sedan and begun to fan out into open country. The expected thrust towards Paris did not develop, however, and the German armies instead pressed westwards, destroying the French Ninth Army and cutting off the French First Army, the British Expeditionary Force (BEF) and the Belgian army in Flanders from the main body of the French forces to the south. On 19 May, the day on which German troops reached the sea at Abbeville, Reynaud dismissed the Commander-in-Chief, Gamelin, and replaced him by General Maxime Weygand, who formulated a plan to cut through the narrow corridor of the German advance and to reunite the Allied armies. This plan proved impossible to carry out, however, and on 25 May Lord Gort, commander of the BEF, began to withdraw his forces. The remnants of the French northern armies followed suit, their retreat being rendered more difficult by the precipitate collapse of the Belgian army on 27–28 May. With the evacuation of the BEF from the Dunkirk beaches between 27 May and 4 June, the first phase of the battle was over.

On 5 June the German offensive was resumed, and within five days had broken through the line of the Somme and the Aisne which Weygand had regarded as his last line of defence. Italy declared war on the same day. From this point co-ordinated resistance ceased. The government left Paris on 10 June, retreating first to Tours and finally, on 14 June, to Bordeaux. Paris fell on the same day. On the night of 16 June Reynaud resigned and was succeeded by Marshal Pétain, whose government immediately sought terms from the enemy. These were made known on 22 June, and the Franco-German Armistice came into force two days later.[14]

Much has been written in an attempt to explain France's astonishing collapse. In the mood of self-criticism which prevailed in France immediately after the débâcle, it became fashionable to ascribe defeat to the fundamental weakness of the national character or to flaws in France's political and social fabric. The generals naturally argued that their defeat had been brought about by overwhelming odds or by the superiority of German equipment, while French politicians of the centre and right were quick to blame Communist subversion for slackness in the ranks.[15] However, there is no reason to believe that the fighting qualities of the Allied armies were seriously deficient when put to the test, and thorough research has similarly revealed that the opposing forces were evenly matched, even in tanks.[16] More convincing explanations have stressed the vastly superior strategic doctrine and command system of the German army in comparison with that of the French. France's military planners of the inter-war period had been totally unreceptive to new ideas and quite unable to grasp the importance of the revolution which had been wrought by the co-ordinated use of air power and mechanised ground forces. A war of rapid movement and attack was beyond the understanding of the French High Command, which remained obsessed with the importance of maintaining the defensive line.[17] The excellent French tanks were frittered away in infantry support work, instead of being concentrated for the purpose of attack and penetration. The Air Force was hardly used. Above all, the French – and the British – were quite unprepared for the speed and intensity of the German thrust. The cumbersome command structure which Gamelin had established broke down immediately. Neither Gamelin nor Weygand established contact with their own force commanders. Orders were issued which could not be carried out, often to forces which had ceased to exist. Liaison with the BEF was appalling.[18]

Initial reverses left the French High Command numbed and

demoralised. Gamelin abdicated direct responsibility the moment the battle had begun. Four days of fighting saw his second-in-command, Georges, weeping before his junior officers, while Bloch describes Blanchard, commander of the First Army, as stunned, 'saying nothing, doing nothing, but just gazing at the map spread on the table between us'. Billotte, commander of the Allied armies in the north, was in a similar condition.[19] Weygand, brought in to save the situation, became in two weeks the most vigorous advocate of surrender. All these men bore a heavy responsibility for France's defeat.

THE STRAINS OF BATTLE

The rapid succession of military disasters quickly brought to the surface the mutual resentment and distrust which the two Allies had held in check during the 'Phoney War'. The British watched the demoralisation in high political and military circles in France with a mixture of horror and contempt. They believed that 'they were fighting harder and better than the French, that the spirit of 1914–18 had gone out of France and that her people were not what they had once been'.[20] The German hammer blows, it seemed, provoked not anger but apathy. Among the French, resentment that Britain had so long thwarted French attempts to restrain Germany, fuelled by Britain's paltry contribution to the common defence, finally exploded as a result of British conduct during the battle. Different national perspectives asserted themselves. To the British, the loss of the Battle of France, although disastrous, was not the end of the war, and the Chiefs of Staff soberly concluded that Britain could hold out with a reasonable chance of victory in the end.[21] The Cabinet therefore refused to commit every resource to the battle. On the other hand the French, whose country was being overrun, were naturally convinced that the decisive battle was being fought and that nothing should be held in reserve.

Particular bitterness was occasioned by the British refusal to commit the whole of Fighter Command to the battle, and these feelings were further intensified by what the French High Command chose to regard as Britain's desertion from the battlefield. The German thrust to the sea had severed the French First Army and the BEF from the main force to the south; if a junction could be effected across the narrow 'Panzer corridor' the spearhead of the German advance might be cut off. The operation hung fire for some days while Gamelin was replaced by

Weygand, and the counter-attack was not finally ordered until 22 May. By this time, however, the German flanks had been strengthened and the plan was incapable of being carried out. A strong counter-offensive in the Arras region had already been launched by a British force under General Franklyn, but by the 22nd his troops were in danger of being surrounded and on the following day Lord Gort, Commander of the BEF, ordered them to withdraw.[22]

This course of action released a flood of recriminations from the French and particularly from Weygand, who insisted that the British retreat had been ordered from London and that the counter-attack would have been successful if the British had not been continually looking over their shoulder to the sea. 'They cannot resist the appeal of the ports,' he remarked to Paul Baudouin, the Secretary to the French Cabinet,* 'Even in March, 1918, they wished to embark.'[23] These accusations were quite unjustified. Gort's forces had been withdrawn (towards the north, not in the direction of the ports) on his own initiative, and Weygand's own forces in the south had made no progress towards effecting a junction. Whatever the truth of the situation, however, what mattered at the time was that the withdrawal was taken by the French as a sign that the British would always seek their own safety and leave their ally to fend for himself. Even when allowance is made for the appalling situation in which the French found themselves, it remains a sad commentary upon Anglo-French relations during the previous twenty years that the myth of British desertion from the battlefield should have gained such ready acceptance.

Worse was soon to come. On 25 May Gort arrived at his fateful decision to abandon the counter-attack and evacuate his forces. Although this decision was endorsed by the British Cabinet and immediately conveyed to Reynaud, the force commanders were kept in ignorance by Weygand and continued to believe as late as 29 May that their orders were to form a defensible bridgehead. The British evacuation was regarded by them as desertion from the battlefield.[24] A further cause of bitterness was that only 15,000 of the 165,000 troops who had been taken off the Dunkirk beaches by 31 May were French, and although Churchill's pledge that evacuation would henceforth proceed on equal terms was largely fulfilled, a further and yet more acrimonious dispute between the British and French commanders at the Dunkirk bridgehead prevented the effecting of his promise that the

* Baudouin was to play a decisive part in the estrangement of the two countries.

British would form the rearguard. British hypocrisy seemed complete: for the second time during the battle the British Prime Minister had ordered one thing and his commanding General had immediately done the opposite. To the reproach that the British had ruined the Weygand counter-attack was now added the accusation that they had left the French behind to cover their own retreat.[25]

The Dunkirk evacuation made clear the inevitability of Allied defeat in the Battle of France and set in motion the events which would lead, three weeks later, to the estrangement of Britain and France. Each side, its forces no longer jointly engaged, looked to its own survival. British policy 'in a certain eventuality', (the defeat and occupation of France by German forces) was considered at intervals by the Chiefs of Staff in late May, and on the 27th the Cabinet approved their conclusion that a German invasion of the British Isles could be held off if air superiority were maintained, and that Germany might eventually be defeated by a combination of economic pressure, air attack, and revolt in the conquered territories.[26] A reasonable hope of survival therefore existed even if France succumbed, and the Cabinet was able to dispose of Reynaud's suggestion that a diplomatic solution might still be found to the conflict with Germany by buying Italian neutrality. Only Halifax, who had told the Cabinet six months before that Britain could not continue the war if France were defeated, and in whom the habits of appeasement died hard, expressed himself willing to 'try out the possibilities of the European equilibrium' and to consider a compromise peace with Hitler if British independence could be ensured. The rest of the Cabinet, strongly led by Churchill and Attlee, recognised that there could be no turning back if the government allowed itself to be drawn into discussion of a general settlement. The integrity of the British position would be fatally compromised. It was better that France should succumb than that she should draw Britain down with her in a dying embrace.[27]

In London, therefore, the military planners believed that resistance could be continued, and the Cabinet was not seriously divided. In France, on the other hand, it was the Commander-in-Chief, Weygand, and Pétain, with all his enormous prestige, who were the loudest advocates of an armistice.* Convinced that the Battle of France was

---

* Pétain was brought into the government on 18 May to lend it the prestige of his name; he had been ambassador in Madrid.

decisive and that the withdrawal of the government to North Africa would simply prolong France's agony without affecting the outcome of the war, they refused to believe that Britain either could, or would, continue the war alone. It therefore followed that France should seek terms with all possible despatch, not only in order to save lives and to preserve internal order (an obsession with Weygand) but also to beat the British to the conference table. Reynaud proved unable – and perhaps in the final analysis unwilling – to take a firm stand against defeatism. The only alternative to capitulation was to remove the government to North Africa, but Reynaud lacked the authority to engineer such a move against Weygand's and Pétain's opposition, even though he might have carried a majority of the Cabinet with him.

Against this background events moved to their conclusion in an atmosphere of rapidly mounting and increasingly overt hostility between the two countries, with every sign of British disengagement being regarded by the French as callous desertion. 'England has coolly assumed that we should succumb in this struggle,' noted Paul Baudouin bitterly.[28] Pétain went further. 'The British intended to permit the French to fight without help until the last available drop of French blood', he told the American ambassador on 4 June. 'With quantities of troops on British soil and plenty of planes and a dominant fleet, the British, after a very brief resistance, or even without resistance, would make a peace of compromise with Hitler which might evolve a British Government under a British Fascist leader.'[29] 'England has got us into this position,' he told the French Cabinet on 9 June. 'It is our duty not to put up with it, but to get out of it.'[30] Many in London, suspecting such sentiments to be widespread among the French leaders, in turn hardened their hearts. The conviction was growing that Britain would be better off alone.[31]

THE 'NO SEPARATE PEACE' AGREEMENT

Defeat being imminent, the two Allies were obliged to consider the question of France's release from the March agreement. This was the rock on which the Alliance finally foundered. As far as the British were concerned, the best solution was for the French armies to capitulate but for the government to withdraw to North Africa or London. In such a situation the question of a separate peace would not arise and the Alliance would be preserved. The chances of this coming about,

however, were slender, as the British knew.[32] They had therefore to
decide how to respond when faced with the French government's
request for release from its undertaking. The question was considered
first by the Chiefs of Staff on 26 May, and by Lord Hankey on the
following day. The latter argued that release should be granted, but
only on certain conditions, which should be met *before* the Germans
were approached for terms. In particular, the French should transfer to
Britain their Navy, merchant ships and Air Force, as well as quantities
of arms, ammunition and machine tools. Oil stocks should be destroyed,
and France's gold reserves placed beyond German reach. The snag
here, of course, was that if the French met these conditions the Germans
would be unlikely to grant an armistice. Nevertheless, Hankey's views
were given wide circulation and determined the course of British
thinking on the matter in the days to come.[33]

For a variety of reasons, the French government was never made
forcefully aware of the British position. Although the *Comité de Guerre*
agreed as early as 25 May that Reynaud should broach the subject of
release from the March agreement with the British, he himself seems to
have felt that by postponing the issue he could buy time in which to
strengthen his hand against the defeatists in his Cabinet. Instead, he
simply enabled the pro-Armistice faction to organise itself and ensured
that the matter was eventually debated in an atmosphere of chaos and
disintegration in which communication between the two governments
had become virtually impossible. To an extraordinary extent, both
sides recoiled from facing the issue squarely. Reynaud flew to London
on 26 May but contented himself with describing the hopelessness of the
military situation and hinting darkly that although he himself would
not sign peace terms, he might be forced to resign by those who would.[34]
Churchill flew to Paris on 31 May, but the discussion centred on the
Dunkirk evacuation, and the possible circumstances of France's
withdrawal from the war were not closely considered. A further
opportunity was missed on 11 June, when Churchill, Anthony Eden
(the Minister of War) and General Dill (Chief of the Imperial General
Staff) flew to Weygand's headquarters near Briare to find out what the
French intended to do. Once again the meeting was inconclusive.
Reynaud still baulked at the question which lay in everybody's mind,
and checked Weygand firmly when the latter tried to insist on the
necessity for an armistice.[35] However, the issue could not be evaded
indefinitely: Pétain had formally demanded that the government
should seek an armistice on 9 June, and on the 12th Weygand gave the

order for a general retreat. With Churchill's insistence upon consultation in mind, Reynaud decided that he must confer again with the British Prime Minister.[36]

A FATEFUL MEETING: TOURS, 13 JUNE 1940

On 13 June, Churchill, Beaverbrook, Halifax and Cadogan* arrived in Tours for the meeting which Reynaud had requested.[37] The question of France's release from the March agreement could no longer be evaded, and Reynaud announced that he had been 'urged by his colleagues' to enquire whether the British government would be willing to release France from her undertaking.

Churchill was evasive. He first dwelt at length, and in warm and generous terms, on France's sufferings. Reynaud arrested the flow of eloquence and put the question afresh. Still Churchill hesitated to give a blunt refusal. He understood that, in her desperate plight, France might be forced to lay down her arms. Whatever happened, Britain would level no reproaches or recriminations at her; but that was a different matter from consenting to release her from her pledge. The first step should be for France to make a further appeal for help to President Roosevelt. At this point the meeting broke off for a few minutes while Churchill consulted with Halifax and Beaverbrook in the garden. On his return he reiterated his position. The British government was not in a position to release France from her obligation. The cause of France would always be dear to Britain; if she won the war she would restore France 'in all her power and dignity'. Britain, however, would fight on, and France, under German occupation, could not hope to avoid the rigours of the British blockade. It was possible that bitter antagonisms might arise between the two countries. The appeal to Roosevelt was discussed once more, and it was agreed that the two premiers would meet again to consider the question in the light of his reply. Shortly afterwards the British party returned to England.

With their departure, personal contact at the highest level between the two countries came to an end. What was or was not said at Tours, and the construction put upon it by each side, was therefore to have a profound influence, not only upon the events of the next few days, but upon the whole course of Anglo-French relations during the rest of the

---

* Sir Alexander Cadogan, Permanent Under-Secretary at the Foreign Office.

war. Neither leader, it is clear, had adopted a firm line. Reynaud was trying to put the question and at the same time personally dissociate himself from it, while Churchill was attempting to soften the firmness of his refusal with professions of his undying devotion to France. The effect of his refusal was further muffled by the suggestion that the question should be deferred until Roosevelt's response to Reynaud's last appeal became known, and by his occasional lapses into erratic French.

Despite this, however, there was little room for doubt about the British attitude. Churchill's mistake had been to underestimate the effect of his warm expressions upon exhausted and defeated men who desperately sought his dispensation and who would, moreover, hear his words only at second hand. It was to be expected that the French minutes of the meeting should have faithfully recorded every magnanimous statement and made the refusal to consent to a separate armistice almost an afterthought. But it was not even this version that gained currency in Bordeaux during the following days. The account which most Frenchmen heard, and which they were eager to believe, originated with Paul Baudouin. Nowhere in his account is there any suggestion that Churchill refused his permission to seek an armistice. His paraphrase of Churchill's reply to Reynaud is that, in the event of an armistice, 'Great Britain will not exhaust herself in useless recriminations, she will continue to cling to France, and if she is victorious she promises to restore France to her power and grandeur, whatever may have been the attitude of France after her defeat.'[38] Baudouin deliberately falsified what Churchill had said, and interpreted the pledge to restore France as a consent that France should sue for an armistice, 'since the British Government had in fact recognised that it would not break the solidarity of the two countries'.[39] What both Baudouin and Churchill really recognised, of course, was that, whether or not Britain gave her formal consent, she could hardly do other than restore France if victory were eventually achieved. Thus, the major disability from which British policy towards the Vichy regime was to suffer stood revealed: the inability to issue long-term threats. On numerous occasions during the ensuing two years the British considered threatening to withdraw their undertaking to restore the greatness and independence of France, but on each occasion they were forced to realise that such a move would conflict with Britain's own best interests. This dilemma was never resolved.

THE FALL OF REYNAUD

For reasons which remain obscure, Reynaud failed to convey to Churchill the French Cabinet's invitation to address its members personally after the meeting at the Tours Préfecture, and the last opportunity to make the British position clear was lost.[40] Baudouin's version of events rapidly gained currency in government circles, Churchill's 'understanding' attitude probably appearing all the more reassuring since, according to Reynaud, the question of release from France's undertaking had not even been put to him. It may even have seemed that Churchill was inviting the French to seek terms. Subsequent denials by the British ambassador and by General Spears, Churchill's personal representative with the French Prime Minister, were not sufficiently authoritative to dispel the impression that Churchill had assented to France's request for release from its undertaking. Reynaud, although unwilling to repudiate the agreement he had himself signed, was equally reluctant to countenance the continued slaughter of French soldiers and civilians, and did not act upon the British ambassador's advice that he should strengthen his hand by making it plain that the British government would not condone a breach of the March agreement.[41] The only solution was for the Army, but not the government, to capitulate, but Weygand refused to follow this course of action, which he contended would bring disgrace upon the flags of the French Army, and Reynaud did not feel sufficiently strong to order the dismissal which this disobedience certainly warranted.[42]

It was at this point, when deadlock appeared to have been reached, that the French Cabinet took the fateful step which precipitated the final capitulation. At their meeting in Bordeaux on 15 June, Camille Chautemps, the Vice-Premier, put forward the insidious proposal that the Germans should be approached to find out the terms of an armistice. If, contrary to expectation, the terms proved moderate, they could be studied. If they were dishonourable, on the other hand, the French people would see that nothing was to be expected from negotiation and would fight to the finish. Before demanding supreme sacrifices, the unacceptability of the terms should be established. Reynaud immediately pointed out that to ask for the conditions of an armistice was the same as asking for the armistice itself; there could be no turning back once talks had begun. But the proposal had the desired effect. It seemed likely that a majority of ministers would support it, if only to preserve the unity of the government. Reynaud's offer to resign was rejected by President Lebrun, and he was persuaded to remain in office to transmit the proposal to the British.[43]

Later that evening Reynaud met Campbell and Spears, and handed over the text of a message to the British government.[44] It had been formally agreed by the French Cabinet that the government could not depart from France without first establishing that the German and Italian armistice terms were unacceptable. If the British government would give its authorisation to this step, Reynaud was empowered to declare that the surrender of the Fleet to the enemy would be regarded as an unacceptable condition. If consent were withheld, however, Reynaud would have no alternative but to resign. To Campbell and Spears he added that he could not, in this event, guarantee that his successors would maintain the decision about the Fleet. It was apparent that he could see no alternative to the Chautemps proposal.

This was certainly the sense in which the British government interpreted the position, in the light of Reynaud's message and the communications from Campbell which accompanied it.[45] The question was no longer whether the armistice would be sought, but who would lead the government which sought it. The Cabinet in London felt that it must above all keep Reynaud in office and that it had therefore to give its conditional assent to release France from the March agreement.[46] At 12.35 p.m. on 16 June the following message (No. 368) was sent to Sir Ronald Campbell:

Our agreement forbidding separate negotiations, whether for armistice or peace, was made with the French Republic and not with any particular administration or statesman. It therefore involves the honour of France. Nevertheless, provided, but only provided, that the French fleet is sailed forthwith to British harbours pending negotiations, His Majesty's Government give their full consent to enquiry by the French Government to ascertain the terms of an armistice for France. His Majesty's Government, being resolved to continue the war, wholly dissociate themselves from all part in the above-mentioned enquiry concerning an armistice.[47]

This was followed by a further telegram (No. 369) which stipulated that Britain expected to be fully consulted when the terms were known.[48]

These communications caused misgivings both in London and in Bordeaux. Neither Campbell nor Spears liked the departure from the principle of the March agreement which they involved, fearing that 'the door once opened would never be closed again'.[49] Reynaud's response was also chilly; the condition about the Fleet, in particular, was 'trop stupide', since the French Navy's removal to Britain would leave North Africa undefended and create enormous problems for the British themselves in the Mediterranean. The conversation was still going on when the telephone call came through from London which conveyed the text of the British proposal for a close and indissoluble union of the two countries.[50]

The two telegrams had aroused disapproval in London also, and de Gaulle* and Corbin, the French ambassador, had expressed their misgivings to Churchill after the morning Cabinet meeting. At the same time, Halifax had been talking to Sir Robert Vansittart of the Foreign Office, who had been working with Jean Monnet, René Pleven and Desmond Morton, Churchill's private secretary, on a dramatic announcement which would keep France in the war. Feeling in the Cabinet was divided. Churchill himself was unenthusiastic at first, but de Gaulle's urgings persuaded him to instruct Campbell to 'delay action' on telegram No. 368 and, later, to 'suspend action' on the second telegram, No. 369.[51] The Cabinet therefore met again at 3 p.m. and agreed with Churchill that 'in this grave crisis we must not let ourselves be accused of lack of imagination'. Some dramatic announcement was clearly necessary to keep the French going.[52] The Cabinet considered the draft, proposed amendments, and agreed that de Gaulle should convey the text immediately by telephone.[53]

It was certainly an ambitious proposal. France and Britain were to form one nation, with joint organs of defence, foreign and economic policies, joint citizenship, a single War Cabinet, and associated parliaments. At de Gaulle's dictation an excited Reynaud scribbled down the proposal with a pencil stub on a scrap of paper which Spears held steady on the marble table-top.[54] The French Prime Minister was jubilant. For a document like that, he exclaimed, he would fight to the last. Presumably the offer superseded the two telegrams which had just been delivered? Campbell and Spears replied that they were convinced that this was the case. Reynaud then departed 'with a light step' to read the British proposal to President Lebrun. Shortly after his departure there arrived from London the two telegrams instructing Campbell to 'delay' action on No. 368 and to 'suspend' action on No. 369. Campbell therefore sent a message after Reynaud, informing him that the two telegrams had been cancelled.[55]

* De Gaulle had been appointed Under-Secretary of the Ministry of National Defence on 5 June.

As mentioned already, the British ambassador had been alarmed at the contents of the two telegrams granting conditional release from the March agreement, and was without doubt delighted to be able to take them back. But in his enthusiasm to speed them into oblivion he exceeded his instructions. The intention of the British government was not that they should be cancelled but that they should be held in suspense pending consideration of the proposal for an Anglo-French union.[56] The distinction, if Campbell was aware of it at the time, probably seemed academic. Surely with this imaginative proposal the French Prime Minister would be able to smother all further talk of an armistice?

Reynaud, too, felt that the proposal would enable him to regain control of the Cabinet. As the meeting opened at 5 p.m. he made only a passing reference to the two telegrams which had been presented and then withdrawn.[57] But the British proposal fell flat. Even the die-hards failed to speak up in its support, while to others in the Cabinet it seemed like a thinly disguised attempt to reduce France to the status of a British dominion. Years of suspicion and resentment, sharpened by the bitter experiences of the previous month, could not be swept aside. There was no serious discussion of the proposal, and the conversation drifted once more in the direction of an armistice. Baudouin returned to his theme of Churchill's 'understanding' attitude at the Tours meeting, and although Reynaud denied that Churchill had given his consent to France's asking for an armistice, he did not take the opportunity to dispose of the lie once and for all. Since Reynaud also omitted to make clear the exact terms of Britain's conditional assent, it appeared to the increasingly distraught Cabinet that the response to the French request to seek terms had been a categorical refusal. The mistakes of Campbell and the machinations of Reynaud and Baudouin all contributed to one result: to make it appear to the French that the British position concerning the French request had moved from assent on 13 June to categorical refusal on 16 June, whereas in fact it had moved in that time from refusal to conditional assent. So uncompromising and unfeeling did this appear that even those in the French government who could not be accused of long-standing anglophobia began to take refuge in the contention that the British, having failed to commit their every resource to the battle, had no moral right to hold France to its engagement. The bitterness aroused so recently by recriminations over the Weygand plan, by the lack of British air support and by the Dunkirk evacuation, was now intensified by what appeared to be the callous indifference of the British.

The meeting broke up in confusion at 7 p.m., without any decision being taken and with ministers in some doubt as to whether the government had resigned. Reynaud had no further stomach for the fight and wished only to set aside a burden which he could no longer sustain. He did not even consult his colleagues, but simply announced that Marshal Pétain would form a government. In so doing, he joined the ranks of those who supported the request for an armistice.[58]

ARMISTICE

Of the political complexion of the new government there could be no doubt. Mandel, Marin and Campinchi, the staunchest advocates of continued resistance, were out. Chautemps remained as Vice-President of the Council of Ministers. Weygand was given the Ministry of National Defence. Colson, Darlan and Pujo were given the Ministries, respectively, of War, of Marine and of Air. Baudouin became Minister of Foreign Affairs, a post which he claimed to have accepted 'on condition of being able to devote all my energies to the maintenance of the Alliance with England and of friendship with the United States'.[59] Pierre Laval was excluded from the Ministry of Foreign Affairs, but on 27 June entered the government as Minister without Portfolio. Bouthillier remained as Minister of Finance. Although eleven of Reynaud's nineteen Cabinet members remained, they were either defeatists or those who had supported the Chautemps proposal. Moreover, the dominating figures in the new government – Pétain, Weygand, Darlan and Baudouin – were also the most strongly anti-British.

The new Cabinet met for the first time just before midnight on 16 June, and decided unanimously that terms must be sought. Baudouin immediately summoned Lequerica, the Spanish ambassador, and asked him to request his government to act as an intermediary with the German government 'with a view to the cessation of hostilities and the settlement of conditions for peace'. Even Lequerica was surprised. Did Baudouin want armistice or peace terms, or both? Baudouin replied that an armistice was always a temporary expedient and his government would like to know the conditions for peace also.[60]

At one o'clock in the morning of 17 June Baudouin met Campbell. It was a difficult meeting. Baudouin argued that no government could leave France without first ascertaining what terms might be offered. If they were dishonouring, they would be refused, and the people would know that their sufferings had been unavoidable. Among such conditions the most dishonouring would be the surrender of the Fleet, and he was authorised to give his government's 'formal assurance' that, although they expected this to be one of the conditions, it would in no circumstances be accepted. Admiral Darlan's appointment as Minister of Marine, he added, provided an additional guarantee of this.[61] Campbell's response was cold, but he decided to avoid a direct confrontation in case Baudouin took this as a sign that the British had washed their hands of France. In so doing, however, he missed the opportunity to make his government's attitude clear. In fact, it seems likely that he had himself misunderstood the existing situation. He did not allude to the two telegrams because he was still under the impression that they had been cancelled and that the 'conditional assent' had been withdrawn. This is the only satisfactory explanation for Campbell's glaring failure, even by his own account, to insist that the French Fleet should sail forthwith to British ports.[62]

In view of the fact that the only person to whom the two telegrams had been given – Reynaud himself – had resigned, it was imperative that they should be unequivocally reinstated. But were they? Campbell's own account is unclear. Just before the meeting of the French Cabinet on the morning of 17 June, he met Pétain and stressed to him that it was vital for the Fleet to be under British control, although it appears that he did not insist that the despatch of the Fleet to British ports was a firm condition of release from the March agreement. It seems that it was not until he received a further telegram from the Foreign Office ordering him, if he had not already done so, to communicate the two telegrams, that he became aware of his mistake. When this instruction arrived is not clear, but it seems likely that it prompted Campbell's next approach to Baudouin, in mid-afternoon on the 17th.[63] Baudouin being busy with the Marshal, the British ambassador was received by Charles-Roux, Secretary-General of the Ministry of Foreign Affairs, to whom he submitted the texts of the two telegrams with instructions that they should be brought formally to the notice of the French Cabinet in writing.[64]

The following morning Baudouin and Chalres-Roux consulted Reynaud, who confirmed that the telegrams had been delivered, and then replaced by the offer of union with Britain. In the circumstances he had not felt empowered to inform the Cabinet of their existence. According to his own account, Baudouin then met Campbell and asked him whether the two telegrams had been resubmitted 'from a desire to clear up completely the successive phases of the Franco-British negotiations of 16 June, or if it gave fresh life to these proposals on the part of the British Government'. The ambassador asked for leave to consult his documents and to re-examine his instructions before replying. At about noon he returned with the answer. He did not consider that the proposals were revived; the two telegrams were the principal part of a negotiation which ended at 4.30 p.m. on Sunday, 16 June, in the only British proposition that was final – the offer of union.[65]

There is no mention in Campbell's messages to London, or in his final despatch, of this second meeting or of the supposed checking of the documents. Charles-Roux was not present, and the account of the meeting in his own memoirs is based entirely on the *note d'audience* which Baudouin susbsequently gave to him. In short, the second meeting between Campbell and Baudouin did not take place, and Baudouin's account is in all probability an elaborate fiction, designed to conceal the British position from the new government and to make sure that no lingering scruples about France's honour should further delay the conclusion of the armistice.[66]

Baudouin had cleverly exploited his position. As Secretary to the Cabinet in Reynaud's government and as Minister of Foreign Affairs under Pétain, he constituted the one slender thread of continuity linking the tortuous negotiations of the previous few days. Ironically, the desperate efforts of Churchill, Reynaud and Campbell to keep France in the war had merely served to lend credence to Baudouin's version of events. Churchill's magnanimous statements at the Tours meeting were twisted into a consent to France's release from the March agreement. Reynaud's lack of candour undermined his credibility when it was most needed. Campbell's fumblings on 16 June enabled the new government to sue for terms without being made quickly and forcefully aware that its action was in violation of the March agreement. Of course, due weight must be given to the dreadful confusion reigning in Bordeaux, to the fear of imminent capture by the advancing Germans, and to a genuine concern for the desperate plight of the millions of refugees who thronged the roads southwards. No doubt many in the government were not as ignorant of the British position as they later professed themselves to have been.[67] But the opportunity to avoid a direct confrontation with their consciences was afforded them by Paul Baudouin. His position in the Ministry of

Foreign Affairs gave little cause for optimism about the future course of Anglo-French relations.[68]

CAMPBELL'S LAST DAYS IN BORDEAUX

In the last days before the signature of the Armistice the situation in Bordeaux remained uncertain. There was no German response to the French overture until 20 June, and the terms themselves were not presented until two days later. In the meantime it seemed likely that they would prove to be unacceptable. It was taken for granted, by both Campbell and the Foreign Office, that the conditions would include a summary demand for the French Fleet, and since the French Cabinet had formally decided that this would be unacceptable it seemed probable that French resistance in some form would be continued; the advance of the German Army towards Bordeaux seemed likely in itself to force the government – although not Pétain himself – to depart for North Africa.

In these circumstances the policy of the British government and of its ambassador proved to be fatally ambivalent. As long as there was a chance that the French might be induced to fight on, or to authorise continued resistance overseas, it seemed unwise to press for the strictest observance of the condition governing British consent to separate negotiations. But anything short of the immediate despatch of the French Fleet to British ports might subject the French government to some brutal demand involving reprisals against the people of France.[69] Besides, as long as the Fleet remained subject to the orders of the government, any guarantees about its fate depended ultimately on the good faith of the government, and in particular of Admiral Darlan. Faced with the appalling prospect of their ally's Fleet falling under German control, it is hardly surprising that the British did not regard such guarantees as sufficient. However, their actions over the next few days all too often had the appearance of nervous interference, made all the more infuriating to the French because every renewed demand for assurances implied a slur upon the honour of those who had already provided solemn undertakings. A hectoring message from Churchill on 18 June, for example, drove Weygand into a fury. Even so, however much the British action was resented, the French Cabinet did reaffirm that negotiations would be broken off if the Germans demanded the surrender of the Fleet. Campbell was told that it had been decided as a matter of honour that the terms should be received while the Fleet was still fighting, but that its ships would sail to Britain when the capitulation on land occurred. If this proved impossible, the Fleet would be scuttled. Although this was not an ideal solution, Campbell reported that he was inclined to believe that Pétain, Weygand and Darlan, all men of honour, were 'playing straight with us'.[70]

In the late afternoon of 18 June the First Sea Lord, Sir Dudley Pound, and the First Lord of the Admiralty, A. V. Alexander, arrived in Bordeaux. Their discussions, especially with Darlan, apparently convinced them that the Fleet would continue to fight as long as possible, and would then either take refuge in British ports or scuttle itself. Pound and Alexander were particularly impressed by the 'sincerity and determination' of Darlan himself.[71] On the following day Lord Lloyd was also despatched by Churchill to Bordeaux. As Secretary of State for the Colonies it was his job to emphasise the importance which the British attached to the continuation of French resistance in North Africa. In particular, he was to promise collaboration in the movement of men and material, and in the future defence of the region. Although the Cabinet's instructions to Lloyd had envisaged a fairly tough approach, Alexander – having in mind particularly the French decision 'in principle' to move to Algeria – persuaded him to adopt a softer line.[72] But Lloyd himself was unimpressed by what he saw and heard. Lebrun was in a pitiable condition, and although Pétain was prepared to give the most categorical assurances about the Fleet, he was evasive about the government's departure. Lloyd found Weygand 'broken' and 'completely finished', and Pétain 'vain, senile and dangerously ga-ga'.[73] None of the three British visitors succeeded in securing any additional guarantees beyond those already given to Campbell, and their presence was bitterly resented; Darlan described them as 'heirs come to make sure that the dying man has made out his will in their favour'.[74]

What restrained the British visitors most of all was the apparent intention of the government to move to North Africa. On 19 June the Cabinet endorsed the suggestion made by Herriot and Jeanneney (the Presidents of the Chamber of Deputies and Senate) that they, Lebrun and a majority of the Cabinet would depart, leaving Pétain behind as a kind of regent.[75] The continuing advance of the German Army, if nothing else, seemed likely to force the government to move again. In fact, however, when the first German response was made known on 19 June, Baudouin, in naming plenipotentiaries, added the request that the German advance be halted to allow the government to deliberate in complete liberty. What this amounted to was a request to the Germans to make it easier for the government not to transfer itself abroad.[76] Lequerica also warned Berlin that Pétain had control of the situation only by the skin of his teeth and that, if the German advance continued, the Reynaud faction might regain control and continue the war overseas.[77] It was prevented from doing so mainly by Raphaël Alibert, who forged an order from Pétain that each minister was to stay put.[78] With that, the prospect of the government's moving overseas fizzled out. Twenty-nine deputies, in accordance with the earlier decision to leave Bordeaux, boarded the *Massilia* on 20 June and set out the next day for Casablanca. Their departure removed from the scene the hard core of those – notably Mandel, Zay, Campinchi and Delbos – who still opposed the Armistice. Lebrun, and with him the French Republic, remained in Bordeaux. On the night of 22 June the Armistice terms were at last received.

2 Armistice

WITH the signature of the Armistice, France entered a period of partial eclipse. The terms were harsh; since France had sustained a heavy defeat they could hardly have been otherwise. But Hitler had not been in a position to make excessive demands and he realised that no more could be achieved without prolonging the conflict indefinitely. There seemed little point in forcing matters to a final conclusion. France had been eliminated as a military power and her remaining resources would be of little significance once the conflict with Britain was over. In short, Hitler's handling of the French accorded well with the smash and grab tactics which he had always found so effective. Ciano likened him to a gambler who had made a big scoop and wished to get up from the table risking nothing more.[1] It seemed unthinkable that the game was not yet over.

Hitler was well aware in the last days before the signature of the Armistice of the advantages of restraint, and made clear to Mussolini that the Italian thirst for booty would not be quenched. Excessive demands would simply drive the French government overseas to continue the war, leaving the Germans with the problem of administering hostile territory. 'Leniency' would neutralise French resources and leave the policing of France largely in French hands. For the French, too, after the shock of defeat, and with the real or imagined threat of anarchy in the air, the prospect of maintaining some control over the national destiny was an attractive one. 'Frenchmen, and in particular the Politicians, the Press, and perhaps even the Generals could live some semblance of their normal lives. However great the trouble which might be anticipated from Controls and Commissions, some part of France was saved from the day to day *réglementation* of the German High Command, and the relation of the French Government with their conquerors would outwardly be that of diplomacy rather than subjection.'[2]

Much has been written on the question of whether the French government should have refused the terms offered and withdrawn to North Africa. Those who were to lend their support to the Vichy government naturally maintained that this would simply have resulted in the final slaughter of the French Armies and in further, needless horrors for the refugees on the roads. Without the 'safeguards' of the Armistice document, no limits could have been placed on the conqueror's will. Up to a point, this was true. The French Army had ceased co-ordinated resistance by 20 June and there was nothing to stop the *Wehrmacht* overrunning the whole of France. Nor is there any reason to feel that France could have avoided the fate of the other countries whose governments had fled abroad. Whether the German Army could have continued its sweep into North Africa is another matter. Supporters of the Armistice naturally argued that this was the case.[3] The best evidence, however, suggests the contrary. Hitler certainly baulked at the prospect, while Churchill always argued that the Allied cause would have been best served by a French government in North Africa, whether or not the Germans pursued it there. 'It passes my comprehension why no French leaders secede to Africa where they have an Empire, the command of the seas and all the frozen French gold in the United States', he wrote in 1940. 'Surely the opportunity is the most splendid ever offered to daring men.'[4] But the aged politicians and military men who now controlled the French government were not daring men; and after an initial show of belligerence, the colonial authorities followed General Noguès, Commander-in-Chief in North Africa, in accepting Vichy's authority.

The deciding factor for men like Noguès was probably the fact that Hitler had made no territorial demands. He was equally astute in not demanding the handover of the Fleet, which he realised would simply prompt its departure to British waters, or to some other point beyond his reach. With this danger in mind, it seemed preferable to neutralise the Fleet, or allow it to be scuttled.[5]

Article 8 was as follows:

The French Navy (with the exception of that part which is left at the disposal of the French Government to safeguard French interests in the French Colonial Empire) is to be assembled in ports to be specified, and is to be demobilised and disarmed under the supervision of Germany or Italy. These ports will be the peace-time naval stations of the ships. The German Government solemnly declare to the French Government that during the war they have no intention of using the French Navy stationed in the ports under German control for their own purposes apart from those units which are necessary for the watching of the coast and for mine-sweeping. The German Government also solemnly and formally declare that they have no intention of formulating claims against the French Fleet at the conclusion of peace.

With the exception of that part of the French Fleet, to be specified, which is set aside to safeguard French interests in the Colonial Empire, all warships which are outside French territorial waters are to be recalled to France.[6]

As the British ambassador remarked, this 'diabolically clever' provision brought about the collapse of all further resistance at Bordeaux.[7] It enabled the government to sign the Armistice without having to reverse the prior decision that the surrender of the Fleet would be an unacceptable condition. At the same time, it drove a neat wedge between Britain and France by enabling the French government to argue that it had given full satisfaction to the British. If they continued to insist on further guarantees, it could only be because they doubted the good faith of the French government.

To the British, the question was less one of good faith – although they entertained grave doubts on that score also – than of the French government's ability to maintain control of its ships. The peacetime ports of most of the French units were in what was to become the Occupied Zone, and disarmament under Axis supervision involved an unacceptable degree of risk that the ships would be seized undamaged. Even the French Cabinet had immediately grasped this when the terms were first received in the early hours of 22 June.[8] But the modification which was proposed – that the Fleet should be stationed in French African ports – hardly improved the situation at all, since disarmament would still take place in Metropolitan France under Axis supervision.[9] In any case, it was not accepted by Keitel, who regarded such questions as 'matters of detail' to be settled by discussion in the Armistice Commission.[10] With that, further objection ceased – not because Keitel's answer provided a basis for negotiation, as Weygand and Baudouin professed to believe, but because all will to resist had evaporated. Honour had been satisfied and obedience to authority assured. Admiral Darlan, conscious of his power under the new regime, dismissed thoughts of rebellion from his mind. Reynaud had been right after all: there could be no turning back once terms had been sought.

The Vichy government's continued control over its colonial and naval resources gave it some negotiating strength in its relations with Germany. Although in the last resort Vichy had to submit to German pressure, there were limits upon the extent to which this could be brought to bear. This was not appreciated in most quarters in the period immediately following the Armistice, and certainly not in London, where the British government too readily accepted the notion that 'that caitiff government', as Churchill liked to call it, had effectively placed its every resource at the disposal of the enemy.[11] The extent of Vichy's freedom of manoeuvre was not fully understood even by Pétain, who threw away his best card, the threat to transfer the government to North Africa, by his insistence that he would remain in France, come what may. As it turned out, Pétain was more concerned to assure the conqueror of his 'good faith' than to employ tactics of this kind. There were, nevertheless, other less drastic measures which could be taken. Even if Pétain himself refused to take back from France 'the gift of his person', he could authorise others to support the Allied cause in his name. Some maintain that he eventually did so. Be that as it may, the unspoken threat of colonial secession was the single most important restraining factor upon Germany in its handling of the Vichy government, especially during General Weygand's period of office as Delegate-General in North Africa, from September 1940 until his dismissal and retirement in November 1941.

The same considerations applied to the Fleet. In the event, the provisions of Article 8 were suspended indefinitely by Hitler after the British attack at Mers-el-Kébir on 3 July. We cannot know, therefore, whether the seizure of the Fleet, even if it were contemplated, would have met with success. It seems, on balance, unlikely that Hitler would have taken such action, if only because its inevitable side-effect would have been to undermine, if not destroy, the control of the Vichy government over the French Empire. By the same token, it was only after the Allied landings in North Africa in November 1942, that Hitler attempted to gain control of that portion of the Fleet which lay at Toulon. There was by then nothing to lose. Until then, however, he was subject to the juggler's dilemma: that by attempting to secure any one of France's assets, the others would fall into Allied hands.

Vichy's power in its relations with Germany therefore rested upon its successful claim to be the legitimate government, and its consequent ability to command the obedience of its Empire and Fleet. But these were wasting assets. The moral authority of the regime, at first high, slumped badly in the latter half of 1940 when it became apparent that the war would not be brought to a rapid conclusion. A basic premise upon which the Armistice had been concluded – that Britain could not continue the war alone – was proved false. Vichy's authority underwent a further, steady decline throughout 1941 and 1942. On the one hand, it failed to secure any alleviation of the plight of the French people, especially in the Occupied Zone. On the other hand, its attempts at half-hearted collaboration spread alarm in the Empire and contributed to the gradual collapse of France's colonial possessions into Allied hands. Vichy was caught in the middle, ground, in Churchill's phrase, 'between the upper and nether millstones of Britain and Germany'.[12] The Allied occupation of North Africa in November 1942 effectively put an end to Vichy as a factor of any significance in international relations. Its only strength had consisted in its maintenance of control over assets which neither Britain nor Germany could afford to let pass into the hands of the other. Many were lost, piecemeal, in 1940 and 1941: vast areas of Africa to de Gaulle, the French West Indies neutralised, St Pierre and Miquelon 'liberated', Syria and Madagascar under Allied control. With TORCH, Vichy lost Morocco and Algeria, its proudest possessions, at a stroke. Tunisia followed by conquest. French West Africa, and with it the vital port of Dakar, adhered to the Allied cause within a matter of weeks. The German response was swift and entirely predictable – the occupation of the Free Zone and an unsuccessful attempt to capture the Toulon Fleet.

Although the decline of Vichy's authority and power was gradual, the decisive challenge to the regime was issued before the Armistice had even been signed. It seemed for a time that Vichy would not succeed in establishing its authority, but in the end, only one man, Charles de Gaulle, proved able to break free of the tight structures of command and obedience which secured the loyalty of the armed forces. Others, notably General Catroux, resumed the struggle when the immediate prospect of British surrender had passed, or when they had lost their jobs under Vichy. Only de Gaulle, the most junior General in the Army, rejected the very notion of an Armistice. His opposition to surrender was not based upon calculations of strategy but upon an obsessive hatred of Germany and upon the conviction that France's honour demanded the continuation of the fight. The conclusion of the Armistice was, to him, an act of baseness which destroyed any claim which the government might make upon the loyalty of Frenchmen.

This uncompromising denunciation, and the violent antipathy which grew up between the Free French movement and the supporters of Vichy, defined the split between the two conceptions of France's role in rigid terms. Post-war apologists of Vichy often claimed that Pétain and de Gaulle simply had different conceptions of France's honour and should have recognised the validity of each other's claim to be serving

France's best interests, and there was a widespread belief in France in 1940 that the two men were hand in glove. In fact, nothing could have been further from the truth. It was entirely characteristic of Baudouin that he should have piously regretted de Gaulle's failure to appreciate that 'the interest of France has two aspects, and her honour two forms', but neither side saw it this way in 1940.[13] Vichy passed sentence of death on de Gaulle, and de Gaulle regarded Vichy as no more than 'un instrument utilisé par les ennemis de la France contre l'honneur et l'intérêt du pays'.[14]

The existence of the Free French movement had a considerable influence upon Vichy's relationship with Germany. In one sense, it weakened Vichy's bargaining position. The Armistice required the French government not only to bring hostilities to an end throughout France and the French Empire, but also to prevent its subjects from enlisting in foreign armies to continue the fight. The existence of the Free French movement challenged Vichy's claim to be able to stop the fighting and deprived it of even the despicable credit of surrender.[15] Although the initial response to de Gaulle's appeal was poor and even the French forces in Britain for the most part chose repatriation, British sponsorship kept alive the alliance which had dissolved amid such bitter recriminations and ensured that France stayed in the war. Later in 1940, the Gaullist movement acquired an extensive territorial base when Chad and the territories of French Equatorial Africa rallied to the cause, and for the next two years, Gaullist and British encroachments steadily nibbled away at the territorial foundations of Vichy's power.

In another sense, however, the existence of the Free French movement strengthened Vichy's hand. As Hitler was aware, de Gaulle would provide a rallying-point for the French colonial authorities if his own intended demands at French expense were to become known. It was precisely this threat which brought Hitler's plans of a grand coalition against Britain to naught in late 1940, since they all depended upon a distribution of spoils which France was expected to provide. Nor were the French slow to appreciate the advantages of the situation. In the Armistice Commission at Wiesbaden, the French delegation constantly stressed that, if Vichy were to counter the Gaullist threat, it must have not only a clear promise that the French Empire would remain French, but also the military means to make its authority effective.[16] The argument applied with equal force to the Navy, and it was by dangling the Anglo-Gaullist threat to the Empire before the Germans that General Huntziger was able to resist the Italian suggestion in September 1940 that the provisions of Article 8 should be implemented.[17]

Although opinion in Vichy was united in a sincere desire to strengthen the Empire against Gaullism, the line of reasoning used by the French at Wiesbaden cut both ways, of course. Weygand insisted in his memoirs that military preparations against Gaullist territories in Africa were a smoke-screen behind which the Empire could build up its resources and eventually re-enter the war against the Axis.[18] Baudouin tried to convey the same point to London in September 1940, and by the end of the year the Foreign Office had come to appreciate the value of de Gaulle in enabling Weygand to re-arm the forces of French Africa on the pretext of defending it against him.[19] Such preparations, however, could equally well have formed the prelude to wholehearted collaboration with Germany, by drawing France into steadily more open conflict with Britain. It was hardly surprising that the British attitude towards the strengthening of French North Africa should have been so ambivalent.

In the final analysis, however, Vichy's possibilities of manoeuvre under the Armistice were as nothing compared to the innumerable means of pressure which the terms placed in German hands. The conditions, harsh on paper, turned out to be almost insupportable in application.[20] Partly, of course, this was because they were not expected to operate except as an interim measure; German confidence that the British would come to terms or be defeated in short order was fully shared by the French government, which had not sought clarification or modification of certain articles – notably those concerning occupation costs and prisoners of war – whose full severity was not to be felt until hopes of an early peace had faded. In the broadest sense, of course, it was precisely because Britain did refuse to capitulate that Vichy enjoyed any freedom of manoeuvre at all. This was not understood at first in Vichy, where the belief was widespread in late June that Hitler would realise his interest in making France his chief conquered province. Vichy's hostility to Britain stemmed to some extent from the fear that continued resistance might instead persuade Hitler to tempt the British to the negotiating table with offers at France's expense, and French politicians were slow to realise that Hitler never intended his peace with France to be anything less than punitive. Gradually, however, Vichy came to appreciate the chance which the conflict offered to play both ends against the middle. As Halifax noted in November 1940, the

French were getting the best of both worlds by using British approaches as a lever in negotiations with Germany.[21]

The full severity of the Armistice terms stemmed not only from their extended duration, but from the harshness with which they were applied. Reynaud had been scornful of Pétain and Weygand in June for imagining that they could sit down around a green baize table to discuss terms. Hitler was not Wilhelm I; he was Genghis Khan.[22] The way in which the Armistice was signed, a set piece designed to feed Hitler's desire to humiliate France, should have made it clear from the outset that, as Chautemps ruefully admitted, one does not negotiate an Armistice.[23] The only French counter-proposal to be accepted concerned the handing over of the Air Force – a provision which it would have proved impossible to enforce. The Germans conceded nothing of substance.

Under Article 2 of the Armistice, about three-fifths of France was placed under German occupation. Although Article 3 preserved French sovereignty over the Occupied Zone in theory, Vichy's authority across the line could never be effectively exercised. Refugees from north-eastern France were not allowed to return to their homes, while many other inhabitants were expelled and their property handed over to German settlers. The departments of the Nord and the Pas-de-Calais were subjected to the German military authorities in Belgium, and thus virtually amputated from France. German intentions in Alsace-Lorraine, too, could hardly have been clearer: Gauleiters were appointed, the frontiers of 1914 restored, and a policy of ruthless Germanisation put in hand.[24]

In purely economic terms, the occupation placed most of France's resources under German control. About 75 per cent of industry, including, of course, coal and steel, was in the Occupied Zone. It was put to work to supply the German war machine. Even more damaging to France's survival was the line of demarcation itself. The Unoccupied Zone depended heavily upon the Occupied north and west for manufactured goods and foodstuffs, and the Germans were able to use the threat to close the line to good effect in extracting further concessions beyond the terms of the Armistice.[25] What was aimed at was nothing less than complete control of the economic life of the country. In the Occupied Zone, resources were simply seized; but even in the so-called 'Free' Zone there was little the government could do except temporise. Most French officials trod the tightrope between *attentisme* and *résistance*. But there was little that could be done to resist outright demands. There were other, more direct means of pressure. Article 18 made the French government liable to pay the occupation costs of the German Army. There was nothing unusual in this. But the amount which the Germans fixed was a staggering 20 million marks a day, a figure which did not even include billeting costs.[26] Furthermore, the exchange rate was fixed at a larcenous twenty francs to the mark. Equally scandalous was the notorious 'clearing account' under which Vichy was to pay for any excess of exports over imports from France to Germany: France was even required to subsidise her own spoliation.

Another highly effective means of pressure upon the Vichy government was afforded by the two million French prisoners of war who, under Article 20, were to remain in captivity until the conclusion of the final peace treaty. The Germans were not slow to realise that threats to worsen their treatment or promises of release constituted a most effective form of blackmail. Despite the considerable ingenuity of the French delegation at Wiesbaden, attempts to secure the release of the prisoners did not meet with much success. There were still over a million men in captivity in August 1942, although Laval's *relève* scheme, implemented in that month, did secure the release of more men in return for skilled labour for the Reich.

However much the French might protest, they had to give in on most points. As a last resort, the Germans could always threaten to exercise the unilateral right of denunciation provided by Article 24 – a measure which would bring about the immediate resumption of hostilities. Any illusions which had existed in June 1940 that France would secure respect through revival were quickly dispelled. It appeared to a disillusioned Baudouin only four months later that the Germans had set about destroying the basis of a Franco-German *rapprochement* 'for fun'.[27] For Weygand, as for many others, one lesson remained clear: if you go to war, especially with Germany, you must make sure not to be beaten.[28]

The full rapacity of the German occupation was not immediately apparent, of course, and in the first few weeks after the defeat there was a widespread belief in the government that Hitler would accord France an honourable, if subordinate, role in the New Europe. Some, like Pierre Laval, viewed the prospect with enthusiasm; most seemed ready to accept it as France's just reward. Frenchmen questioned themselves deeply in 1940 on the causes of their country's defeat, and a general feeling prevailed that France had fallen because her strength had been sapped by years of political and social strife, and by the habits of easy living. In the words of Drieu la Rochelle, France had become a nation of 'idlers, Pernod-drinkers and river-bank fishermen'. In the urgent desire for change, hardly a murmur was heard as the Third Republic voted itself out of existence. As before in moments of national crisis, France sought salvation through unquestioning obedience to one man's authority.[29]

This desire to cut loose from the past found expression also in a reaction against the foreign policy of the Third Republic and against the alliance with Britain which had formed its basis. The long-stifled resentments of the inter-war period combined with anger at British conduct during the Battle of France to produce a violent outburst of anglophobia. Laval told the Chamber of Deputies that France was at the bottom of the abyss into which Britain had led her, while Darlan spoke with apparent relish of the destruction of British morale by German bombing raids. Many, fearing that Britain's prolonged resistance would enable her to come to terms at France's expense, looked forward to a speedy collapse and to a general peace settlement.[30] There were few 'resisters of the first hour'. Most Frenchmen longed for a return to the normal tempo of life. Of England, they asked only to be left alone. But, as Churchill had warned on 13 June, this was not to be.

3 Picking up the Pieces: Britain's Response to the Armistice

JUST as the hopes and ambitions of the men in Bordeaux were shaped by the mood of urgent self-examination and doubt which held France in its grip, so too were the responses of the British policy-makers an expression of the very different mood which had prevailed in London since the time of Dunkirk – one of profound relief at having escaped from a campaign which had been viewed from the start with so little enthusiasm, and at having been freed from the continued obligation to support a crippled ally. This feeling of relief and elation was only lightly tinged with regret at the fate which had befallen France. General Brooke, for example, had deplored the decision to send the BEF back to France after Dunkirk, and made it plain to Eden before he left that he entertained no hope of success.[1] When Air Marshal Dowding heard of the Armistice, he fell to his knees and thanked God.[2] Even Churchill, who had been more willing than anybody else in the Cabinet to commit increasing numbers of fighters to the battle, decided finally that he had been 'throwing snowballs into hell'.[3] As early as 26 May, he had even suggested that Britain might be better off without France.[4] Cadogan, at first sceptical, soon came round to the same view. 'If we keep them in the fight, we've got to give them air protection and drain away our defences and so fall between two stools. Better to say "All right: if you can't stick it, get out or give in: we go on alone." '[5]

Cadogan's attitude was prompted by more than just bravado. If France had to abandon the struggle, there was much to be said for the view that she should do so sooner rather than later. As Churchill pointed out, France would be more able to resist German demands as a powerful neutral than as a no-man's-land.[6] But the mood of elation in London owed little to sober calculations of military advantage. With the onset of disaster doubt, at least, had been removed, and with it the tiresome necessity of keeping alive the spirit of resistance in France. Many shared the King's relief that there remained no more Allies 'to

38

be polite to and to pamper', and that Britain stood alone, 'come the four quarters of the world in arms'.[7] Some even seemed to think that this in itself brought victory closer.[8] The mood of the country as a whole was well summed up by the *New Statesman* on 22 June: the British public, although appalled by the French defeat, felt that 'the ring was now clear for the bout everyone had been waiting for, the heavyweight championship of Europe'.[9]

Inspired by such patriotic fervour, the British looked with mingled regret and contempt upon those who had proved unequal to the challenge, and overlooked, as Weygand bitterly remarked, that the Channel was a very good anti-tank trap.[10] This sentiment was particularly strong in military circles. Brooke returned from France convinced that the French High Command, knowing that its own forces were doomed, had not cared how many British troops were 'sucked down with them in the whirlpool of this catastrophe'. Even those who rejected defeat could not be sure of a welcome in Britain. 'We don't want any Frenchmen over here,' the CIGS told Churchill. 'I shall think my honour satisfied if I say to the French Generals "Any man that wants to stay here and fight can do so," and then I hope they will all go back.'[11] Churchill's reply was scathing, but even he, in a tirade to the Defence Committee on 27 May, had dwelt upon 'the misfortune into which our Allies have landed us, while we have loyally carried out our obligations and undertakings to them'.[12] Many gave free rein to their prejudices about the French national character. 'Their insularity and non-travelling habits are coming out with a rush', noted Hugh Dalton on hearing of the French refusal to continue the struggle abroad. 'They are too much attached to their mistresses, and their soup, and their little properties.' Lord Hankey was more genteel but no less patronising. The French, he wrote to Lord Halifax, were more responsible for Britain's troubles than anyone else; they had been 'our evil genius' since the Paris Peace Conference, with their inflexible attitude to Germany and their fondness for collective security and 'other impracticable projects of this kind'. An attractive people but most unstable, he concluded. As for the future, 'we shall have to envisage a new orientation after the war . . . some time may elapse before we can fit France in.'[13]

It was against this background of disintegrated trust and mounting francophobia that far-reaching policy decisions were to be made in June 1940. Long-standing antagonisms, aggravated by the months of uneasy alliance during the 'Phoney War', and by the harrowing experience of swift defeat on the battlefield, played as important a part in determining the posture which Britain adopted towards the new French regime as any rational and ordered process of policy-making. The resignation of Reynaud on the 16th had removed from the scene the one French politican whom the British felt they could trust, and the bad faith of the new government seemed amply confirmed, firstly by their action in requesting terms without meeting the firm condition laid down by the British, and then by concluding an Armistice without consulting London. A careful consideration of the Armistice terms would have revealed, as we have seen, that the French government could expect to maintain some degree of independence. No such appraisal of the situation was carried out in London, however, where the prevailing mood of Churchillian pugnacity ensured that the problem of France would be approached in fairly rudimentary, black-and-white terms. It was an atmosphere in which fine points of argument looked like quibbling, and in which measured responses smacked of appeasement. This is not to suggest that the policy which emerged was seriously misguided, or that the assumptions upon which it was based were necessarily unsound. It is simply to point out that, for better or worse, the British government's initial, uncompromising definition of the situation, and the sometimes ruthless actions which resulted from this definition, were to determine the future course of its relations with the Vichy government within narrow limits. When policy towards Vichy was eventually subjected to careful scrutiny after the failure of Operation MENACE, in late September and October, it was realised that policy alternatives had become rigidly circumscribed within the framework so arbitrarily constructed in the heady atmosphere of late June.

The British, in the first place, took for granted the bad faith of 'the most miserable lot of very old men' who now controlled the French government.[14] In this respect, the influence of the small group of soldiers and diplomats who had been first-hand witnesses of the French collapse was paramount. Spears, who enjoyed considerable influence in Downing Street, gave lurid descriptions of the last days of the Third Republic and poured scorn on France's new leaders, confirming in Churchill's mind the impression of moral disintegration which he had gained on his own visits to France. In the Foreign Office, too, the former ambassador was painting a bleak picture of the new government, now controlled, in his opinion, by a 'crook' (Baudouin) and 'an old dotard' (Pétain). Campbell was in no doubt that the government had violated the March agreement, that it had ignored the clear conditions laid down on the 16th, and that there had been an 'organised conspiracy' to prevent him from ascertaining the facts.[15]

Deep-seated moral disintegration and consequent bad faith – it followed from such a view of the French collapse that the Bordeaux government, which had already failed to honour its treaty obligations, would not hesitate to surrender itself entirely to the enemy. There was little dissent within the government from Churchill's view, broadcast on 23 June, that the Armistice could not have been signed by a government 'which possessed freedom, independence, and constitutional authority'. The terms placed France and the French Empire entirely in the power of the German and Italian dictators.[16] This bold pronouncement did not stem from a close reading of the Armistice terms, which were regarded as secondary. What mattered was that the French government had signed an Armistice at all. This alone was enough to reduce it 'to a state of complete subjection to the enemy and deprive it of all liberty and of all right to represent free French citizens'. This was an extreme position to adopt and Halifax, already alarmed by Churchill's encouragement of de Gaulle, tried to have it modified, but without success.[17] The spirit of the Tours meeting was as dead in London as its letter had become in Bordeaux. 'They had broken their solemn treaty obligations with us and were now completely under the thumb of Germany,' declared Churchill on 24 June. 'They would allow all their resources to fall into the hands of the enemy and be used against their previous allies.'[18] On the following day it was decided to treat Unoccupied France for blockade purposes as territory 'which is in the occupation of or under the control of the enemy'.[19]

Whatever the exact circumstances of her defeat, and whatever terms she might secure in negotiations, it was obvious that the cessation of French resistance would upset every calculation upon which Allied strategy had been built and might fatally impair Britain's chances of continuing the fight. Only a week after the beginning of the battle in the west, urgent consideration was being given to 'British Strategy in a Certain Eventuality', and on 27 May the Cabinet considered the report of the Chiefs of Staff (see above, p. 13). The French collapse held wide-ranging implications for the future conduct of the war and the report did not attempt to explore these thoroughly. It was more concerned to establish that survival, and perhaps even victory, was still possible. In many respects, the report was wide of the mark, giving little weight to the possible role of large ground forces in the future conduct of the war, and too readily assuming that economic pressure, air attack, and the creation of revolt in the conquered territories would provide an adequate substitute for military methods.[20] On the whole, however, the report was remarkable for the dispassionate manner in which it weighed up the chances of survival and reached, as it turned out, sound conclusions. In the short run, there was no doubt about the most immediate questions posed by the Armistice: the fate of France's Fleet and colonial Empire.

CRUEL NECESSITY: THE FRENCH NAVY

In the last days before the signature of the Armistice, the fate of the French Fleet became the major concern of the British government.[21] Although it was recognised that the chances of its being handed over to the Germans willingly were remote, it was taken for granted that its surrender would be a condition of the Armistice.[22] If the Fleet was still under French control, the French government might be subjected to the most brutal blackmail.[23] For this reason, the repeated assurances of Darlan, Pétain and Baudouin could do nothing to allay British fears, and only the despatch of the Fleet to British ports before negotiations had begun could have persuaded them to consent to the French request for terms.

From the British point of view, Article 8 could hardly have been worse. An outright demand for the Fleet would have prompted either the French government's departure to North Africa or spontaneous action on the part of the Fleet itself. Instead, it now seemed practically certain that, sooner or later, the Fleet would pass under German control. If the ships were not seized during demobilisation, large numbers might in any case be made available to the enemy on the pretext that they were required for minesweeping. Even the flimsy safeguards of Article 8 could be removed at a stroke if Germany exercised its unilateral right of denunciation. They rested, in any case, upon Hitler's word of honour, and, as Churchill pointed out, 'What is the value of that? Ask half a dozen countries what is the value of such a solemn assurance.'[24]

It has been argued that the British should have accepted the French government's assurances that adequate measures had been taken to ensure that no vessels could be seized by the Germans. Admiral Darlan

had indeed attempted to ensure that under no circumstances would the
French Navy be allowed to fall into German hands. As a last resort it
was ordered to sail to the United States or to scuttle itself.[25] The British
Cabinet appears to have been unaware of those orders, and of the
Italian government's concession of 30 June in allowing demobilisation
to be carried out in North African ports.[26] It is most unlikely, however,
that this information would have affected the decisions taken in
London. As Churchill told the Cabinet on 1 July, 'discussions as to the
Armistice conditions could not affect the real facts of the situation'.[27]
Even the texts of the orders themselves could not have stilled British
fears where all Darlan's assurances had failed, especially since the
British had evidence that the Germans were in possession of the French
naval codes and could therefore issue orders purporting to come from
Darlan himself.[28] Even if it were able to do so, it was felt to be
increasingly unlikely that the French government, or its possible
successors, would stand by its guarantees. Sir Ronald Campbell, for
one, left Bordeaux unsure of whether Darlan could be trusted and
convinced that French assurances about the Fleet expressed 'a pious
hope rather than a sacred pledge', while Duff Cooper, the Minister of
Information, feared that the French Admirals were too stunned to be
capable of resisting a takeover.[29]

As the month of June drew to a close, the British Cabinet moved
steadily towards an uncompromising position, although it recoiled from
attacking its recent ally and also realised that such a course of action
would probably destroy any chance of rallying the French Empire.[30]
There existed also the more alarming prospect that the French
government might be provoked into active hostilities against Britain,
and the Joint Planning Sub-Committee concluded as late as 29 June
that if there was a genuine danger of this, it could not regard the action
contemplated as justifiable.[31] On the following day, however, the Chiefs
of Staff decided to recommend the use of force, if necessary, to immobilise
the French Fleet.[32] The very real danger of French hostilities was
dismissed for the somewhat implausible reason that the strict imposition
of the blockade would in any case eventually bring them about. 'In the
light of recent events,' the Chiefs of Staffs concluded, 'we can no longer
place any faith in French assurances, nor could we be certain that any
measures, which we were given to understand the French would take to
render their ships unserviceable before reaching French Metropolitan
ports, would, in fact, be taken. Once the ships have reached French
Metropolitan ports we are under no illusions as to the certainty that,

sooner or later, the Germans will employ them against us.'[33]

The story of Operation CATAPULT has often been told and its details are not in dispute. Its purpose was the 'simultaneous seizure, control or effective disablement or destruction of all the accessible French Fleet'. The dispositions of the Fleet on 3 July were as follows:

British ports	2 old battleships, *Courbet* and *Paris*
	2 large destroyers, *Léopard* and *Triomphant*
	2 smaller destroyers
	7 submarines (including *Surcouf*)
	6 torpedo boats
	various minesweepers and other craft
Casablanca	*Jean Bart* (without guns)
Dakar	*Richelieu* (incomplete but could fire guns)
Mers – el – Kébir	
and Oran	2 modern battlecruisers, *Dunkerque* and *Strasbourg*
	2 old battleships *Bretagne* and *Provence*
	6 large new destroyers and a seaplane carrier
	7 destroyers and 4 submarines
Algiers	6 cruisers
Toulon	4 cruisers
Alexandria	1 old battleship, the *Lorraine*
	4 cruisers and some light craft
West Indies	various ships[34]

The ships in British harbours were seized in the early hours of 3 July without much difficulty. In Alexandria, the negotiating skill of Admiral Cunningham succeeded in bringing about the demobilisation of the French squadron in a situation where strict adherence to the Cabinet's orders might have resulted in disaster, and the French ships eventually rejoined the fight on the Allied side in 1943.[35] The main action, however, was to take place at Mers-el-Kébir, the main port of Oran on the Algerian coast. Admiral Somerville's Force H arrived off the port on the same day and through an emissary, Captain Holland, conveyed the following alternatives to Admiral Gensoul: firstly, to sail for British harbours and continue the fight; secondly, to sail to a British port with reduced crews, who would be repatriated when desired. If Gensoul accepted either of these alternatives, but insisted that the ships should not be used during the war, the Cabinet authorised Somerville to agree 'for so long as Germany and Italy abide by the Armistice terms', but he was not to raise this point himself. Thirdly, the ships might be sent with reduced crews to a French port in the West Indies, where they could be demilitarised or perhaps entrusted to the United States for the duration of the war. If none of these alternatives were acceptable, the French ships must scuttle themselves. Failing this, they would be destroyed.[36] Somerville was authorised to accept any French alternative which would bring about the demilitarisation of the ships, provided this could be carried out within six hours and remain effective for at least a year. In fact, this provision added nothing since it ruled out anything short of immediate scuttling.[37] In the event, Gensoul refused to consider these alternatives and informed his government only that he had been commanded to scuttle his ships or he would be compelled to do so by force.[38] Weygand and Bouthillier later suggested that the course of events might have been different if Gensoul had conveyed the ultimatum in full. This seems unlikely. All the alternatives, as Gensoul pointed out to the Parliamentary Commission of Inquiry after the war, were part of an ultimatum, and 'It was absolutely inadmissible that I accept any term of this ultimatum under such pressure.'[39] Acceptance of any would have constituted a violation of the Armistice.

Gensoul's delaying tactics during the course of the day did not signify that he was considering the alternatives. On the contrary, he was simply buying time until reinforcements arrived. Indeed, it was the British Admiralty's interception of the French Admiralty's order to answer force with force and to summon submarine and air reinforcements if necessary which brought negotiations to an end and decided the reluctant Somerville to open fire.[40] Events had assumed their own momentum. The British Admiral's mining of the harbour entrance at 1 p.m. effectively closed all options except scuttling. Confusion and time-lag also played their part. The French government had only just arrived in Vichy, and radio communication had been forbidden by Article 14 of the Armistice. Convinced that the attack had already been launched, the French government took no further action after 2 p.m. Somerville eventually opened fire at 5.54 p.m. The *Bretagne* was blown up and capsized, the *Dunkerque* run aground and the *Provence* beached. The *Strasbourg*, with two destroyers and four flotilla leaders, escaped from the harbour against all the odds. 1297 French sailors died. The British force returned on 6 July and inflicted further damage upon the *Dunkerque*. On the following day, the *Richelieu*, the most powerful vessel in the French

Navy and perhaps in the world, was immobilised, but not sunk, at Dakar.

The adoption of such a drastic course of action against a recent ally was bound to provoke controversy. As Churchill's message to Somerville on 2 July recognised, he had been charged 'with one of the most disagreeable and difficult tasks that a British Admiral has ever been faced with'. It was only with great reluctance that the admirals obeyed their orders. They, more than anybody, had been prepared to accept the word of honour of their French colleagues; none of them was ever persuaded that their faith had been misplaced. Even if one sets aside the objections of those who naturally resented the obligation to carry out so hateful a task, however, it is by no means certain that CATAPULT was a wise decision. On the credit side, there can be no doubt that the attack, as Churchill claimed, did more than anything to demonstrate British resolve to continue the war. Certainly the action met with general approval in the government, and Churchill's speech to the Commons on 4 July was constantly interrupted by applause.[41] The reception abroad was mixed. Hitler was unconvinced by British determination to prosecute the war 'with the utmost vigour by all means that are open to us until the righteous purposes for which we have entered it have been fulfilled', and went ahead with his appeal for peace on 19 July. Ciano was more impressed, and concluded that the British Fleet 'still has the aggressive ruthlessness of the captains and pirates of the seventeenth century'.[42] Cordell Hull, the American Secretary of State, thought CATAPULT a 'tragic blunder', but Roosevelt approved of the action, and the American press was for the most part favourable.[43] If indeed the action was decisive in persuading the American President of British determination to continue, it can be fully justified on this ground alone.

Against this, however, must be placed the disastrous effects of CATAPULT upon the already strained relations of Britain with the Vichy government. Formal diplomatic relations were severed, and the memory of Mers-el-Kébir poisoned all future dealings between London and Vichy. For a time, it seemed likely that open hostilities might result.[44] But the attack, while it undoubtedly increased bitterness against the British in Vichy, did not cause it: feelings had been running high for some time before 3 July.[45] It nevertheless certainly strengthened the hands of those who sought a closer *rapprochement* with Germany.[46] There was a revulsion of feeling in the French Empire also, and recruitment into de Gaulle's forces, never brisk, slowed to a trickle.

These drawbacks might have been less apparent if the operation had met with complete success. In fact, as Cadogan noted, the results were 'not too good', and in no way justified Churchill's claim that 'a large portion of the French Fleet has . . . passed into our hands or has been put out of action or otherwise withheld from Germany'.[47] One old battleship, the *Bretagne*, had been destroyed. The *Dunkerque* and *Provence* were seriously damaged. Neither the *Richelieu* nor the *Jean Bart*, which Churchill regarded as the main targets, had been sunk. The *Richelieu* was immobilised at Dakar, but had been repaired within twelve months. She could put to sea at short notice and her guns played their part in frustrating Operation MENACE two and a half months later. The *Jean Bart* was beyond reach at Casablanca. The *Strasbourg* and five destroyers escaped from Somerville's guns and reached Toulon. On the other hand, the vessels seized in British ports were a useful addition to naval strength.

The most fortunate result of CATAPULT was unforeseen: Hitler, delighted by the turn of events, agreed to the indefinite suspension of Article 8. Thus the immediate danger that the French Fleet might fall into Axis hands during demobilisation was removed. But even this cut both ways. The lifting of restrictions upon the movement of French ships enabled the Vichy government to despatch to Dakar in September the six ships which played some part in preventing a Gaullist landing. The same concession enabled the guns of the *Jean Bart* to be turned against the Allied forces during Operation TORCH two years later. At the same time, the brutality of the British action, while it indirectly removed the threat of an Axis takeover, considerably increased, if it did not create, the risk that the remaining units of the French Navy might be used against Britain on French initiative, while the removal of the Fleet from French African ports to the safety of Toulon *increased* the ever-present risks of a German takeover.

With the benefit of hindsight it is not difficult to make out a case that CATAPULT was a blunder. No evidence has ever come to light that the French would have surrendered their Fleet to Germany and the eventual fate of the ships in Toulon harbour in November 1942 was a striking demonstration of French determination that the Fleet should not pass under foreign control. There is likewise no evidence that Germany planned to seize the ships, while in the unlikely event of her being able to do so, it would have taken perhaps eighteen months to put them into service. It can also be argued that the memory of Mers-el-Kébir increased French resistance to the British at Dakar in September, and again to the Allied invasion of North Africa in November 1942. In the situation as it appeared in July 1940, however, it is difficult to see what alternative course of action could have been adopted. Above all, the British could not allow questions affecting national survival to be dependent upon the word of honour of a government whose first action had been to violate its solemn pledge to its ally. In such a situation, no degree of risk, however small, could be accepted.[48]

THE FRENCH EMPIRE

France's far-flung and strategically vital Empire was Britain's other major preoccupation when the French collapse became inevitable, and on 14 June the Chiefs of Staff drew up a report on the likely situation in France's colonial possessions in the aftermath of defeat. This proved to be unduly pessimistic. It was assumed that the Germans would be able to make what use they liked of French North Africa, and in view of the prevailing belief that Britain's ability to defeat Germany rested mainly upon the effectiveness of the blockade, access to French colonial sources of supply seemed to present a grave threat. At the same time, it was apparent that the normal methods of enforcing the blockade would no longer be effective with diminished naval resources over a vastly increased area. It was now necessary to control Europe's essential external resources at their source, and for this to be achieved key strategic positions in the French Empire had to be denied to the enemy. The attitude of the French colonial authorities would therefore be vital. The Chiefs of Staff suggested that they might continue the war independently, adopt an attitude of complete acquiescence, or actively resist neither side. They failed to predict what turned out to be the most widespread response – obedience to the government, and a resolve to fight *both* sides in defence of France's 'neutrality'.[49]

The report took for granted that every effort should be made to keep the French Empire in the war. Pétain's broadcast on 17 June calling for an end to hostilities removed any possibility that it would do so on the government's orders, and British consular officials were therefore instructed to make individual approaches to the French colonial authorities.[50] The response was mixed. Although most officials expressed the desire to continue the struggle, it was soon apparent that they would be reluctant to do so if the French government itself did not give its authorisation, or if no other governmental authority were established to which they could transfer their allegiance.[51] It was in an attempt to meet this urgent need that the British government, in the next few days, began to search for some authority which would ensure the continuance of the war in the French Empire. Unfortunately, their attempts in this direction were seen in Bordeaux as attempts to seduce the Empire from its obedience to the government – which indeed they were – and played their part in further exacerbating the hostility and mistrust of Britain in the French government. This in itself was a small price to pay since London and Bordeaux were already on a collision course over the French Fleet. More serious was the resentment of the colonial officials themselves, steeped in the anglophobe traditions of the French colonial service and chronically suspicious of British designs, especially in the Middle East. To some extent, their reluctance to cut loose stemmed from simple pecuniary interest. An even stronger influence, however, was the French tradition of obedience to the legal government, an attitude which the British tended to discount, or to dismiss as defeatism.

The obvious contenders for the role of alternative French government were the die-hard politicians who had departed from Bordeaux on 21 June aboard the *Massilia*. On the 24th, the Cabinet decided to despatch Lord Gort and Duff Cooper to Rabat to establish contact with them. The uncertain attitude of Noguès made it seem likely that Morocco might become the focal point for continued resistance to the Armistice.[52] The mission failed utterly to achieve its objective. Access to the French politicians, who were in detention, was denied, and Noguès refused to meet the British delegation. In an interview with M. Morize, his deputy, Cooper was told that France's only hope lay in preventing a division in the ranks. What yet remained must stick together. He, Morize, was merely an official who must obey his instructions, however distasteful. If General Noguès ordered him to shoot himself, he would obey, but the orders he had were even more cruel.[53]

Morize spoke for many uneasy French consciences which sought refuge from choice in unquestioning obedience. Cooper was unconvinced, however, and reported on his return that obedience to Bordeaux was merely the result of 'passing panic' and lacked roots.[54] The Cabinet accordingly decided, upon his advice, to prepare plans for an expedition to Morocco. The idea, however, did not find favour with the Chiefs of Staff, who argued that although it was to Britain's advantage that the French should continue the war in all possible theatres, resistance in North Africa, without the support of Metropolitan France, could only be a wasting asset, since it could not be prolonged without British assistance. They concluded that an Allied force in North Africa would not be a profitable detachment, and the continuation of French resistance there was not essential to the prosecution of the war.[55] The idea was therefore dropped. Churchill's own enthusiasm to bring French North Africa back into the war was only temporarily dampened, however, and he was to return to the project at frequent intervals during the next two years.

DE GAULLE: THE POST OF HONOUR

What signalled most clearly the increasingly intransigent attitude of the British government towards the Pétain regime during the Armistice period was the steadily growing measure of support extended to General de Gaulle. As things turned out, the failure of any senior military or civilian authority to emerge after the fall of France left de Gaulle in a position that was as unassailable morally as it was feeble militarily. His was the only voice raised in defiance of defeat and surrender – and that, it should be remembered, *before* the Armistice had been signed. In time, this action was to confer upon him a unique claim, of which he was both well aware and increasingly jealous, to speak on behalf of undefeated France. Since it was the basis of British long-term policy in Europe to seek the restoration of France as a Great Power, de Gaulle's movement clearly had an essential role to perform in Britain's post-war planning. Nowhere was this to be appreciated more than in the Foreign Office, his staunchest supporter in the years ahead, when the General's own unflinching pursuit of French interests had combined with his autocratic temper and his inveterate suspicion of British designs to bring his relations with Churchill into a condition of more or less permanent crisis.

In view of these later developments, it is important to stress that in June 1940 de Gaulle was accepted in London as an additional means of securing immediate objectives, not as a foundation stone upon which to rebuild the authority and prestige of France.[56] This should not be exaggerated, however. There was much support in London for Dalton's view that Britain should 'disrecognise' Bordeaux and recognise 'anything else that can be collected'.[57] At the same time, it was understood that the future of the Alliance might not be well served by the resurrection of discredited politicians like Daladier.[58] In view of later fears, widespread in France, that the British sought the restoration of the Third Republic, it was fortunate that no such men came forward. Even so, until the failure of the Cooper–Gort mission, British hopes were centred upon the inmates of the *Massilia*, not upon the lowest-ranking General in the French Army: de Gaulle was supported in his early days in London not by the Foreign Office or the Cabinet, which both did their utmost to restrain him, but by Churchill.

On 17 June, with little hesitation, the Prime Minister authorised de Gaulle to broadcast an appeal for continued resistance. The Cabinet, however, had serious misgivings about extending facilities to the General, 'so long as it was still possible that the French Government would act in a way conformable to the Alliance', and decided on the 18th that de Gaulle should remain silent. Pressure upon individual Cabinet members later in the day secured the reversal of this decision, and de Gaulle's famous appeal was broadcast that night.[59] Although it called for continued resistance, the speech did not directly challenge the authority of the Bordeaux government. Even so, it was poorly received in the Foreign Office, Cadogan complaining that 'No. 10 Hall is like behind the scenes at the circus and every crank in the world is getting hold of P.M. and getting half-baked decisions'. Halifax pressed Churchill and, this time with Duff Cooper's support, was able to prevent a further broadcast asserting that the Bordeaux government no longer represented France and that a new government had been set up in London.[60]

The de Gaulle issue is an excellent illustration of Churchill's style of leadership. The decision to support de Gaulle was an individual one owing much to the influence of General Spears. The Cabinet was called in afterwards, and its decision was in any case informally reversed. The Foreign Office had not been consulted at all. For a short time, however, the Foreign Office was able to restrain the Prime Minister. The Alexander–Lloyd mission seemed to indicate that there still remained some chance that the Bordeaux government would move overseas, and de Gaulle's first broadcast had been poorly received in France. It seemed unwise to 'ride two horses at the same time'.[61] Everything changed with the signing of the Armistice, and the committee formed to study the possible continuation of French resistance concluded on 22 June that de Gaulle should go ahead once more. In the Cabinet meeting that day, only the First Lord of the Admiralty, deeply concerned with the fate of the French Fleet, raised any objection to the decision to allow de Gaulle to issue further appeals.[62] Even so, the misgivings of the Foreign Office had not been stilled, and a last-minute attempt, inspired by the French ambassador, M. Corbin, was made on the evening of the 23rd to have the General's statement modified.[63] This was to little avail. On the same occasion, a statement was issued by the government taking note of the formation of a French National Committee representing independent French elements, and declaring that it would deal with it in all matters concerning the prosecution of the war as long as it continued to represent all French elements resolved to fight the common enemy.[64] This fell far short of recognising de Gaulle's movement as anything like an alternative to the government in Bordeaux; it was rather envisaged as the first step in a process which, it was hoped, would lead to the formation of a more representative civilian authority.[65] Again, it was only after the evident collapse of all further resistance in the French Empire on 28 July that de Gaulle secured recognition as 'the leader of all free Frenchmen, wherever they may be, who rally to him in support of the Allied cause'.[66] Nevertheless, however cautious the British government's policy, and however divided its counsels, it had taken an irrevocable step. If they abandoned de Gaulle, without at the same time finding a viable alternative, the British would abandon also the elaborate fiction that 'France' remained in the fight. By continuing to support him, however, they rendered infinitely more difficult the task of re-establishing relations with the government in Vichy – the importance of which, at first discounted even in the Foreign Office, was to become increasingly apparent as that regime moved into steadily closer collaboration with Germany.

4   Vichy France, de Gaulle France, Weygand France

I N the months after the signature of the Armistice, the full complexity of the dilemma facing the British government gradually emerged. On the one hand, Vichy's bad faith in reneging on its engagements combined with the bitterness caused by the attack at Mers-el-Kébir to make it impossible for relations to be established on a basis of mutual trust, while the democratic solidarity which had existed with the Third Republic was swept away when the regime voted itself out of existence on 10 July and established under Marshal Pétain a form of government which seemed to bring it into close ideological accord with the Axis powers. The Vichy regime appeared to many to be a form of National Socialism with which the British should have no dealings in principle. On the other hand, it soon became apparent that Vichy would continue to wield a significant degree of power as long as it retained its Fleet and Empire. Some form of contact could therefore be regarded as essential if these were to be denied to the enemy or even, perhaps, secured for the Allied cause.

The need to maintain relations with the Vichy government brought the British government into conflict, not only with the ill-defined principles on behalf of which the war was being fought, but also with its undertakings to de Gaulle. One difficulty has already been touched upon: the impossibility of issuing threats which Vichy would be likely to take seriously. Having promised France, in the person of de Gaulle, that it would do its best to restore the French Empire after the war, the British government could hardly deny this intention in a threat to Vichy. As W. H. B. Mack, the head of the Foreign Office's French department, pointed out in late 1941, the withdrawal of the promise to

The words of the chapter title were used by Churchill as the heading to a minute to the Foreign Secretary and Chiefs of Staff on 8 November 1940: see Minute M. 279 in PREM 3/178/5.

restore France would do more harm than good since it would strengthen the hand of the collaborators, lend colour to French suspicions of British colonial ambitions, and involve, above all, a 'real crisis' with de Gaulle.[1] This should not be exaggerated, however. Long-term threats and promises of this nature carried little weight in Vichy until the British had demonstrated their ability, if not to win, at least to force the Germans to a negotiated peace. More serious in the short term was the fact that by September 1940 de Gaulle appeared to have outlived his usefulness as an instrument for bringing the French Empire back into the war. Supporting heroic resistance suited the mood of June 1940, and fitted in with the assumption that Pétain's government would give way on every point to the Germans. The vigorous resistance of the Vichy authorities to Operation MENACE, however, demonstrated that Vichy was determined to maintain its neutrality and that the British might after all have an interest in the maintenance of the French colonial *status quo*. From September 1940 onwards, the complete identity of interests between the British and the Free French broke down. Although unwilling – and perhaps unable – to abandon de Gaulle altogether, the British came to regard Free France as an obstacle to the establishment of a discreet understanding with Vichy which would keep the French Fleet, bases and colonial produce out of German hands. The fierce fighting which took place in Syria in 1941 also revealed the full extent of the bitterness which forces loyal to Vichy felt for the Free French, and reinforced the British determination to keep de Gaulle firmly in the background in all its dealings with Vichy, and to exclude the Free French from military operations altogether. It was this divergence of interest, more than the clash of personalities, which kept Anglo-Gaullist relations in a state of tension.

Vichy and de Gaulle, then, represent the two major dimensions of the British dilemma. But the issue was further complicated in late 1940 and early 1941, and again in 1942, by British efforts to resolve the problem by establishing an alternative to both: an authority which would rally the French Empire, and perhaps also the Fleet, to the Allied cause, thus relieving them of the embarrassing need to maintain contact with Vichy; and which would at the same time inherit the mantle of de Gaulle and subordinate French resistance to more pliable leadership. This approach, which was mainly favoured by Churchill himself, had as its aim to persuade at least a section of the Vichy government to raise the standard of revolt in North Africa. Hopes rested mainly upon Weygand.[2] Churchill had begun to consider using the General as early as July 1940, and his interest in stimulating him to action was given an enormous impetus when he was removed from the Vichy government in the Cabinet reshuffle in early September and appointed Delegate-General in North Africa. In view of Weygand's undoubted opposition to collaboration with Germany, it did not seem unrealistic to hope that he might be persuaded to bring French North Africa back into the war, and it is clear that if he had done so the British would have obliged de Gaulle to accept his leadership. In the event, however, Churchill's attempt to square the circle failed; he underestimated not only the General's aversion to all forms of dissidence, but also the extent of the military assistance which would be required to goad him into action.

The dilemma posed by France's collapse was therefore a three-sided one. On the one hand, the British government found itself committed in a moral sense to supporting de Gaulle. On the other hand, it was obliged to attend to the distasteful but necessary task of using diplomacy to prevent the Vichy government from drifting too far into a policy of collaboration with Germany. And finally, it sought to escape this contradiction by setting up some alternative body which, although it might derive its authority from Vichy, would establish by its actions a claim to speak for France. From 1940 to 1942 British policy vacillated between these three alternatives without finding a solution in exclusive pursuit of any of them. As Douglas Johnson has noted, there was 'a constant reserve in British policy, a persistent refusal to commit Britain absolutely'.[3] It was the constant awareness of the contradictory demands of principle and expediency which gave to British policy this appearance of hesitancy and uncertainty.

VICHY FRANCE: DIPLOMATIC TWILIGHT, JUNE, 1940 TO FEBRUARY, 1941

Britain's dealings with the Vichy government in the months following the Armistice confront the historian with special problems which stem from the very nature of the relationship which existed between the two countries and from the character and methods of Marshal Pétain and his associates. 'The normal rules of conduct did not apply to our relations with France at the present time', Churchill told the Cabinet in 1940. In the following year he told Eden that nothing like this relationship had ever been seen before in diplomatic history.[4] To some extent, the tortuous nature of British dealings with Vichy reflected the latter's anomalous position in relation to Germany: the fear of reprisals and the desire to establish a basis for collaboration with Germany made Vichy unwilling to enter openly into negotiations with London. At the same time, however, the British blockade and the successes of the Gaullist movement in French Equatorial Africa during the autumn of 1940 awakened Vichy to the need to trim its sails to 'the incipient breeze blowing across the Channel'.[5] As 1940 wore on, Baudouin in particular, his illusions of an early peace destroyed, became increasingly eager to safeguard France's uneasy neutrality by entering into discreet negotiations with the British.

The British were unable to decide what tactics to adopt to meet this situation. On the one hand it could be argued that restraining de Gaulle, relaxing the blockade, and reaffirming the promise to restore the greatness of France in the event of a British victory would re-establish good will and contribute to the re-entry of France and her Empire into the war, while at the same time strengthening the hand of those elements in Vichy which opposed collaboration with Germany. On the other hand, this policy might simply enable Vichy to sit out the war in the minimum of discomfort without committing itself to any action in support of the Allied cause. 'I have an uncomfortable feeling that the French Government are getting the best of both worlds', wrote Halifax in December 1940. Eden, his successor at the Foreign Office, expressed the same view more vigorously. 'The French want us to win the war to rescue them, but they still want to receive the produce of their colonies, even including wine, though they pay toll 80% to the enemy, who will then be better placed to fight us.'[6] Two months later, similar arguments inspired a Foreign Office telegram to Lord Halifax, then British ambassador in Washington: 'Neither the Vichy Government nor their agents in North Africa show any spark of nobility or courage or any active will to resist. They may hope for our victory but will do nothing to help, since if we lose, they may have acquired merit in German eyes, while if we win they assume we shall in any event restore France.'[7]

All the clandestine negotiations conducted between London and Vichy in the late autumn of 1940 foundered on the question of ratification. Marshal Pétain could hardly have been expected to conclude a formal agreement with the British government. The best that could be achieved was to arrive at tacit understandings, which might lapse as circumstances changed. It need come as no surprise that Vichy and London failed to reach a common understanding of their respective positions, or that their tangled negotiations should have given rise to elaborate theories regarding the existence of secret treaties or 'gentlemen's agreements'. Such theories, which were to form the basis of post-war attempts to justify the policy of Marshal Pétain, should be treated with great reserve. Equally without foundation is the argument that, even if formal agreements are absent from the record, their existence can be inferred from a supposed relaxation of the blockade in early 1941. In reality, the blockade was not lifted, but proved impossible to enforce for lack of ships. In the same way, the 'artificial tension' which Pétain is reported to have proposed as a smoke-screen behind which Anglo-French negotiations could be carried forward became real enough in early 1941 as the pace of collaboration quickened.[8]

The problems created by the need for secrecy in dealing with the Vichy government were aggravated by the physical conditions in which Pétain and his ministers were forced to operate. Vichy, a genteel spa in central France, offered no facilities for the efficient conduct of affairs, and the chaos of its surroundings reflected the disarray within the government itself.[9] On 10 July 1940 the Senate and Chamber of Deputies voted to give full constitutional powers to Marshal Pétain. Cabinet solidarity, and with it, responsible control of foreign affairs, became a thing of the past.[10] Pétain, whose deafness put him at a disadvantage in free discussion among large groups, chose instead to work through small, sometimes informal groups in which discussion was not encouraged. Cabinet meetings were held once a week, but the real decisions were made either in private meetings between a minister and Pétain, or in the daily meetings of the *Conseil restreint*, which itself ceased to function after October 1940. It was government by clique.[11]

This arrangement suited Pétain's temperament. By nature secretive and opportunist, he disliked the adoption of clear policies and preferred to allow his ministers to pursue their own, often contradictory, courses, disavowing or even dismissing them if they threatened to commit him irrevocably to their policy. He was helped in this by his mastery of dissimulation. Immured by deafness and great age, he appeared at once a sage and a dotard. It was often difficult for his interlocutors to know if he was listening, or even if he was awake. Nobody enjoyed his confidence, although his habit of agreeing with the point of view of the last person to whom he had spoken gave many the impression that they did. He often gave in to pressure through sheer fatigue.[12] Many have borne witness to his impressive, magisterial bearing, and his calm dignity. Those in frequent contact with him, however, detected the sly peasant behind the mask, Even Admiral Leahy, the American ambassador, who was no judge of men, realised that Pétain might be 'a proud old man, showing amity and confidence for the purpose of getting what he could from America while favouring collaboration'.[13] The conduct of diplomacy with a man of such Buddha-like passivity proved to be virtually impossible. Foreign representatives saw nothing absurd in trying to divine his true feelings from veiled allusions to his 'intimate thoughts', from nods, smiles, gestures, or simply the 'frank, imperturbable gaze of his extraordinary blue eyes'.[14]

Nowhere was the confusion more evident than in the field of foreign affairs. In 1940 Vichy had two Foreign Ministers and two foreign policies conducted without reference to each other – one for the Axis powers, conducted through the Armistice Commission and by Laval's frequent trips to Paris to confer with Otto Abetz, Hitler's 'Ambassador', and the other for Britain and the neutral states, conducted by Baudouin and Charles-Roux through third states or any personal intermediaries who came to hand. Pétain gave tacit approval to both. Much of the inconsistency of Vichy's policy in the latter half of 1940 was a reflection of the bitter struggle between Laval and Baudouin. On the one hand, Baudouin could exploit Pétain's fear of being drawn too far towards collaboration with Germany. On the other hand, he was aware that too obvious an improvement in relations with London would incur the wrath of the Germans and bring about his dismissal. His function, to Pétain, was the essential complement to that of Laval in maintaining a 'prudent balance' between Germany and Britain.[15] It was an intolerable situation, and Laval's *coup* in bringing about the Montoire meeting with Hitler in October eventually forced Baudouin to resign. But Laval's formal assumption of the office of Foreign Minister made little difference. Baudouin continued to involve himself with relations with Britain, and in December helped to engineer Laval's downfall.

Even when allowance is made for the difficulties of his position, however, it remains true that Baudouin's own devious character, and his aversion to clear-cut positions, rendered even more impenetrable the dense jungle of Anglo-French relations. His previous experience of diplomacy was limited, and his amateurism bred contempt among his subordinates. In London he was regarded with universal antipathy, and the profound suspicion aroused by his conduct in June was heightened by the squabble which ensued immediately after the Armistice over his part in smothering the British objections to the terms. By the end of October, dislike had matured into contempt. The Foreign

Office viewed with scorn his attempts to maintain his position by issuing anglophobe statements in public and following them up through diplomatic channels with professions of good will,[16] and there was general agreement with Hankey that these tactics were simply intended to enable Baudouin 'to keep a foot on each side of the ditch'.[17] A suggestion from the Madrid embassy in September that Baudouin was not, perhaps, as anglophobe as he appeared was dismissed by Vansittart as rubbish: 'M. Baudouin has always been our enemy, but we aren't dead yet and he is doing a little reinsurance.' Cadogan also confessed himself unable to detect any signs of grace in the Minister of Foreign Affairs.[18] Nevertheless, however unsatisfactory were London's exchanges with Baudouin, some form of contact was at least possible until his resignation from the Ministry of Foreign Affairs – and indeed for some time afterwards. Laval's arrival at the 'Quai d'Orsay' brought to an end all possibility of negotiation through the normal channels. From November 1940 onwards, the only way to establish contact with the Marshal was by using intermediaries of varying reliability, or by seeking the intervention of the United States. Pierre Flandin's brief period in control of foreign affairs did nothing to restore communications with London, and the ascendancy of Darlan in early 1941 brought all semblance of normal diplomatic intercourse to an end.

Direct communication between the two governments did not long survive the signing of the Armistice. Campbell left Bordeaux on the 24th and although he stressed that this did not constitute a severance of relations it was taken as such by Baudouin. Relations were formally broken off after CATAPULT, on 8 July, by the Marquis de Castellane; Corbin, the French ambassador, and Cambon, the Chargé d'Affaires, had resigned in rapid succession to avoid this heartbreaking task. The Foreign Office had little enthusiasm for maintaining further contact and Cadogan and Strang both argued that the imposition of the blockade, the support of de Gaulle, and the launching of CATAPULT, made it unlikely that exchanges with Bordeaux would be very fruitful.[19] Only Halifax's influence prevented the further estrangement of the two countries. In his reply to Castellane on the 9th he expressed the hope that the French government would not feel constrained 'to widen the breach between the two countries by bringing to an end all diplomatic contacts', and suggested that a representative might be sent to Vichy to settle outstanding matters. For the future, 'His Majesty's Government are firmly convinced that a continuance of relations between the two

Governments is in accord both with the sentiments and with the interests of the British and French peoples.'[20] This was only the first of several occasions on which Halifax was to adopt the position almost of a mediator between the two governments.

Baudouin grudgingly agreed to an exchange of representatives, but the effect of this was nullified by repeated assertions that the British had agreed to France's release from the March agreement and that Campbell had been initially responsible for severing relations. To forestall further conciliatory moves by Halifax, he imposed conditions upon the full resumption of diplomatic relations which he admitted after the war were intended to be unacceptable.[21] Even the exchange of agents proved impossible, for reasons which are difficult to determine. Paul Morand had been accepted as French agent by the British Cabinet on 11 July, and this was confirmed by Castellane on the 15th. Then, on the 25th M. Chartier, the French Consul-General, told the Foreign Office that the British nominee, Nevile Bland, could not be received until fifty French officials detained in London had been released and the dropping of propaganda leaflets over Morocco stopped.[22] At the same time, Morand, apparently on his own initiative, returned to Vichy with the remaining staff of the French mission, including Castellane, who was later to confirm, not only that the two conditions had been pretexts, but also that Morand's return to London had been prevented by German pressure.[23]

What little enthusiasm had existed in the Foreign Office for the maintenance of contact with Vichy was rapidly dissipated by these developments. 'We shall be working the whole time against this Vichy Government,' wrote Cadogan on 26 July, 'for we shall never wean them from German tutelage, and while that remains the situation, I do not think that representation at Vichy would be useful or indeed practicable.' The government should put its money on some other horse. Although this had been done to some extent with de Gaulle, the ultimate aim should be the establishment of an alternative government in North Africa. Strang, too, dwelt on the conflict of aims in policy towards France; the attempt to keep on speaking terms with Vichy while at the same time subjecting it to propaganda attacks, attempting to suborn its troops and detach its colonies: he doubted whether Bland could serve any useful purpose even if he could be got to France.[24] Roger Makins, on the other hand, advanced the argument which was to become all too familiar later in the mouth of the American Secretary of State. If the attempt to maintain contact were abandoned, he suggested, Vichy would drift 'right into the enemy camp'. If it were not, 'we may keep the French somewhere near neutrality and gradually build up a spirit of resistance in France'.[25] This was a plausible line of reasoning, but one which too readily assumed that conciliation – for that was what contact meant – would ignite, rather than extinguish, the flame of resistance. It equally ignored the danger of being led by piecemeal concessions to a policy of appeasement. Once again, however, Halifax was inclined to compromise, and he urged the Cabinet to adopt a conciliatory line in order to maintain contact and gather information as to the real aims and policy of the Vichy government.[26]

This was to no avail. Baudouin's reply on 10 August made it plain that contact would not be resumed unless the British were prepared to refrain from their attempts to detach the French Empire. This was out of the question: as Churchill wrote to Halifax on the 4th, 'Anxious as I am to establish contacts of all kinds, official and unofficial, with defeated France, I hope we shall not be turned at all from the main lines of our war policy.'[27] Baudouin's public utterances were even more un-satisfactory than his diplomatic notes, and on the 24th, Cadogan replied through the Madrid embassy that the Foreign Office was unable to find in the French note any indication of a desire to maintain relations. Even Halifax gave up hope.[28]

Ironically, it was at almost the same time as hope of further contact had been abandoned in London that new initiatives began to be taken in Vichy. The diary of Paul Baudouin, which creates the quite false impression that its author had consistently sought to maintain contact with a reluctant and obstructive Foreign Office since late June, does little to explain the apparent volte-face. It seems to have been partly an attempt to regain the initiative in the struggle with Laval and partly a response to Gaullist successes in Africa and to the threat to French colonial lines of communication posed by the British blockade. Nor could Baudouin fail to be influenced on the one hand by evidence of increasingly anglophile sentiment in France, and on the other hand by the evident failure of the Germans to appreciate the possibility of reconciliation. The true character of Nazi rule had become sufficiently clear by late August to dispel any illusions which Baudouin had entertained on that score.[29]

Baudouin's new approaches were made through Madrid. This was an astute move; the British ambassador, Sir Samuel Hoare, was widely believed to favour a compromise peace and he also enjoyed a cordial relationship with the French ambassador, Count Renom de la Baume, a convinced anglophile. In early September, Hoare began to report signs of a new willingness on the part of the French in Madrid to keep in touch with him.[30] On 3 September de la Baume conveyed a personal message to Halifax pointing out that the encouragement of de Gaulle could only draw the Axis into Morocco and might also drive Spain into the German camp, and on the 13th, this was opened out into a general request for some form of colonial *modus vivendi*.[31]

DE GAULLE FRANCE: OPERATION MENACE[32]

There was little possibility of resuming even unofficial relations with Vichy as long as the British maintained their support of de Gaulle and entertained hopes of the French Empire rallying to his cause. It was only when these had been dashed that the Cabinet was prepared to consider reaching some accommodation with Vichy. And, just as Halifax's temperament made him seek to maintain contact with Vichy, so Churchill's led him to support de Gaulle wholeheartedly in his attempt to bring France back into the war. Neither man enjoyed much departmental support. The permanent officials of the Foreign Office were as sceptical of Halifax's desire to appease Vichy as the Chiefs of Staff were of Churchill's plans to establish de Gaulle in West Africa.

It seemed incomprehensible to Churchill that the French colonial authorities would not seize any opportunity to resume the fight, and there were many indications in early July that the situation was developing favourably, particularly in West Africa, where the civilian population was reported to be strongly pro-Gaullist. The port of Dakar was an attractive prize and in enemy hands would threaten Freetown, a vital convoy assembly point. For de Gaulle, too, possession of Dakar would provide a territorial base as well as control of the French gold which had been deposited there at the time of the collapse. However, it proved impossible for vigorous action to be taken with the necessary speed, and what chance there may have been for a bloodless *coup* rapidly disappeared as Vichy consolidated its authority in the region. On 4 August the Joint Planning Sub-Committee reported that the situation had deteriorated to the point where there was now little chance of the local authorities breaking with Vichy.[33] The Colonial Office and the Chiefs of Staff therefore felt that some sort of local accommodation with the Vichy authorities would provide the best solution, especially since the latter appeared willing to reciprocate. Departmental objections were circumvented, however, and Morton, Spears and de Gaulle drew up a plan to establish the Free French in West Africa to which Churchill gave his approval on 3 August.[34] The Foreign Office was not informed and even the Chiefs of Staff were consulted only as an afterthought.[35]

From the outset, Operation SCIPIO was moved by Churchill's initiative, and imposed upon reluctant planners. There was no definition of the aim of the expedition, and much confusion about the methods it would use. While de Gaulle advocated a show of force off Dakar, with strong naval backing, the Chiefs of Staff were thinking in terms of strictly limited assistance for a primarily Free French expedition which would be abandoned if it met resistance.[36] On 7 August they argued that there was no reasonable prospect of success and warned against the danger of provoking hostilities in a theatre which was not essential to the prosecution of the war and where the further commitments resulting from success or failure were to be avoided at all costs.[37] Churchill responded by taking the chair at the Chiefs of Staff meeting the same night and stifling all further objections at their source.[38] On the following day he issued a firm directive confirming Dakar as the main objective and pledging full British military backing. The risk of a French declaration of war and whether it should be courted was reserved for the Cabinet: it was not for the Chiefs of Staff to concern themselves with the political implications of the military operations they were called upon to plan.[39]

The Joint Planning Staff drew up a plan of action on 9 August which received the endorsement of the Chiefs of Staff the same day. War Cabinet approval followed on the 13th, and with it a change of name, from SCIPIO to MENACE.[40] The Cabinet did not consider it very likely that Vichy would declare war, and even thought it would not matter much if it did – an extraordinary conclusion. As Churchill later wrote, 'I had now become set upon this venture'.[41] Yet the tactical assumptions upon which its success depended proved as dubious as the strategical ones. The military and naval commanders pointed out that, for a variety of technical reasons, the achievement of surprise, and with it, the hope of a bloodless landing, was out of the question. The Chiefs of Staff, thus armed, reverted to their earlier objections. Was MENACE a friendly force to rally the colony, or an expeditionary force to invade it? If this were not decided, they warned, the expedition would fall between two stools. Churchill intervened again, with the Chiefs of Staff on the 20th and the Vice-Chiefs of Staff on the 22nd.[42] Surprise being out of the question, the colony would be invited to rally. If this were rejected, an opposed landing would be carried out. The whole plan had become absurd.

Churchill was determined that the project would be carried through, however, and reports received on the 28th indicating that resistance was to be expected were overshadowed by the rallying of Chad and French Equatorial Africa to de Gaulle on the 26th and 28th, which seemed to show that the French colonies were not as anti-British as had been supposed and that 'resolute action by a few strong men determined to continue the fight will succeed in seeing that others do so'.[43] This optimism was short-lived, however. On 9 September six French cruisers left Toulon harbour, and by the 14th, the three fastest ships were anchored at Dakar. Oddly, it was now Churchill who felt that the fate of the expedition had been sealed and that it should be abandoned forthwith, while the Force Commanders urged continuance. On the 15th, Churchill telephoned Morton and urged that MENACE should revert to SCIPIO – a landing at Conakry. Even this project was abandoned after consultation with the Chiefs of Staff, and on the 16th the Cabinet accepted Churchill's recommendation that de Gaulle should proceed instead to Duala in order to consolidate his recent gains.[44] On the following day, the 17th, the Cabinet met twice to consider unexpectedly vehement appeals from Major-General Irwin and John Cunningham that the expedition should not be called off simply because the odds against success had lengthened still further. Churchill brought the question back to the Cabinet, and on the 18th authority was given to the Force Commanders to 'go ahead and do what you think is best in order to give effect to the original purpose of the expedition'.[45]

It is not proposed to describe the expedition in detail.[46] On the 23rd, the Anglo-Gaullist force arrived off Dakar. Heavy fog prevented it from overawing the garrison. Two of de Gaulle's aeroplanes landed at the airfield and their pilots were arrested. Emissaries, despatched by boat under a flag of truce, were fired upon from the shore. A general engagement ensued in which two British destroyers were slightly damaged and the *Cumberland* was hit in the engine room. When this was reported to Churchill that night, he replied, 'Having begun we must go through to the end. Stop at nothing.'[47] Boisson, in his turn, replied to an ultimatum that he would fight to the last. On the 24th the engagement was resumed in slightly improved visibility. The *Richelieu* sustained further damage and a Vichy submarine was sunk. On the following day, the *Barham* and the *Resolution* were both hit, the latter with serious effect. Around the middle of the day, the Force Commanders and the Cabinet came independently to the conclusion that the action should be called off, and the expedition returned to Freetown on the 29th.

The project was a complete fiasco. Appalling mistakes had been made. Equipment was unsuitable. There were constant postponements because of technical difficulties of the most elementary kind, such as faulty loading and miscalculations concerning the speed of the supply ships. Worst of all, security had broken down almost completely. It later became fashionable in British circles to blame the Free French for this, and de Gaulle's movement was never able to shake off the reputation for 'leakiness' which it acquired at this time. But British indiscretions had been as marked, as the British records make clear.[48] Nevertheless, such mistakes, however shocking, do not go to the root of the failure of MENACE, for which responsibility must be laid at Churchill's door. His own account, stressing bad luck and bad planning, ignores the most fundamental cause of failure – his refusal to be swayed by the advice of the Chiefs of Staff. On any dispassionate calculation of the odds, the plan had no chance of success and should have been dismissed on this basis alone. As Marder concludes, ' "Menace" is an object lesson on how a combined operation should *not* be conducted by politicians and High Command in Whitehall.'[49]

RETHINKING POLICY, SEPTEMBER–OCTOBER 1940

The main lines of British policy towards Vichy had been formed as a spontaneous reaction to the circumstances surrounding the signature of the Armistice. The Cabinet had never been called upon to consider whether contact with Vichy should be maintained, and no attempt had been made to resolve the contradiction which existed between the support of the Free French and the continuance of relations with Vichy. The British policy before the Armistice of securing the maximum French resistance had continued into the period after the collapse without any serious discussion of whether widespread revolt against Vichy's authority would really be in Britain's interest or not.

The British attitude of uncompromising belligerence in the summer and autumn of 1940 encouraged the government, and Churchill in particular, to view the French situation in terms of heroic resistance or abject surrender. It followed from this that the authorities in Dakar were expected either to rally enthusiastically to de Gaulle or remain supine. Intelligence reports received in August and September about feeling in West Africa had been mixed, and some had indicated that vigorous resistance might be met. These warning notes had been ignored, however, and the violent reaction of the Dakar garrison had come as a severe shock. 'We had, perhaps, accepted too readily the rosy estimate of the operation which had been given by General de Gaulle's supporters, and we had been misled by people on the spot as to the feeling of the French Forces at Dakar,' wrote Halifax.[50] It was apparent for the first time that loyalty to Vichy did not necessarily imply any lack of fighting spirit and that the French colonial authorities might after all be relied upon to resist Axis encroachments. It also followed that resistance to the Axis might not be synonymous with support for de Gaulle.

The failure of MENACE, in short, lent powerful support to the view that the British government had a common interest with Vichy in maintaining, instead of undermining, Vichy's authority in the French Empire. For some time before the expedition, support had been growing in London for a less belligerent policy. Halifax had always been inclined personally towards moderation and the Foreign Office as a whole, although less sanguine about the possibilities of maintaining useful contact with Vichy, was as yet unconvinced of the wisdom of supporting de Gaulle. 'All the Dakar and Libreville schemes will only do us harm, even if they did succeed,' wrote Cadogan.[51] The Chiefs of Staff had urged from the outset that Britain should avoid being drawn into conflicts which could have only a marginal effect upon the outcome of the war and which might involve hostilities with the French, and they were supported in this by the Admiralty, which lacked the resources to make the blockade of France and the French Empire effective and feared that its efforts to enforce it would lead to naval conflict. At the beginning of September, for example, the Chiefs of Staff argued that 'for the present our aim should be to maintain the stability of any Government not actively hostile to us, particularly in West Africa, where any upheaval might endanger our interests, while we ourselves are so weak in that area'.[52]

After MENACE, the case for a *modus vivendi* with Vichy was put forward even more urgently. On 30 September the Admiralty argued that British policy towards Vichy 'should be largely governed by the need to keep the calls upon our naval forces (other than for operations against

Germany or Italy) down to a minimum'. Vichy forces in North Africa could easily render Gibraltar untenable, thereby destroying Britain's naval position in the Western Mediterranean and with it all hopes of striking at Italy or of preventing supplies from West Africa reaching ports in Unoccupied France.[53] Halifax in his turn warned the Cabinet on 1 October that 'if we did not play our cards wisely we might find ourselves drifting into something like hostilities with the Vichy Government. . . . The line of country that we had to ride was tricky; none of us wished to start eating out of the hand of an uncertain Vichy, yet there was a considerable case for informing Vichy of what we wanted, what we would stand and what we would not stand.' Halifax argued that the present blockade policy was getting the worst of both worlds. Tunisia, Algeria and Morocco were nominally subject to contraband and enemy export control in the same way as Metropolitan France, but the blockade was not in fact effective. 'Cargoes pass from Algiers to Marseilles and from Casablanca to Bordeaux, and yet we continue to incur the odium of the so-called blockade among the population in North Africa and it is made a cause of grievance by the authorities.' In the rest of the Empire, the general policy was to exert economic pressure upon those French colonies which did not elect to join de Gaulle – 'join de Gaulle or starve' – with exceptions in special cases. In fact, however, if Vichy were organising the French Empire for resistance, 'it would plainly be to our advantage that the economic position of the French Empire should be strengthened rather than weakened'. 'Our main purpose in all this must surely be clear', he concluded. 'It is to secure that the French Colonial Empire should be healthily anti-German and anti-Italian and be got to act accordingly. Provided it will so act, it is immaterial to us whether it be under leaders that will not break with Vichy, or under de Gaulle.'[54]

These arguments brought about a significant change of emphasis in British policy. From henceforth it came to be accepted, albeit grudgingly, that an aggressive policy based on subversion or attack would not be fruitful. The British were discouraging towards further Free French adventures and the Gaullist liberation of Gabon in November was brought off without direct British assistance.[55] For the next few months, the main impetus of British policy towards the French Empire was in the direction of bringing it back into the war under its own leadership. Even when this, in its turn, had failed to bear fruit, there was no question of reverting to the aggressive policy of the pre-Dakar period. Action against Vichy's overseas possessions was taken only in response to what were regarded as pressing strategic demands, as was the case in Syria in May 1941.

For the rest, Halifax's enthusiasm for a *modus vivendi* won little support in the Cabinet, and Churchill's own attitude was defiant. 'It would be a great mistake', he argued, 'to fall into a mood of being afraid of offending Vichy, or trying to "kiss and make friends".'[56] Although he grudgingly agreed to the resumption of negotiations in Madrid, Churchill opposed any general softening of approach and insisted that Vichy, far from drifting into hostilities with Britain, would actually respond better to a policy of toughness. He expanded upon this theme in a minute to the Chiefs of Staff on 15 October.

We cannot accept that we must yield to the wishes of Vichy out of fear, lest they make air raids upon Gibraltar; for there would be no end to that. . . . Of course, if we could be assured that Vichy, or part of Vichy, were genuinely moving in our direction, we could ease up on them to a very large extent. It seems probable that they will be increasingly inclined to move as we desire, and I personally do not believe that hard pressure from us will prevent this favourable movement. It is becoming more difficult every day for Vichy to lead France into war with us. We must not be too afraid of checking this process, because the tide in our favour will master and overwhelm the disturbing eddies of the blockade, de Gaulle and possible sea incidents.

I agree with the Admiralty suggestion that, if unhappily Vichy should attack Gibraltar again by air, we should reply by attacking not Casablanca, but Vichy itself, or any other place to which that caitiff government might resort.[57]

As far as the blockade was concerned, the outcome of the Cabinet discussions was mixed, for while it was agreed to pursue negotiations with Vichy which might lead to its relaxation, it was at the same time decided to enforce the blockade of the Straits more rigidly. On the 18th the Cabinet agreed in principle to apply contraband control even to escorted convoys passing Gibraltar, although no interceptions actually took place until January 1941.[58] Negotiations over a possible *modus vivendi* proved to be equally inconclusive, and the situation in Vichy steadily worsened towards the year's end. On 24 October, Pétain's meeting with Hitler at Montoire made it clear that Vichy's main aim was to reach an accommodation with Germany, not with Britain. The replacement of de la Baume by François Piétri as ambassador in Madrid underlined this. In November and December 1940, with Laval and then Pierre Flandin in charge of foreign affairs, official exchanges over a proposed colonial *modus vivendi* ceased altogether, to be resumed in January with the quite unacceptable French demand for navicerts to import enormous quantities of wheat and maize into France. At the same time, it was revealed that the Germans had been informed of the negotiations, which the British took as a sign of bad faith.[59] Anthony Eden, the new Foreign Secretary, refused to consider any request for supplies to Metropolitan France and insisted that the discussions should be confined to Morocco. The Madrid negotiations had thus virtually ground to a halt even before the Germans ordered them to be broken off on 13 February. 'It seems almost impossible to establish contact with these people', remarked Strang.[60]

BACKSTAIRS DIPLOMACY, OCTOBER, 1940 – JANUARY, 1941

While negotiations went forward in a somewhat desultory fashion in Madrid, relations between Britain and Vichy France became considerably complicated by parallel negotiations conducted in London, Algiers and Vichy which intertwined bewilderingly with the exchanges through the two ambassadors in Spain. After the war, a number of accounts appeared which claimed that the British government had reached agreements with Vichy which had been embodied in secret treaties or 'gentlemen's agreements'. In reality, the negotiations which aroused the greatest interest after the war were those of least significance at the time. This comment applies in particular to the mission of Professor Louis Rougier, who came to London in late October with Pétain's knowledge and consent and held discussions with Churchill and Halifax. Rougier had no power to negotiate and the Prime Minister conveyed no message to Pétain by his hand. He was thought to be useful, however, in persuading General Weygand of the high state of morale in Britain and the certainty of British victory. The professor therefore drew up an *aide-mémoire* of points which he proposed to make to Weygand and which he submitted to the Foreign Office for approval. He then returned, first to Algiers and then to Vichy.

After the war, Rougier published a number of accounts of his mission in which he claimed to have been the negotiator of a 'gentlemen's agreement' between Britain and France. According to him, Vichy undertook to defend its colonies and bases from German control and to refrain from any attempt to win back its dissident colonies by force or to interfere with those which declared spontaneously for de Gaulle. At an opportune moment, France would re-enter the war at England's side. In return, the British government was alleged to have agreed to abstain from interference in colonies loyal to Vichy and from personal attacks upon the Marshal himself. Trade between French North Africa and Unoccupied France would be treated as coastal trade and effectively exempted from the blockade. After the war, Britain would effect the full restoration of France and its overseas possessions. To lend colour to his story, Rougier published a number of documents, including a photostat copy of the first page of the *aide-mémoire*, altered in a small but vital sense to give it the appearance of a draft treaty. He then concocted additional pages in which the British made undertakings to relax the blockade and to restrain de Gaulle from further activities in Africa, in return for assurances from Pétain about the future of the French Fleet and colonial bases. These allegations were a source of considerable embarrassment to the British government when they were published in 1945 because they appeared to demonstrate that it had condoned and even encouraged the 'double game' with the Germans which Pétain was supposed to have played and which formed the basis of the defence at his trial. A White Paper was eventually produced refuting Rougier's allegations, and the whole mythology of secret treaties and gentlemen's agreements was later dismantled by General Schmitt. Despite this, however, the retrospective incorporation of Rougier's fictions into numerous later accounts has lent them a quite spurious authority which repeated debunkings have never quite removed.[61]

This is partly because, like all convincing lies, Rougier's story contained a leavening of truth. The British blockade *had* been virtually suspended, and radio attacks on Pétain had been stopped because they were thought to be counter-productive. Similarly, the British had no intention of trying to enlarge de Gaulle's conquests: a tacit agreement not to upset the colonial *status quo* was in fact the basis of the policy which Halifax had urged on the Cabinet after the failure of MENACE. However, the important point is that none of these issues formed the subject of any express agreement with Vichy, and that Vichy made no commitments to the British in return. The Rougier mission added nothing of substance to the abortive negotiations in Madrid.

It is only fair to add, however, that the most damaging of Rougier's allegations – that the British had agreed with Vichy to keep de Gaulle on a tight leash – was very seriously considered by the Foreign Office. Halifax, Cadogan and Strang all agreed in November on an *aide-*

mémoire proposing that 'we will hold back de Gaulle if Vichy does not attack him or any other French territories that may spontaneously come over in the future'. Cadogan, in particular, felt that de Gaulle was a 'loser' and should be played down, and that the promise to restrain him might be worth making.[62] This was as far as the matter went, however; de Gaulle would certainly not have agreed to such a formal undertaking, and he made clear to Halifax and Cadogan on 28 November that in his view, the attempt to negotiate a *modus vivendi* could postpone, but not prevent, the taking of 'irrevocable decisions' by Vichy. In the meantime, the British attempts to improve relations with Vichy would cause grave offence to the vast majority of French people.[63] What really caused the question to be dropped, however, was the attitude of the Prime Minister. Although the suggestion that de Gaulle might be restrained was twice put forward in draft telegrams to Madrid, on each occasion Churchill struck it out.[64] No formal assurance to hold back de Gaulle was made at this or any other time.

The main importance of the Rougier mission was that it gave an added impetus to Lord Halifax's efforts to establish some form of direct contact with Pétain which would circumvent the blockage in the Madrid negotiations caused by the return of Laval to the Ministry of Foreign Affairs after the Montoire meeting. As long as Laval remained in power, no useful purpose could be served by exchanging messages through Madrid. The Foreign Office telegram of 27 November inviting Vichy's participation in economic discussions was blocked by him, and did not become known to the rest of the government until after his fall.[65] Similarly, the appeal which was sent to Pétain in the King's name at the time of Montoire, although drawn up by Halifax and Cadogan in almost obsequious terms, received an abrupt and ungracious reply which Laval had drafted.[66]

Even after his dramatic removal from power on 13 December, little progress was made towards improving the climate between the two governments. Pierre Flandin, whose appointment was welcomed cautiously by the Foreign Office and with misplaced enthusiasm by Churchill, did nothing to restore communications with London. It seems likely that his appointment was intended as a gesture of compromise towards both London and Berlin, and Pétain insisted in his speech on 14 December that Laval's removal would not affect relations with Germany. Measures set in train by Laval were continued, discussions about the recapture of Chad went on as before and the Armistice Commission functioned without interruption. The real reason for Laval's dismissal had been the incompatibility of his temperament with that of the Marshal. To keep him out of office, Pétain was willing to give way on every point of substance.

Flandin's appointment aroused little comment in London although, as Cadogan remarked, it could not possibly be a change for the worse.[67] The Foreign Office hoped that Laval's removal might enable relations to be resumed in Berne (where de la Baume had been transferred), but nothing came of this. In Madrid, David Eccles, the representative of the Ministry of Economic Warfare, had some contact with Captain Delaye, the French Naval Attaché, but their exchanges were fruitless. Despite these setbacks, however, Halifax remained willing to put the best possible interpretation upon the actions of the Vichy government, and in an important memorandum to the Cabinet on 19 December he called for a policy which would combine firmness with a 'sympathetic understanding' of Vichy's difficulties. In particular, he suggested that Vichy's reluctance to enter into paper commitments was really intended only to prevent German suspicions from being aroused. Like Hoare in Madrid, Halifax had become convinced that new techniques of diplomacy had to be devised to deal with 'these captive and semi-captive Governments', and the Foreign Office began in November to explore more unorthodox methods of making contact with Vichy.[68] The Rougier mission pointed the way, by demonstrating how direct access to the Marshal might be gained by the use of personal intermediaries who could short-circuit diplomatic channels.[69] At the same time, Mr Frankowski, who had been Polish Chargé d'Affaires in Vichy, arrived in London and urged the Foreign Office to adopt a more conciliatory line with the Vichy government.

This approach was exactly what Halifax sought to adopt, and one which the Montoire meeting seemed to him to make more, not less, desirable. The difficulty was to secure the Prime Minister's endorsement. A preliminary skirmish took place at the beginning of November, when it was rumoured that the Vichy government intended to move the *Jean Bart* and *Richelieu* into the Mediterranean. Churchill, irked by the inbuilt tendency towards appeasement of Halifax's Vichy policy, warned that 'we must not allow ourselves to become obsessed with the idea that we must never in any circumstances offer provocation to the Vichy Government. That obsession might bring great dangers in its train.' Halifax replied rather lamely that 'we were conducting our relations with the Vichy Government in a kind of twilight, in which we have to balance opposing risks'.[70] A week later Halifax again warned of the danger of French reprisals if the ships were sunk.[71] A full discussion of policy was obviously needed; de Gaulle was becoming restive at the growing signs of Halifax's willingness to appease Vichy, while at the same time a conflict was developing within the government between the Foreign Office and the Admiralty, who were concerned at all costs to avoid a naval conflict with Vichy, and the Minister of Economic Warfare, angry at what he saw as efforts to dismantle the blockade behind his back.[72] On 15 November the matter was brought before the Cabinet.

Sir Ronald Campbell's minute covering his discussions with Mr Frankowski was the starting point for the discussion. Frankowski first dwelt on the way in which the state of mind of the men of Vichy had changed since the capitulation. The early expectation of a British defeat had given way to a mood of heart-searching and indecision. Some hoped for a British victory. Others, such as Laval, were convinced that, whatever the outcome, France would have to seek an accommodation with Germany. The French people had faith in the Marshal and tolerated Laval because they believed him capable of 'wangling' concessions from the Germans. Pétain was still in control and constantly acted without informing Laval. Frankowski recommended that the British should 'rigidly abstain' from abuse of the Vichy government, even including Laval. Verbal attacks could embitter them, but not remove them from office. In any case, the alternatives were so much worse. At the same time, although it would be wrong to withdraw support from de Gaulle, it would be advisable to refrain from throwing into relief the conflict between him and the Vichy government. Some relaxation of the blockade, if only symbolic, should be made.

The most important recommendation was that Britain should establish contacts with Vichy 'through one or more carefully selected unofficial agents who could go there inconspicuously on some plausible pretext or other'. In this way, they could be encouraged gradually to show greater resistance to German pressure. Campbell added his personal endorsement to these views: 'We must get at them individually.' The right policy would be to try to lead them gradually along. 'They will be shy and timid at first, but if we can persuade them individually that we have no personal animus against them, and as our prospects of destroying the Nazi regime improve, there is at least a chance that they may come round.' The Vichy government was not as hostile to Britain as it had to pretend to be. 'We should try to persuade them that we realise their difficulties, just as we expect them to realise ours. If we can do this we may get to a position where we can discuss things (very secretly) with a measure at least of mutual understanding.' The alternative was to drift into a virtual state of war.[73]

Churchill's response sums up his attitude to Vichy so well that it is given here in full:

Although revenge has no part in politics, and we should always be looking forward rather than looking back, it would be a mistake to suppose that a solution of our difficulties with Vichy will be reached by a policy of mere conciliation and forgiveness. The Vichy Government is under heavy pressure from Germany, and there is nothing that they would like better than to feel a nice, soft, cosy, forgiving England on their other side. This would enable them to win minor favours from Germany at our expense, and hang on as long as possible to see how the war goes. We, on the contrary, should not hesitate when our interests require it, to confront them with difficult and rough situations, and make them feel that we have teeth as well as Hitler.

It must be remembered that these men have committed acts of baseness which have earned them the lasting contempt of the world, and that they have done this without the slightest authority from the French people. Laval is certainly filled with the bitterest hatred of England, and is reported to have said that he would like to see us *crabouillés*, which means squashed so as to leave only a grease spot. Undoubtedly, if he had the power, he would have marketed the unexpected British resistance with his German masters to secure a better price for French help in finishing us off. Darlan is mortally envenomed by the injury we have done to his fleet. Pétain has always been an anti-British defeatist, and is now a dotard. The idea that we can build on such men is vain. They may, however, be forced by rising opinion in France, and by German severities, to change their line in our favour. Certainly we should have contacts with them. But in order to promote such favourable tendencies, we must make sure the Vichy folk are kept well ground between the upper and nether millstones of Germany and Britain. In this way they are most likely to be brought into a more serviceable mood during the short run which remains to them.[74]

The difference of view expressed in these memoranda was never resolved, and policy towards Vichy was to remain, as it had been from the outset, pragmatic and opportunistic, a series of *ad hoc* responses rather than a consistently pursued policy. Within two years, Churchill himself was to put forward with equal conviction the views he so eloquently condemned on this occasion (see pp. 134–7).

THE DUPUY MISSIONS TO VICHY, 1940–2

The decision to approach individuals within the Vichy government, which the Cabinet sanctioned, gave rise to a number of suggestions in the closing weeks of 1940. The most drastic, a proposal by Lord Swinton to bribe Laval himself, met with an unenthusiastic response. As Cadogan pointed out, Laval's attitude was dictated by the belief that Germany would win the war; it would therefore take a very large sum to persuade him to throw over his German friends. In any case, what useful service could Laval provide, once bought? Even if he could be coaxed into the British camp in this way, 'we should have handicapped ourselves with an incubus'. The matter was resolved on the following day by Laval's dismissal from office, and Churchill wrote on 15 December that he was no longer worth buying.[75] The bribing of members of the Vichy government held little attraction for the Foreign Office. When Malvy, the father-in-law of Marcel Peyrouton, the Vichy Minister of the Interior, suggested in January 1941 that for a million dollars his son-in-law would work for the Allied cause, Cadogan retorted: 'What sort of resurrection of France do we expect to buy for a million dollars a month? Can we expect that for cash M. Malvy can deliver to us the soul of France?'[76]

None of the proposals considered by the Foreign Office in the autumn of 1940 came to fruition because an apparently more reliable intermediary came to hand in the person of Pierre Dupuy, a French Canadian who had lived and worked in France since 1919, first in the office of the Canadian High Commissioner in Paris, and from 1931 to 1940 as Secretary of the Canadian Legation. In 1940, as Chargé d'Affaires, he began to press the Foreign Office to use him as an intermediary with the Vichy government, and at British prompting, the Canadian government agreed in October that Dupuy should proceed to Vichy to act on behalf of the British government. Exactly what he was supposed to convey to Vichy is difficult to establish. At the same time it was later to form part of the evidence put forward at the Pétain trial in support of yet another 'secret agreement' with London, although for some reason, perhaps because Rougier's allegations had acted as a lightning conductor, the evidence of an agreement produced by Jacques Chevalier, Secretary-General of the Vichy Ministry of Education in 1940, failed to cause much stir in 1945.[77]

Before Dupuy's departure for Vichy on 13 November, he had at least two meetings with Halifax, although the British record does not disclose exactly what was said. The minutes of the Cabinet meeting on 12 November suggest that Dupuy's brief extended no further than 'to cultivate good relations with Vichy and report at once any promising openings'.[78] Dupuy, however, had a somewhat larger view of his task. He explained in 1945 that he understood his mission to be to enquire into the state of mind of Pétain and his entourage, to tell the French that Britain was determined to continue the fight and that there was no question of a compromise peace, to say that His Majesty's Government's requirements would be met if the French Fleet and Empire remained under French control, and to find out whether Vichy intended to recapture the colonies which had rallied to de Gaulle.[79] The visit was therefore intended to be of an exploratory nature only.

On 20 November Dupuy arrived in Vichy and on the 24th had the first of four interviews with the Marshal. The latter seemed tired and sleepy at the start of the conversation, although on other occasions when Dupuy met him, he appeared alert and decisive. More seriously, although he assured Dupuy that 'I am obliged officially to maintain the balance between both sides, but you know where my sympathies lie', Pétain seemed willing to contemplate the surrender of colonial bases to the Germans, regarding this as only 'passive' collaboration.[80] After this first meeting, it proved difficult for Dupuy to gain access to the Marshal. He therefore looked around for somebody who enjoyed his confidence and with whom he was in regular communication, settling finally upon Jacques Chevalier, the Secretary-General of the Ministry of Education, who had been a close friend of Halifax's at Oxford. Dupuy established contact by saying that Halifax wished to be remembered to him.[81] According to Dupuy, therefore, the idea of using Chevalier as an intermediary was his own. This is difficult to accept. Halifax was pressing the Cabinet to endorse a policy of pursuing individual contacts with the Vichy government, and with such a strategy in mind, it seems incredible that he did not propose to Dupuy the use of his old friend Chevalier as an intermediary. No record of Halifax's talks with Dupuy was kept, however, so the question remains open.

On 4 December Dupuy approached Chevalier. According to the latter's testimony at the Pétain trial, he wrote down, at Dupuy's dictation, a verbal message from Lord Halifax, calling for the resumption of Anglo-French contacts behind a façade of 'artificial tension'. All that the British asked was that the French should defend their colonies and Fleet from the Germans. ('Vous avez deux poumons, les colonies et la marine.') Vichy should also refrain from trying to reconquer the Gaullist territories. In return, the British would agree to a *modus vivendi* allowing the passage through the blockade of foodstuffs, medical supplies, petrol, lubricants, and coal.[82] It is not possible to establish from the available evidence the origin of this message in either of its forms. Schmitt suggests that Chevalier and Dupuy 'camouflaged' the hint ('toute l'aide et tout l'appui') of support for a French resumption of hostilities in order to obtain the Marshal's agreement to a *projet d'accord* which they submitted to him on 6 December.[83] The British record, however, which of course depends entirely upon the accounts provided by Dupuy on his return and later, in 1945, makes no mention of any written proposals. The suggestion that a state of artificial tension should be maintained between the two countries is made to originate, not in a proposal of Halifax's, but from Pétain, Darlan and Huntziger.[84] Even the metaphor about France's two lungs, which in Chevalier's account is contained in Halifax's message, appears in Dupuy's report as a statement by Pétain.[85] In short, the Chevalier account suggests a strong British initiative, while the Dupuy account suggests precisely the opposite.

It seems most likely that Dupuy, like Rougier, allowed his eagerness to play a part to get the better of his judgement. There is little doubt that Halifax did speak to Dupuy along the lines of the verbal account which Dupuy is alleged to have given to Chevalier (see pp. 78–9). Whether he was authorised to present Halifax's views so frankly and fully, however, is unclear. It is even possible that Halifax presented the Dupuy mission to the Cabinet as a purely exploratory one, but intimated to Dupuy that he himself favoured a conciliatory line and that if satisfactory assurances were given, the blockade would be relaxed. Some support is given to this conjecture by the fact that, as the Foreign Office remarked, Pétain seemed to be under the impression that he was dealing with Lord Halifax personally and not with the British government.[86] On arrival in Vichy, Dupuy probably became alarmed by Pétain's vagueness on the question of the colonial bases, and by rumours of the discussions then taking place in Paris concerning the recapture of Chad.[87] In what appeared to be a critical situation, he may have created the impression that he was empowered to negotiate, and have made suggestions – such as that petroleum products would be allowed through the blockade into Unoccupied France – which Halifax probably conveyed to him for his own information but which went beyond what the Cabinet was prepared to concede. Since Dupuy is our main witness, this is difficult to prove, but it seems the most likely explanation.

The rest of the 'negotiation' is equally difficult to unravel. According to Chevalier, Pétain approved the memorandum which he had copied out at Dupuy's dictation, with the single reservation that the word 'tension' should be replaced by 'coldness'.[88] Chevalier therefore drew up, with Dupuy, a long 'report or memorandum' which was included in a *projet d'accord*. The long report has never been produced: no copy was kept. At Pétain's trial, however, Chevalier indicated that it included an agreement to maintain the colonial *status quo* in return for a vague promise of British 'support'. The BBC was to abstain from interfering in France's affairs (in fact, radio attacks on Marshal Pétain had already been stopped in November because they were thought to be counter-productive) and, most important, it was agreed to allow petrol to pass through the blockade into France.[89] On 6 December, according to Chevalier, Pétain expressed his full agreement with the *projet d'accord*. Nothing, however, was signed. On the following day, Dupuy left for London, and on the 9th Vichy received from him a telegram, 'Tout va bien.' Chevalier claimed that this, by prior agreement, was meant to convey the British government's assent. This was absurd: the text could not have been conveyed to London, deciphered, discussed and agreed to in three days. In fact, there was no text of a *projet d'accord* any more than there was a text of a Halifax memorandum. If Dupuy intimated to Pétain that satisfactory assurances concerning the Fleet, the Empire and the Gaullist colonies would bring about the cessation of anti-Vichy propaganda and the exemption of petrol supplies from the blockade, he exceeded his authority.

Nevertheless there is a fairly close correspondence between the assurances which Chevalier claimed Pétain had given and those which Dupuy conveyed to Halifax on his return to England. The main difference is that Dupuy's report did not reveal what hints or suggestions Dupuy may have made in order to elicit those assurances. The other significant difference is that whereas Chevalier's post-war account gave the impression that only he and Pétain had been involved, Dupuy made it clear that both Darlan and Huntziger played an active part. On 19 December Halifax gave the following account to the Cabinet:

I saw Mr. Dupuy before he left London for Vichy and informed him fully of our exchanges with the Vichy Government and what our requirements were. Mr. Dupuy, who is now on his way back to London, saw Marshal Pétain twice. On the second occasion he saw the Marshal and Admiral Darlan together. Admiral Darlan told him that the French Government would resist German pressure on them to attack the de Gaulle colonies, anyway until February, and possibly longer. . . .
He added that there was now no question of Germany being granted the use of French metropolitan or African bases. If the German pressure became irresistible, they would invite us in time to take the bases over. Admiral Darlan was confident that the French ships would have time to leave metropolitan harbours, but if not they would scuttle themselves. Mr. Dupuy asked Marshal Pétain if he agreed with these views and the Marshal said 'Yes.' Darlan also gave a definite assurance that the French Fleet would not become embroiled with the British Fleet and in particular that it would not attack French colonies. Mr. Dupuy has formed the opinion that Marshal Pétain is genuinely anxious for a British victory. . . .
Mr. Dupuy points out that it is inevitable that, outwardly at least, a deterioration of relations should continue between His Majesty's Government and the French Government. If it looked as if we were working together Germany would intervene. Behind this outward tension France is praying for a British victory. It is, however, essential to move with caution and to avoid premature action.

Halifax concluded that the policy of firmness tempered with a sympathetic understanding of France's plight had been the correct one to adopt.[90]

THE FINAL BREAK, JANUARY–FEBRUARY 1941

The Dupuy mission, which at the end of 1940 seemed likely to usher in a period of renewed clandestine contact with Vichy, instead helped to hasten the final rupture. By exaggerating the desire for agreement existing in both governments, Dupuy had hoped to establish the basis for further exchanges. Instead, he succeeded only in convincing the Vichy government that no further exchanges were necessary. It seemed in Vichy that the British were prepared to allow France to seek as comfortable a position as possible, and that the 'British problem' had been to a large extent stabilised. There seemed everything to lose and nothing to gain by continued exchanges, since the British would simply press for a more vigorous defence of the French Empire against Axis encroachments, and in return would offer only to relax a blockade which was in any case ineffective. The highest priority for Vichy in late 1940 and early 1941 was the normalisation of relations with Germany, not the continuation of negotiations with Britain.

If Dupuy had unwittingly succeeded in persuading Pétain that all was well with London, he had at the same time aroused expectations in the British government which stood no chance of fulfilment. On 21 December he reported to Churchill that Pétain, Darlan and Huntziger had spoken to him about the possibility of co-operation in North Africa and continental France 'under this vital condition – that the present atmosphere of tension between Great Britain and France be maintained as a smoke screen, behind which contacts could be made and information exchanged'.[91] The suggestion was seized upon by Churchill with an enthusiasm which put Dupuy in an extremely awkward position, since he was well aware that an offer of military assistance in North Africa stood no chance of acceptance. However, apart from suggesting rather weakly that Pétain should not be 'rushed', there was nothing he could do to reverse the new initiative which his own report had prompted.[92]

On the 24th Churchill put the question of offering military aid in North Africa to the Chiefs of Staff, who suggested that a force of six divisions should be specified. Even if the offer were not immediately taken up, as Cadogan pointed out, it might 'ferment'.[93] It was communicated by two separate channels to General Weygand in January, and fell upon deaf ears. It met with a similar response from Pétain, as might have been expected. The Chiefs of Staff had pointed out that there was not much point in communicating such a message through Flandin. It was therefore telegraphed to Washington and transmitted to the American Embassy in Vichy for delivery to the Marshal by Chevalier. This whole manoeuvre, however, was rendered futile by the latter's supreme *gaffe* in delivering the message in Flandin's presence. Pétain, deeply embarrassed, burnt the text and announced, 'We have not received it.'[94] The offer was repeated at the end of January, once more without result. Pétain never deviated from his resolve not to leave the soil of France. As Chevalier himself made clear to the American Chargé d'Affaires, not even the total occupation of France would persuade Pétain to depart for North Africa.[95]

Although Dupuy was to retain a measure of personal support from Churchill, Halifax's departure for Washington, and the evident failure of his efforts to maintain discreet but reliable channels of communication with Vichy, caused a sudden and permanent decline in his standing in the Foreign Office. To a certain extent this stemmed from Eden's natural desire, on assuming office, to have done with the whole apparatus of backstairs diplomacy which had reduced Britain's policy towards Vichy to such an unsatisfactory muddle. Although willing to improve contacts with Vichy, Eden was more inclined at first to do so by conventional means, by sending a Treasury representative to France to settle outstanding financial matters and to maintain contact at the same time.[96] Eden was equally unhappy with the maintenance of 'artificial tension' with Vichy, and with the notion that British dealings with Vichy should, behind this smoke-screen, be basically cordial. The aim of British policy was not to make the Marshal's life easier.[97] There were abundant signs also that Dupuy was poorly suited to the delicate task which he had undertaken, and the Foreign Office soon began to suspect that he had exceeded his brief. Eden expressed his irritation that Dupuy had suggested in Vichy that the blockade might be relaxed, and Cadogan noted with disapproval his desire to be a negotiator rather than a postman.[98] Equally damaging was his lack of discretion; within days of his return from Vichy, news of his interviews had reached the pages of the Chicago *Daily News*. Later in 1941 the Foreign Office, the Dominions Office, and the three Services were ordered to exercise extreme caution in all their dealings with him.[99]

After his first visit to Vichy, therefore, the British had no further use for Dupuy. His assessment of the situation in Vichy had been too optimistic and his main contact, Chevalier, had proved himself to be inept.[100] His usefulness diminished still further in 1941. Chevalier, hopelessly compromised, was eventually dismissed from office. Huntziger was killed in an air crash in November. More important, Darlan, who replaced Flandin in February, and who dominated Vichy for the next twelve months, refused to see him – as, eventually, did Pétain also.[101] Since Dupuy was a Canadian and not a British diplomat, there was little the Foreign Office could do to prevent his frequent trips to Vichy. Very little attention was given to his views, however, and the voluminous reports which he produced from time to time were greeted with mounting irritation in London. A shrewd Cadogan observed, after meeting Dupuy on his return from his second trip to Vichy in March, that he was inclined to paint a rather rosy picture and to report things as he would wish them to be, and Morton commented scathingly that Dupuy's assessments of personalities and events were so wrong as to be dangerous, and he should be allowed further contact with Vichy only for the purpose of misleading them.[102]

By early 1941, therefore, all efforts to establish contact with the Vichy government had failed and the policy of approaching individuals had largely gone by default because no reliable intermediaries had come to hand. Both Rougier and Dupuy, because of their sympathy with Pétain and their eagerness to gain the credit for restoring Anglo-French relations, had forfeited the confidence of the Foreign Office. In Madrid, the economic discussions came to a confused and ragged end. In view of post-war claims to the contrary, it is worth emphasising that contact ceased not because agreements had been reached but precisely because they no longer seemed possible. Six months of diplomacy, however confused, had not been altogether without effect, and repeated exchanges had resulted in a certain degree of mutual comprehension. Both governments had come to appreciate that their best interests would not be served by open conflict. An uneasy equilibrium had been reached; no more.

'WEYGAND FRANCE', JULY 1940–MARCH 1941

The third major strand in British policy towards France in the period after the Armistice was composed of attempts to coax North Africa back into the war under its own leaders, with or without Vichy's blessing. Ingrained traditions of obedience to authority had held the French Empire together after the collapse, and Dakar demonstrated the limits of subversion. If the chain of command could be broken at a sufficiently high level, however, the same traditions of obedience might enable a large proportion of the French Empire to be hived off with relatively little effort. Churchill in particular, although he yielded to no man in his contempt for what Morton called 'that pitiable crew' in Vichy, and although he was usually in favour of toughness in dealing with them, was also an opportunist for whom the side door exerted a powerful attraction. As early as 23 July he was talking of 'a kind of collusive conspiracy' in Vichy, 'whereby certain members of that Government, perhaps with the consent of those who remain, will levant to North Africa in order to make a better bargain for France from the North African shore and from a position of independence', and on the 25th the Cabinet agreed that this should be the main objective of policy towards Vichy.[103]

Civilian leadership for such an initiative was out of the question in the prevailing reaction against the Third Republic. As Cadogan wrote, 'No ex-French politicians need apply.'[104] The only serious candidate was Weygand, who had emerged from the *débâcle* with considerable prestige and who, after a short period in the government, became Delegate-General in North Africa in September. From henceforward, coaxing him back into the war became 'the big object in view'.[105] Whether this policy enjoyed any prospect of success seems doubtful, however. Although wielding absolute power as Pétain's deputy, Weygand probably lacked the authority to act independently. Working as Foch's second-in-command during his best years seems to have blunted his initiative. What is certain is that he supported Pétain's authoritarian style of government to the hilt, despised republican democracy, and would do nothing to speed its restoration. Furthermore, although he detested the Germans, he hated the British almost equally; it was he who had predicted in June 1940 that Britain's neck would be wrung like a chicken's.[106]

Nevertheless the situation seemed urgent enough at the time of Montoire to warrant a direct approach to Weygand, and the fortuitous presence of Rougier in London provided the means to effect this. Rougier was urged to impress on the General the enormous responsibility which rested on his shoulders, and the determination of the British to fight on. If he would 'raise the standard' in North Africa, 'he can count on the renewal of the whole-hearted collaboration of the Government and peoples of the British Empire, and on a share of the assistance afforded by the United States'.[107] This message was delivered by Rougier in Algiers on 6 November and was reinforced by other messages sent from London, the most important of which affirmed the British Government's sincere desire to 'bury the past' and its confidence in eventual victory. It continued:

Mr. Churchill does not understand the reason that deters the leaders of France, or some of them, from a policy of secession in Africa, where they would find an Empire and would have at the same time the control of the seas and of all the French financial resources now in the United States of America. The Prime Minister is convinced that the opportunity that presents itself is the most brilliant ever offered to men of courage.[108]

Rougier reported that Weygand's reaction to these proposals was nil and that he was determined to defend North Africa against all comers.

Other reports were more encouraging, however, and the climate of optimism created at the end of the year by successes in the desert campaign and by the fall of Laval made more concrete proposals seem worthwhile. The Dupuy report, in particular, suggested that a 'collusive conspiracy' was in Pétain's mind also. As we have seen, however, the offer of military support had no effect (see above, p. 80).

Despite these setbacks, Eden's return to the Foreign Office in December gave an added impetus to efforts to seduce Weygand, this time through Colonel Mittelman, a French naval officer who had put himself at British disposal after the Armistice. Mittelman had met Eden in Cairo in November and went from there to Algiers. Weygand refused to meet him on principle so he was housed next door, the conversation being conducted through the General's personal staff, who 'faisaient la navette' between them: an apt illustration of Vichy's reliance upon bogus principles.[109] There was inevitably some confusion about the outcome of this curious conversation. Mittelman told the British Consul General in Tangier that Weygand was willing to 'continue the war' subject to assurances from the British, particularly regarding petrol supplies. But this meant very little because Weygand always argued that the Armistice was a 'simple suspension d'armes' and that he was continuing the war by doing nothing. Mittelman's reports were received with considerable scepticism when he arrived in London shortly afterwards, particularly by Morton.[110] Nevertheless, on 6 January the Prime Minister dwelt upon the effect on Vichy of recent victories in Libya in a minute to the Chiefs of Staff.

The probabilities of delay in Spain until the spring give rise to the hope that the Vichy Government, under German pressure or actual German incursion, may either proceed to North Africa and resume the war from there, or authorise General Weygand to do so. . . .

We have therefore thought it right to assure Marshal Pétain and General Weygand that we will assist them with up to six divisions, substantial air forces, and the necessary naval power from the moment they feel able to take the all-important step we so greatly desire. We have also impressed upon them the danger of delaying their action until the Germans have made their way through Spain and become masters of the Straits and of Northern Morocco. We can but wait and see what Vichy will do. Meanwhile we enforce the blockade of France fitfully and as naval convenience offers, partly to assert the principle, partly to provide a 'smoke-screen' of Anglo-French friction, and especially not to let the Vichy Government feel that if they do nothing life will be tolerable for them so far as we are concerned. It is greatly to our interest that events should develop rapidly in France. . . .[111]

On 9 January Churchill and Eden decided that Mittelman should return to Algiers with a copy of the offer of six divisions which had been sent to Pétain and with a cordial personal message asking Weygand what grades and quantities of petrol he required, and for what purpose. 'You may be confident', Churchill concluded, 'that we have a full understanding of the difficulties which surround you; but as the days pass and the prospects of victory broaden out before our eyes, we look forward with greater assurance to the resumption of active collaboration between British and French arms in what is still the common cause.'[112]

In fact, Weygand had simply been using people like Mittelman and Léon Marchal, a pro-British member of his staff, to cast flies over the noses of the British to see what offers would be forthcoming without having the slightest intention of acting. After the war he endorsed a remark attributed to him by Rougier: if the British came to North Africa with twenty divisions, he would embrace them; if they came with four, he would fire on them.[113] His reaction to the British offer is therefore not difficult to imagine. He demanded supplies before action, while the British demanded action before supplies. Neither acted in good faith. 'I am sorry to appear unhelpful,' wrote Brigadier Hollis, Secretary of the Chiefs of Staff Committee, 'but the stuff, which Weygand wants, is literally non-existent.'[114] When considering the matter two weeks later, the Chiefs of Staff were only willing to assume that two divisions, not six, would be available to help Weygand.[115]

The General's inaction soon created a mood of disillusion in London. 'Are we not going to have any direct answer from Weygand?' asked Churchill on 27 January. 'Surely we ought to have something better than what we have got before lavishing our supplies.' 'We have made Weygand great offers, to which we have had no reply,' he told the Foreign Office in February. 'It is clear that he will be activated only by forces set in motion by pressure of Nazis on Vichy. . . . Not one scrap of nobility or courage has been shown by these people so far, and they had better go on short commons till they come to their senses.'[116] 'He seeks peace not war; peace at any price without justice or honour', wrote Morton. 'Have not those stupid British promised to restore the greatness of France if they win?' 'During the battle for France,' he concluded,

'Weygand sent a message to Mr. Churchill; "Cut my head off if I fail."
Is it not time he paid forfeit?'[117]

These developments forced the British to consider how they could
reconcile their efforts to create a successor regime to Vichy with their
support of de Gaulle. Although they had made no exclusive commitment to support him, and although he himself had been willing at first
to submit to any senior authority which stepped forward, the British
had to take account of the growing spiritual importance of Gaullism. De
Gaulle's unique claim to have been the first to reject dishonour was one
which they would disregard at their peril if they wished to preserve the
fiction that France had never left the battlefield. Robert Parr, Consul
General in Brazzaville and therefore in close contact with de Gaulle,
was arguing even before the end of 1940 that he would eventually have
to be recognised as the head of the French State rather than just as the
leader of 'a colonial adventure, controlled by us'.[118] The British
government was very far from accepting this view, however, and every
discussion of policy took for granted that the Free French movement
would occupy a subordinate position in relation to the North African
regime which it was hoped to establish.[119]

The failure of MENACE marked the beginning of a period of great
danger for the Free French. On the one hand, the Foreign Office was
considering making an undertaking to restrain de Gaulle as part of a
modus vivendi with Vichy. On the other hand, it defined its policy in
November as being to effect a *rapprochement* between Weygand, Catroux
and de Gaulle in which he would occupy third place; Churchill had
already offered the leadership of the Free French movement to Catroux
in September.[120] Hoare was informed that what was aimed for was not a
conflict but 'such an evolution on the part of Weygand as would enable
us to bring de Gaulle to his standard . . . this is the end that we are
seeking in our present contacts with the Vichy Government and its
agents'.[121] Even Churchill, de Gaulle's supporter at first, began to have
second thoughts after MENACE. 'We must put frankly before him the
facts which are developing and the position of his movement in relation
to them', he wrote on 8 November. 'He and his movement may now
become an obstacle to a very considerable hiving off of the French
Empire to our side. There is no doubt that men like Weygand and
Noguès when searching their souls about their own misdeeds harden
themselves against us by dwelling on the insubordination of de Gaulle.'
Morton was writing as late as February 1941 that the time might soon
come when de Gaulle would be obliged to tell Frenchmen to accept the

direction of Pétain or his deputies in North Africa.[122] Two weeks after this, feeling in Number Ten had changed again with Weygand's refusal to respond to British offers, and Churchill was describing de Gaulle as 'much the best Frenchman now in the arena' whom he wanted taken care of as much as possible.[123] But this mood also passed. The British were no less willing to subordinate the Gaullist movement to considerations of immediate military and political expediency in 1941 and 1942 than they had been in 1940, and the most serious threats to Gaullist integrity were yet to come.

5 Britain and America's 'Vichy Gamble'

WITH the breakdown of the economic discussions in Madrid and the failure of attempts to draw North Africa back into the war, most of the momentum had gone out of British policy towards Vichy in the early months of 1941, and a pessimistic appreciation of likely developments in Franco-German relations which Eden submitted to the Cabinet in early February had little to offer in terms of an effective British response.[1] Even when the danger of Laval's return to power had passed, the ascendancy of Darlan removed any hope of a favourable evolution on the part of the Vichy government. Darlan, indeed, was thought to be even more dangerous than Laval, partly because he was the more 'respectable' politician and partly because of his feelings of bitter animosity towards the British.[2]

The government's attitude towards Vichy was summarised in a telegram despatched to Lord Halifax on 3 March. The government's hopes, it pointed out, had been largely placed in Pétain's stubbornness and sense of honour, and in the belief that he would hold to his promise not to surrender the Fleet or bases to the Axis. But recent events had considerably shaken his hold on the government, effective control of which lay in the hands of the 'anglophobe and ambitious' Darlan, and of Bouthillier, the Minister of Finance. Vichy did not wish to have economic discussions with Britain, and was actively discussing economic collaboration with Germany.

The Vichy Government has shown no desire to establish effective contact with us. They have refused to accept a Treasury representative at Vichy, pleading that this was contrary to the Armistice. They thought fit to inform the Armistice Commission in December that they would have to engage in economic discussions with us. They apparently consult the Armistice Commission on every detail concerning their foreign relations and can it appears carry on no discussions with us without the explicit approval of that Commission. . . . This present policy of subservience to Germany and the tolerance of German commissions at important bases in France and North Africa bids fair to nullify his [Pétain's] undertaking that in no circumstances will bases be surrendered to the enemy. Neither the Vichy Government nor their agents in North Africa show any spark of nobility or courage or any active will to resist.[3]

In short, there seemed to be no reasonable prospect either of establishing contact with Vichy or of achieving any useful result from such contact. M. Chartier, acting head of the French liquidation mission, who had been attempting for some time to establish semi-official relations, was told to leave the country in April in retaliation against Vichy's closure of the remaining British consular missions in the Unoccupied Zone. 'We will be well rid of M. Chartier who is not doing anyone any good here', remarked Cadogan.[4] There was thus nothing resembling a 'Chartier mission', as Hytier suggests.[5]

The Foreign Office did maintain clandestine contacts with Allied sympathisers in Vichy and North Africa, but these were at too low a level to be of use in influencing Vichy's policy. The exception to this was the visit to London in June of Colonel Groussard, Inspector-General of the Sûreté Nationale, who held discussions with Eden, Churchill and Morton. But again the outcome was inconclusive. It was doubtful whether Groussard's mission had Pétain's approval, and his only authority stemmed from a rather vague *accord passif* given by General Huntziger. The latter agreed to convey to the Marshal any acceptable proposals which Groussard might bring back, but made it clear that if his mission came to light, he would be disavowed.[6]

Groussard's reception was frosty. Morton, who met him first, was contemptuous of his suggestion that Vichy favoured the Allied cause and pointed out that Vichy had not done any of the small, practical things which lay within its power to aid the Allies.[7] Groussard's meeting with Churchill was more cordial but nothing came of further meetings with Eden and Winant, the American ambassador.[8] Eden was disagreeably impressed by Groussard and the Joint Planning Staff concluded that the main purpose of his visit was to reinsure French interests with the United States, rather than with Britain, to find out the extent of America's commitment to the Allied cause, and to assess Britain's chances of winning. The Colonel had brought no information about France, no hope of assistance to the Allied cause and no sign of French readiness to make sacrifices, and his suggestions 'seem little more than might be expected from the present German-controlled French Government'.[9] Despite this, the Foreign Office provided Groussard with a cypher and invited him to maintain contact.[10] He then returned to Vichy, where, according to his own account, he secured Pétain's agreement to the continuation of his talks with London. However, plans for his return were thwarted by a security leak which alerted Darlan to his activities and resulted in his arrest on 15 July. Pétain took no steps to secure his release, and all contact between London and Vichy petered out.[11]

AMERICAN INITIATIVES IN VICHY

British pessimism about the value of maintaining contact with Vichy in the opening months of 1941 was not shared by the American government, and during this period the initiative in dealings with Pétain's government passed by tacit consent from London to Washington. This development was welcomed by the British government, and especially by Churchill himself. However much the British may have disagreed with the application of American policy, and however reluctant they may have been to support it publicly, they were completely agreeable in principle to a powerful American presence in Vichy and Algiers. The need for a strong American initiative in French affairs was a constant refrain of Churchill's in his personal correspondence with Roosevelt throughout the year.[12]

These constant reminders of course served the broad purpose of levering the American government into a more active involvement in Europe, but they also stemmed from a belief that Vichy would be more responsive to pressure from Washington than from any other quarter except Berlin. There was some truth in this. No French politician, even Laval, wished to risk the hostility of the United States. American recognition was Vichy's strongest link with the free world and gave the regime a mark of respectability.[13] More urgently, the United States was the most obvious source of supply for all those commodities which France so desperately needed, and her most effective intermediary in persuading the British to relax their blockade. In the long term also, it was felt that the United States was, as Roosevelt himself put it, 'just about the best friend that France has got', and that she could be relied upon to defend the interests of France, in particular by restraining the colonial ambitions which Britain entertained at her expense in the Middle East and West Africa.

The maintenance of the link between Washington and Vichy fitted in not only with the interests of Britain and Vichy France, but also with those of the United States. The collapse of French resistance carried serious implications for the security of the western hemisphere and for the balance of power in south-east Asia, and the fate of the French Fleet, in particular, was a matter of great concern to the American government. From the very outset, however, the American attitude towards Vichy was fundamentally different from that of the British. In place of the traditional rivalries of Britain and France, there existed the so-called 'Lafayette tradition'. Franco-American relations had been spared the corrosive effects of appeasement, the tensions of alliance, and the bitterness of defeat. Many Americans were angered by Vichy's submission to Japan in Indo-China, but it was hardly open to them to reproach France, as the British did, for withdrawing from a struggle which they had not even entered. Finally, it was Britain, not the United States, which supported de Gaulle, and British, not American guns which sounded at Oran. The British regarded the Armistice as a betrayal, and Vichy as Hitler's glove-puppet. The American government, however, was much more willing to take Vichy at its own estimation and to regard the signature of the Armistice as a legitimate response to defeat. Pétain's role as the defender of France from Germany and from the dangers of anarchy was, by and large, accepted.

This difference of perspective was reflected also in the tactics which each country adopted in its dealings with Vichy. Both Britain and the United States had the same aims: to prevent the French Fleet and colonies falling under enemy control, to prevent Vichy from becoming abjectly collaborationist, and, ultimately, to bring France back into the war.[14] For the most part, the British government, and in particular the Prime Minister, held to the view that a policy of toughness was best calculated to make the Vichy government co-operative, and that the force of public opinion in France combined with Pétain's and Weygand's sense of honour and hatred of Germany would always prevent Vichy from declaring war upon Britain, however severe the provocation offered (see p. 68). The real danger, it was felt, lay not only in the policy of outright collaboration favoured by Darlan, but in the mood of flaccid defeatism which brought about piecemeal concessions to Germany. Severe British pressure would demonstrate to Vichy that the government was determined to win, while any relaxation of that pressure would simply enable Vichy to 'browse on chocolates', and to sit out the war with the minimum of discomfort.[15] In practice, the British were far from consistent in pursuing this line, and tended to vacillate uncertainly between the position that Vichy enabled Germany to rule Europe cheaply and should therefore be undermined, and the grudging acceptance of the argument that Vichy's quasi-neutrality was in fact more advantageous to the Allies and should be preserved.

The American outlook was much more consistent. There had been little sign of indulgence towards the Vichy regime in 1940, and the American response to the Montoire meeting was a great deal more stern than that of the British. By the end of the year, however, it had been decided to put into effect a policy of moral and material support for the Vichy government. As Hull explained it after the war, 'It seemed to us to be the part of common sense to continue full contact with Vichy, particularly since the British had no contact at all. By maintaining our relations we could buttress the Pétain Government during a future which we knew would inevitably be marked by more excessive demands from the Germans. We could encourage the French people by convincing them we were still behind them.'[16] In December 1940 this endorsement was given added emphasis by the appointment to Vichy as American ambassador of Admiral William D. Leahy, whom Roosevelt was to make his Chief of Staff when the latter left his Vichy post, and who was to exercise no little influence in that capacity.

American policy took as its starting point the assumption that the Marshal was firmly opposed to collaboration and was often ignorant of the policies pursued by his ministers. Thus Roosevelt's instructions to Leahy described Pétain as 'the one powerful element in the French Government who is standing firm against selling out to Germany'.[17] This assumption, although erroneous in fact, had the virtue of enabling the American government to exonerate the Marshal from the policies of collaboration conducted in his name. Every misdemeanour could be laid at the door of the collaborationist 'element'. Whenever Vichy's policy demanded a vigorous response from the American government, this tired formula ensured instead renewed assurances of American support, and Pétain was not slow to appreciate the advantages of being cast in the role which Washington had ascribed to him and which suited his own purposes so well.

Post-war defences of the 'Vichy Gamble' were mainly concerned to establish that American contacts did not imply a moral judgement on the regime, and that the policy had been all along 'sensibly opportunistic'.[18] The first part of the argument is easily disposed of. The issue in 1940 was not whether or not relations should be maintained, as Langer suggests, but the degree of cordiality which should be shown. If America's decision to support Vichy had been devoid of moral significance, there would have been no point in it. The second part of the argument presents more problems, however, for although a case can be made out for American policy on the grounds of pure opportunism, it is difficult to come away from a study of American attitudes without suspecting that the American government approved of Vichy.

The explanation for this is complex. In the first place, of course, the American political tradition is much more tolerant of military heroes in high political office than the British. Rallying to the leader was accepted by Americans as a legitimate reaction to a national crisis. In a wider context, however, American attitudes to Vichy were a reflection of that government's estimate of France's position after the war. As de Gaulle later wrote, 'At bottom, what the American policy makers took for granted was the effacement of France. They therefore came to terms with Vichy.'[19] This was true in the sense that, unlike the British, the American government accepted without demur the demotion of France from the first rank. It was also consistent with Roosevelt's desire to place parts of the French Empire under international supervision after the war.

The same considerations determined American attitudes towards de Gaulle. Again, post-war defences of American policy which argue the impossibility of 'recognising' de Gaulle miss the point. Recognition did not become an issue until 1943. American policy is open to criticism not for failure to recognise de Gaulle as the government of France, which nobody did, but for failing to grasp the moral significance of his movement. American policy towards France was largely shaped by men of Roosevelt's, Leahy's and Robert Murphy's stamp; men of right-wing, patrician views who saw France's future in terms of paternalistic capitalism and who viewed the growing appeal of Gaullism to the left-wing and to radical nationalism with mounting distrust. At bottom, the objection of these men to de Gaulle was the same as that of Pétain; that he had disobeyed orders. According to Robert Murphy, for example, Roosevelt's own distrust of the General dated from the Dakar expedition, when de Gaulle had started 'what amounted to a French civil war, putting his own ambitions above French and Allied interests'.[20] It seems that, for these men, the duty of all Frenchmen was to rally to the Marshal. Leahy later recounted with relish his refusal to meet anybody of a Gaullist persuasion in France.[21] Only by bearing in mind such attitudes can one understand the tenacity with which the

American government clung to its position on the French problem during the four years after the Armistice.

THE BRITISH BLOCKADE, 1940–1

The moral aspects of the Vichy problem, although of growing importance, did not become critical until 1942, when the projected invasion of North Africa forced Britain and the United States to consider how far military advantage could justify coming to terms with that regime or its successors. During 1941 the problem presented itself more as an issue of expediency, since the American government wished to lend substance to its support of Vichy's authority in France and North Africa by launching a programme of relief and economic aid, while the British, sceptical of the political benefits to be gained by such a policy, sought above all to keep the blockade intact.

In theory, British policy was straightforward and consisted of applying the most rigid blockade possible of German-occupied Europe and the French possessions of North and West Africa. On 26 July 1940 the Cabinet agreed to treat France for blockade purposes as being under enemy control, and on 13 July contraband control was extended to all ships, French or neutral, bound for ports in French Morocco, Algeria and Tunisia.[22] During the following months, however, a vigorous debate took place within the government on the question of whether the blockade should be maintained in its full force. On the one hand, as we have seen, the Foreign Office under Halifax's direction became increasingly willing to negotiate a *modus vivendi* which would involve the relaxation of the blockade in return for assurances about the fate of the French Fleet and colonial bases. Churchill was also willing to relax the blockade, although he was more inclined to press for a firm commitment to enter the war as the price of any concession. The mounting agitation for relief measures in the United States and the possibly adverse effect of a rigid policy upon American public opinion and upon the maintenance of the President's good will weighed more heavily with him.[23] The Admiralty also supported a policy which would relieve the burden upon the Mediterranean Fleet and enable it to concentrate upon its primary objective of destroying Italian naval power.[24]

Against all efforts to dismantle the blockade the Ministry of Economic Warfare under the redoubtable Hugh Dalton maintained a vigorous and single-minded opposition. Although his relations with

Halifax were cordial enough in spite of their different views on the blockade, Dalton had little regard for the permanent officials of the Foreign Office, whom he regarded as appeasers, while any suggestion from within his own Ministry that a relaxation of the blockade might after all win valuable political concessions was regarded as defeatism or worse.[25] During the second half of 1940, Dalton maintained a steady flow of memoranda which were among the most forceful which the Cabinet had to consider. The basis of the Ministry's case was that the Germans were legally responsible for maintaining the economic life of the countries which they had enslaved and that any relaxation of the blockade would be of direct or indirect assistance to them in doing so. Europe's food problem was one of distribution rather than supply and there would be no starvation if Germany shared out available resources equitably. It followed that any relaxation of the blockade would have the effect of releasing for hostile purposes transport and fuel which would otherwise be tied up.[26] Never forgetting that he was a Socialist in a predominantly Conservative Cabinet, Dalton could not resist the temptation to point out that the food situation in Unoccupied France and French North Africa was better than it had been for some years among the British unemployed.[27]

From the time of the failure of Operation MENACE Dalton had to fight a rearguard action against the combined opposition of the Foreign Office and the Admiralty to the maintenance of a rigid blockade. In Halifax's opinion, 'the Economic Warfare boys' were 'constantly losing any sense of proportion' over the blockade and Dalton, in particular, had to make a physical effort to keep his hands off any French ship on which he could lay them.[28] The fact that the shortage of ships made the blockade almost completely ineffective added further weight to the Foreign Office argument that it should be traded off against political concessions.[29] In view of the unlikelihood of further Gaullist successes, there was also a lot to be said for the view that French North Africa should be strengthened rather than weakened. This position was supported by Sir Samuel Hoare in Madrid and in the Foreign Office by Strang and Cadogan.[30] The Ministry of Economic Warfare drew a different conclusion from the situation and argued that a willingness to negotiate carried with it the danger that the blockade might be seen to be completely in abeyance. 'We have already drifted, though I suspect that many of my colleagues do not realise the facts, into a sort of half-surrender which, unless we now reverse it, will have the most disastrous consequences', he informed the Cabinet on 18 October.[31] Although he had been willing to make a virtue of necessity and agree that ships passing between North Africa and Unoccupied France should not in practice be interfered with, he insisted that the blockade of French West Africa should be strengthened. It was clearly desirable that the Gaullist colonies in West Africa should find themselves relatively better off as a result of their action in rallying to the Allied cause, while on economic warfare grounds the autumn was the most effective time to apply the blockade, when the groundnut crop, which accounted for 50 per cent of Europe's peacetime needs, had been gathered and would rot if it were not moved.[32]

Although Churchill gave Dalton initial support, the Cabinet's decision to enforce a strict blockade for a time was soon suspended, and in the middle of November Dalton brought the question squarely before the Cabinet again.[33] The breach in the blockade at Gibralta was enormous and the Vichy government itself had announced that from 15 September to 15 October more than 200,000 tons of goods from North Africa, Casablanca and Dakar had entered France.[34] Dalton complained bitterly that the present position 'reduced economic warfare to a farce'.[35] Although the First Lord still held out for a *modus vivendi*, even Halifax had come to agree that the situation could not be allowed to continue. However, although the Cabinet agreed to effect a strict blockade of the Straits, the necessary ships were simply not available to enforce it. In spite of signs towards the end of the year that the Vichy government regarded the non-imposition of the blockade as the result of indulgence rather than weakness, it seems more likely that the economic discussions in Madrid finally broke down because the obvious weakness of Britain's position encouraged Vichy to put forward demands which were quite unacceptable.[36] Halifax's replacement by Eden in late December brought about a marked stiffening of attitude in the Foreign Office and at the end of the year Dalton could feel some satisfaction that his first line of defence had been maintained in principle even if it could not be enforced in practice.

The mood of disillusionment which had set in in London after six months of fruitless negotiation, however, was not shared in Washington, where the 'new policy' was about to germinate. It is necessary to distinguish two separate strands in American opposition to the blockade. First, and less dangerous from the point of view of the Ministry of Economic Warfare, was the agitation which took place outside the government for a programme of widespread relief in

Occupied Europe along the lines of the Belgian Relief Programme in the First World War. Although humanitarian motives were to some extent involved, the movement was really an expression of political isolationism and was widely supported by elements which favoured a compromise peace. The attitude of the British government towards this question was clearly stated by the Prime Minister in a speech to the Commons on 20 August 1940, which placed responsibility for feeding the conquered territories firmly upon Germany. A Gallup poll on 1 September revealed that the majority of Americans were in sympathy with this attitude, and the Administration did not take issue with the government in London over the blockade of the occupied countries.[37]

Unoccupied France, however, presented a different case. The Ministry of Economic Warfare's view was that a valid distinction between the two zones could not be maintained. The natural interdependence of Occupied and Unoccupied France meant that goods had to cross the line and that the Germans were therefore free to siphon off from the north whatever was allowed through the blockade in the south. Here the American view diverged. In August Roosevelt informed the British ambassador that he was definitely and strongly of the opinion that a scheme should be established under American supervision for distributing medical supplies and milk to children in the Unoccupied Zone. The Gallup poll and the British reply on 3 September caused the President to drop the question for the time being, but it was taken up again in November when Norman Davies, the Chairman of the American Red Cross, put forward definite proposals to London. A Cabinet meeting on 6 December rejected these, on the grounds that the distinction between the zones could not be maintained and that if the principle of German responsibility were weakened, it would be impossible to refuse similar treatment to Holland, Belgium, Poland and Norway, 'which countries have established a good deal stronger claims [sic] on our sympathy than France'. Relief measures would serve only to prolong the war, and with it the misery and suffering of the very people whom it was supposed to assist. It would also arouse strong criticism in Parliament and among the public at large.[38]

At the end of 1940, the President himself put forward relief proposals very similar to those of Mr Davies, and the British government felt that it was no longer possible to refuse. On 31 December Roosevelt formally proposed that supplies of milk and vitamin concentrates should be sent to the Unoccupied Zone, arguing that the likely political gains far outweighed the risk of loss to Germany and that a distinction between the zones could be maintained.[39] Admiral Leahy arrived in Vichy on 5 January and added his voice in support.[40] Since the President had made a point of linking the question with that of Spain, where the British were seeking American support for exactly the policy which that government now wished to apply to France, agreement could hardly be withheld, and on 3 January Churchill conveyed the government's conditional assent.[41]

American plans for French North Africa were of even greater importance from the point of view of the blockade. Washington's policy towards Vichy France and French North Africa had a common basis in the belief that the provision of supplies and the maintenance of French authority would be best calculated to encourage resistance to German demands, maintain the independence of the Empire, and, eventually, draw France's possessions back into the war. 'To us', wrote Hull, 'it seemed that Weygand in North Africa might become a cornerstone around which to build a policy of resistance to Germany.'[42] The British had also pursued this line, but the failure of their approaches left them effectively without a policy towards North Africa. Churchill himself seems to have favoured the maintenance of a strict blockade, partly because he never fully gave up hope that Weygand might thus be goaded to action, and partly from a suspicion that stability in North Africa favoured Germany and that chaos would therefore favour Britain. In practice, however, the government was reluctant to pursue its policy to a logical conclusion and undermine French authority in the Maghreb by economic pressure. 'Of course we must maintain the blockade,' argued Sir Samuel Hoare in October 1940, 'but nonetheless if we want France and the French colonies in North Africa to come in with us in the end, we must in the meanwhile keep them alive.'[43] The same point was made by David Eccles of the Ministry of Economic Warfare, who from early September had been arguing for a more flexible attitude towards the export of phosphates from Morocco. 'Can it be right to starve an invalid', he asked, 'in the hope that he will, in yet greater misery, crawl back to you?'[44] The Chiefs of Staff were equally reluctant to upset the *status quo*, pointing out that Algeria and Tunisia could not be defended against the inevitable Axis reaction, and that any unrest in Morocco might be exploited by Spain.[45] As a result of this, it was agreed in November to allow limited quantities of sugar and green tea through the blockade to avoid internal disturbances in Morocco.[46] Despite these measures, there was no declared change of policy, and the Foreign Office was forced to admit to the State Department, when asked to elucidate its policy, that the need to encourage resistance in the French colonies and the need to prevent supplies getting to Germany 'may seem to involve inconsistencies between principle and practice'. Although the blockade would be maintained in principle, it would be relaxed if local political circumstances seemed to justify it.[47]

The American government's view was quite different. It assumed that the neutralisation of French North Africa benefited the Allies and that the authority of the Vichy government in the area should therefore be supported. A supply of essential commodities would maintain the economy on a sound footing, prevent unrest, and ensure that the French authorities continued to look to the United States rather than to Germany for supplies. It was also felt that Weygand's position would be compromised by staff talks and that economic aid should not be made conditional upon any promise of immediate action on his part. While the British concluded that Weygand would never act independently of the Marshal, American policy was based upon the supposition, which Weygand encouraged, that when the time was ripe he would rally to the Allied cause. This was important because it enabled Washington to separate its North African from its Vichy policy, and to maintain that the argument for the provisioning of North Africa held good regardless of the policy of collaboration pursued by the government in Metropolitan France or in other parts of the Empire.[48]

In late December 1940 Robert Murphy, formerly United States Consul-General and Counsellor of Embassy in Paris, was despatched by the President on a fact-finding tour of North Africa, meeting Weygand for the first time in Dakar on the 21st and later in Rabat.[49] He conveyed his findings to Washington on 14 January. The situation, he reported, was desperate: essential supplies were running low and French authority was being undermined. He reported with approval the General's view that the British should build him up rather than deprive him of the means to strengthen North Africa and bring it back into the war. The French High Command expected a German advance on North Africa within the following three or four months and Murphy supported their demand for the speedy despatch of paraffin, petrol and motor oil.[50] Three days later he reported personally to Roosevelt. With presidential endorsement, internal debate on the merits and demerits of the policy virtually ceased and Murphy's personal position became almost unassailable.

The State Department lost no time in informing the British government of its intentions, and made clear that it was determined to proceed with the implementation of its policy. It had become a point of American policy, Halifax was told, to see that North Africa did not disintegrate.[51] The determination of the State Department made protest seem fruitless, and the Foreign Office therefore accepted the American initiative philosophically and attempted to make the best of the situation. On 3 February Washington was informed that the British government welcomed American influence in Morocco. Although they had less confidence in Weygand they would support the American gamble so long as no serious breach was made in the blockade. Algeria and Tunisia – but not French West Africa – could be included in the supply programme so long as stocks were not accumulated or re-exported, and American observers were admitted to supervise distribution. The message ended with a mild protest that American negotiations should have proceeded without consultation, since this had upset similar plans which the British had entertained for trading supplies against the release of the 250,000 tons of British shipping held by the French authorities in North Africa. If the latter could get all they needed from the Americans, hope of securing the release of the ships would vanish.[52] The American response to this was stiff. Hull told Halifax on 10 February that the American policy of conciliation was more important than the ships and refused to make any American offers conditional on their release. To the British suggestion that the United States had been proceeding without consultation, the State Department responded that, on the contrary, it was the British who had failed to explain their policy to the United States. On the same day it announced its intention to commence supplies forthwith by sending a tanker of petroleum products to Casablanca.[53]

American determination to proceed with the new policy come what may gave rise to considerable unease in London in early 1941, not least because it coincided with a sharp deterioration in the political situation in Vichy. Darlan succeeded Flandin on 9 February, and at his first meeting with Leahy expressed himself frankly in favour of collaboration with Germany.[54] There were increasing signs of Axis infiltration into French North Africa, while from the point of view of the blockade, the situation could hardly have been worse. Increasing quantities of goods were passing up the West African coast into France and there were signs of the beginning of a French transatlantic trade. In the previous three months 200,000 tons of produce – meat, groundnuts, rubber, tea and sugar – had reached France through the Straits. From 1 October 1940 to 1 March 1941, the Ministry calculated later, 2,650,000 tons of shipping carrying 1,750,000 tons of cargo were unloaded at Marseilles. In the first three months of 1941, of 108 French ships passing Gibraltar on their way to France, the British intercepted only eight.[55] This was all the more alarming in view of the accumulating evidence that a large proportion of French colonial produce was finding its way across the demarcation line. Most reports received in London in early 1941 suggested that as much as 80 per cent of imports into Unoccupied France found its way into Axis hands.[56]

These developments served only to reinforce the State Department's conviction that rapid measures of economic support were the appropriate response to the quickening pace of Vichy's collaboration with Germany. The British, on the other hand, drew the opposite conclusion, and regarded American enthusiasm to supply North Africa not only as dangerous from the economic warfare point of view, but as highly suspicious politically. The new prominence of the urbane Irish-American Murphy seemed particularly menacing. David Eccles, the Ministry of Economic Warfare's representative in Morocco, reported that he was a dangerous element: personally anglophobe, he thought more of helping France than of defeating Germany. The British Consul-General in Tangier came to the same conclusion. 'Murphy seemed to me a pronounced "Vichyphil",' he wrote on 13 January, 'and his pronouncements are mostly concerned with the misfortunes of the Vichy Government and the misunderstanding of it by Great Britain.'[57] Despite assurances that the British would be fully consulted during negotiations with the North African authorities, Eccles found himself firmly excluded, while even American observers expressed their alarm at Murphy's apparent freedom from control.[58] The first round of negotiations with the North African authorities was brought to a swift and successful conclusion, and in early February the American government agreed to despatch a tanker of fuel oil to Casablanca and two shiploads of grain to Unoccupied France.[59] On the 26th Murphy and Weygand initialled in Algiers an agreement bearing their names which set out the conditions under which the American government would facilitate the passage of supplies to French North Africa. It was ratified by Darlan on 10 March.[60]

The British had little alternative but to fall in with American wishes. An open break was clearly to be avoided while the Lend-Lease Act was before the Senate. At the same time, to Churchill's chagrin, the President had not overlooked the fact that it was British pressure which was being exerted upon Washington to provide economic support for the Franco regime in Spain.[61] The British argued that there was a difference between a regime which had declared its non-belligerency and one which, although technically *hors de combat*, was lending Germany tangible support. The American position was that what was good for Spain could hardly be bad for North Africa. At a confused and inconclusive Cabinet meeting on 4 March, the Cabinet decided that although the blockade must be upheld in principle, American pressure could only be resisted up to a point and that from time to time it would therefore have to be relaxed. All such concessions, however, were to be kept to a minimum.[62] Halifax was in the meantime to continue to 'reason patiently' with the American government, a task which he found increasingly difficult to discharge effectively since his own views were so much closer to those of the State Department than they were to those of his own government.[63]

Within a few days, however, Churchill had had second thoughts. Until early March his policy had been, in his own words, 'to maintain our blockade in its full rigour as long as possible and then, at the last possible date, to allow the least possible infraction of it'.[64] It now seemed that American pressure would in any case force substantial blockade concessions, and that the credit for these would accrue solely to the United States. 'I am becoming ready to ease up about letting food into Unoccupied France,' he cabled Halifax on 9 March, 'provided and as long as they will prevent German infiltration into North Africa, and especially if they would send some more of their warships from Toulon to Atlantic Moroccan ports.'[65] There were signs that even Dalton was prepared to consider abandoning his rearguard action in defence of the blockade in favour of a rationing agreement which would secure solid political guarantees, if only as 'the least lousy of all the lousy alternatives'.[66]

On 10 March – the same day on which he ratified the Murphy–Weygand agreement – Darlan broadcast a threat to convoy supplies across the Atlantic, a measure which would either bring about the collapse of the blockade or would involve possibly large-scale naval clashes with the British. Berlin was delighted.[67] The British were gravely alarmed. It had been assumed that Vichy's policy would be to avoid unnecessary clashes with the Royal Navy and that the Cabinet could afford to take risks in dealing with Vichy.[68] This complacent assumption no longer held good. With setbacks in the western desert and in the Balkans, with the neutrality of Spain unassured, and with naval resources stretched to the limit, an aggressive policy on the part of

Vichy might tip the scales of the war in Germany's favour. For all these reasons, Darlan's announcement, far from causing the return to the hard line which one might have expected, instead made the British all the more eager to reach some discreet basis of agreement with Vichy. On the 12th Churchill proposed that Roosevelt should accept a mediator's role to bring about a working agreement between Britain and Vichy under which a ration of wheat would go month by month to Unoccupied France and 'something for French Africa so long as other things were satisfactory'. 'These other things [he went on] might form the subject of a secret arrangement . . . by which German infiltration into Morocco and French African ports would be limited to bare Armistice terms, and by which an increasing number of French warships would gradually be moving from Toulon to Casablanca or Dakar.' In the meantime American agents would be installed in North Africa and the Unoccupied Zone.[69]

Churchill's message demonstrated the serious alarm which could be occasioned by threats from Vichy at a critical period, and showed the persistence with which Churchill clung to the idea of a secret accommodation with Vichy. It also bore witness to the remarkable extent to which British expectations had been lowered. Churchill was now asking little more than that Vichy should abide by the Armistice terms, in return for which she would be granted approximately the quantity of wheat which had been demanded in Madrid a few weeks before and which the Foreign Office had rejected as 'preposterous'.[70] Ironically, the proposal was coolly received in Washington. Hull said that he disliked being placed formally in a mediator's position and that he preferred to move more gradually. He was also reluctant to put his policy towards Vichy on a quid pro quo basis.[71] Hull's real objection to the British proposal was, of course, that it would reassert British initiative. The good will which Hull hoped to win by gratuitous offers of supplies would be lost if rigid conditions were attached, while an attitude of intransigence on the part of the British was required in order to counterpoint American generosity. It was important, in short, that British concessions should be seen to have been achieved by American pressure. This interpretation of Hull's motives may seem harsh, but is borne out by the fact that he combined his rejection of Churchill's plan with the request that the British should nevertheless be 'a bit lighter' on French shipping generally – that is, that they should fall in more readily with American wishes.[72] This, as Churchill told Halifax on the 18th, was 'very baffling'. When the American view was accepted, they recoiled. When we tried to enforce the blockade we were asked to be 'lighter'. What did the Americans want?[73] In the event, however, little was to be achieved by continued argument and Churchill, as always concerned to avoid quibbling with the United States when greater things were at issue, instructed that the Americans should be allowed to go their own way for a while.[74]

With this exchange of views, British and American policies became fairly clearly defined: on the one hand, a determination to proceed with a supply programme for North Africa which would be entirely American in character, and on the other hand, a desire to maintain the blockade mitigated by a grudging acceptance that, with more important issues at stake, London would be forced to yield from time to time to American pressure. As things turned out, however, political developments in Vichy and in other theatres of war constantly interrupted the implementation of American policy and involved all three governments throughout 1941 and 1942 in negotiations which were, in the Official Historian's words, 'prolonged, exasperating, and intermittent'.[75] Darlan's actions in attempting to align Vichy with Germany and to secure for France a favoured place in German-dominated Europe threw American policy into disarray time after time. The policy of support turned out to be self-defeating. Every move on Darlan's part to hasten Franco-German collaboration was greeted with hesitation or even alarm, and subsequently with renewed offers of support to strengthen the 'pro-Allied faction' which was alleged to exist around the Marshal. It acted, therefore, not as a deterrent, but as a spur to further measures of collaboration. From the material standpoint, as well, the American supply programme was of trifling importance. Very little, in the end, got through. Such measures, in any case, hardly affected the attitudes of the Vichy leaders. Those who believed in or hoped for an Allied victory were not strengthened in their belief by shiploads of wheat or oil. Those who saw no alternative to a German victory were equally unmoved by such trifles. In the first half of 1941, Vichy's policies were dictated by a belief in German victory which British reverses in the Balkans and the western desert could only reinforce, and in late 1941 and 1942 by a growing uncertainty about the war's outcome created by the failure of BARBAROSSA and the entry of the United States into the war. Nothing else really mattered.

British acquiescence in the American supply programme had hardly been given before the first of many interruptions took place. In late

March evidence came to light of a massive barter deal between Germany and France under which 800,000 tons of wheat was to be supplied from the Occupied to the Unoccupied Zone in return for livestock and vegetable oil (which could only have come from French West Africa).[76] As the Foreign Office told Halifax on the 29th, 'Darlan's latest deal with his German masters shows he is unaffected by friendly offers from this country or the United States and now little is to be gained by a policy of continual concession'.[77] On the same day, Churchill telegraphed Roosevelt, 'Parliament and the public will ask me why, when we are ourselves suffering a grievous blockade and British rations are reduced week by week, the French and Germans should have these advantages, thus prolonging the war.' The Admiralty had been instructed to tighten up the blockade as far as naval resources permitted. 'I hope you will not think this unwise or unreasonable.'[78] At the same time, on 28 March, an Italian tanker arrived in Algiers to collect 5000 tons of petrol for the use of the German army in Libya, while news also arrived that a shipment of rubber from the Far East was on its way to Metropolitan France. Most alarming of all, news reached London on 2 April that Vichy intended to move the *Dunkerque* and *Strasbourg* to Toulon for repairs, 'the exact opposite', as Churchill pointed out to the Cabinet on the following day, 'of the course which we and President Roosevelt had asked the French to adopt in regard to their fleet'.[79] In the event, the American government, under fire from the press on both sides of the Atlantic over its supply programme and already sensitive to the accusation of appeasement, responded satisfactorily enough to British pressure. On 3 April Hull despatched a strong message to Pétain, stating that if any such movement of ships took place, American help and sympathy would be forfeited. This eventually produced the assurance that the *Dunkerque* would be moved only with American agreement.[80]

These events, while they confirmed London's and Washington's worst fears of Darlan, lent simultaneous support to the view that American intervention could strengthen Pétain's resistance to his policies, a view which was receiving support from other quarters also.[81] Far from being deterred by evidence of Vichy's assistance to the Axis forces in Libya or the ease with which supplies from French West Africa were reaching the Occupied Zone, the American government resumed its policy with renewed zeal. In late April, discussions commenced between the State Department and the British embassy in Washington over the extension of the supply programme to French West Africa.[82] Leahy went so far as to recommend that supplies should be sent to the Unoccupied Zone regardless of the quantities of raw materials and supplies moving northwards across the demarcation line.[83] Although supplies destined for North Africa had been delayed by wrangling over shipping, a request for a further two ships a month, beginning in July, had been submitted by Vichy and accepted 'in principle' by the American government without reference to London.[84] When Halifax asked what would be the American government's reaction if Britain refused to agree to this, Sumner Welles replied that they would have to drop the scheme. 'He also implied, however, that if the United States government were thus compelled to drop the scheme, they would drop a good deal else besides.'[85] Welles's threat gave substance to Churchill's constant fear that arguments over French affairs would interfere with the more serious concerns of Atlantic co-operation and should be avoided at all costs, and Dalton's objections to the American proposal to operate a shuttle service were overruled. The Cabinet agreed with Churchill on 5 May that apart from asking the United States to avoid publicity and to insist on the speedy admission of observers to North Africa and Unoccupied France, no firm action should be taken.[86]

THE CRISIS OF MAY 1941

In the middle of May, negotiations were again temporarily halted by alarming signs of renewed Franco-German collaboration. Throughout April there had been a steady thaw between Berlin and Vichy and a number of measures of economic collaboration had been launched.[87] At the same time, Britain's position, especially in the Middle East and the Balkans, was such that Vichy was in a position to assist Germany in making vast gains at relatively little expense.

The opportunity soon presented itself. In late April the pro-Axis government of Iraq under Raschid Ali appealed to Berlin for German aid, and Ribbentrop suggested that this could be provided by supplying his government with French arms from Syria and allowing German aeroplanes to refuel en route to Iraq.[88] Darlan accepted these suggestions, hoping, it seems, to establish a new basis of collaboration on a broad front. On 11 May he met Hitler at Berchtesgaden and declared his resolve to enter the war against Britain in the near future.[89] Darlan then proposed a fourfold programme of collaboration to the Vichy Cabinet, involving military co-operation in Syria, the cession of bases and military facilities in North Africa, and the eventual open support of France for the war against England. Darlan told the Cabinet that this was France's last chance of a *rapprochement* with Germany. If France followed a pro-British policy she would be 'crushed, dismembered and cease to be a nation'. If she vacillated, Germany would create a thousand difficulties for her in the exercise of her sovereignty and would foment unrest. The peace negotiations would be disastrous. But 'if we collaborate with Germany, without thereby ranging ourselves along-side her to make deliberate war on England, that is to say work for her in our factories, and if we give her certain facilities, we can save the French nation, reduce our territorial losses to a minimum at home and in the colonies, and play an honourable if not important part in the Europe of the future. My choice is made, and I shall not allow myself to be turned away from it by the conditional offer of a cargo of wheat and a cargo of petrol.'[90]

It could hardly have been expected that the American programme of aid would sway a man so convinced of German victory as Darlan himself, and not even the defenders of that policy have claimed that it did. What it was intended to do, however, was to encourage Pétain and his supporters to resist his policies. In this, too, it failed. While Darlan was making his proposals to the French Cabinet, two American flour ships were docking at Marseilles. Their effect upon the Marshal can be gauged from the fact that on the following day he made the most unambiguously collaborationist speech of his career.[91] The events of May and June have nevertheless been taken as proof of the success of American policy. America supported Weygand, and it was Weygand, supported by Boisson and Estéva, Governor-General of Tunis, who arrived in Vichy on 2 June and blocked the 'Paris Protocols'. There is little contemporary support for this view. Weygand's outlook was as much based upon long-term strategic possibilities as Darlan's and was as little affected by shiploads of flour. His intervention was a good deal less spirited than he later claimed, and he was even willing to accept the Paris Protocols in return for wider political counter-concessions. It has been claimed that Weygand adopted this tactic because it gave Vichy a way out of the negotiations, and even that Darlan relied upon Weygand's opposition to enable him to backpedal on a policy which had got out of control.[92] These were post-war rationalisations. The French demands, although wide, were by no means preposterous and were only a basis of negotiation for the broad political settlement which Darlan sought.

The urgent pace of collaboration in the middle of 1941 was brought
to a halt not by Darlan's reluctance, nor by Weygand's posturings, and
least of all by the influence of Washington, but by a reversal of policy in
Berlin. Prompt British action in Iraq prevented Germany from
exploiting the situation, while the launching of Operation
BARBAROSSA on 22 June made Ribbentrop seek stability in the west
rather than an open Anglo-French conflict which might lose French
West Africa to the British and bring about increased French demands
for political concessions. A swift and successful campaign in the east
would enable Germany to impose its terms upon France before the end
of the year without the need for tiresome negotiations.[93] The image of a
frightened Darlan seeking an escape from negotiations which had run
away with him will not bear scrutiny. The loss of Syria made him more
determined to seek political concessions before courting hostilities with
the British once more, but it left his desire for a broad settlement
undimmed; it was Vichy, not Berlin, which strove for the remainder of
1941 to establish high-level contact, while Pétain himself abandoned
much of his reserve towards a policy of collaboration in what had
become a crusade against Bolshevism.

There is no evidence that American policy, when put to the test, was
able to exert any significant influence upon Vichy. Mesmerised by
German successes in the Balkans, the Vichy government paid no
attention to suggestions of a distant American participation in the war.
'My friends', wrote Leahy later, 'either refused to believe in the
existence of the great military power of the United States, or if it did
exist, they thought it would never be employed.'[94] Welles refused to
pass on a strong British message to Pétain, whom he felt was 'fighting a
lone hand against Darlan, de Brinon and company'.[95] On 8 May
Roosevelt made it clear to Pétain that American good will would be lost
if aid were given to Germany but received in return only the
unsatisfactory assurance that no 'voluntary active military aid' would
be given. Leahy thought that nothing short of this would be refused.
The trend in Vichy was strongly collaborationist and no serious
resistance was to be expected. Only a British victory in the Middle East
or concrete signs of American participation in the war could reverse
this. It was unlikely that either Pétain or Weygand would offer
resistance to a German descent on North Africa and there was no sign
that Pétain was willing to play his trump cards – the threat to resign or
to despatch the Fleet to the British side.[96] Roosevelt's speech expressing
disbelief that France would 'willingly' accept an agreement to col-

laborate with Germany, far from being 'tough', as Hytier implies, rather demonstrated Washington's continued reluctance to accept that Vichy was seeking collaboration rather than having it thrust upon her.[97]

Langer claimed after the war that during the crisis the British 'all but lost their nerve' and 'blew now hot, now cold towards attempts to keep France in line'. American policy, however, remained 'steadfast and consistent'.[98] The contemporary evidence suggests quite the contrary. While the British took a carefully calculated risk in acting with speed and despatch in the Middle East, American policy-makers had suffered a severe reverse. (On British action in Syria see below, Appendix I, pp. 183–4.) Having little faith in Pétain, the British saw in his new public posture only the confirmation of their long-standing mistrust. American policy, on the other hand, was based upon the assumption that Pétain resisted all measures of collaboration, and the 15 May speech was a severe reversal. Confusion and indecision were more apparent in Washington than in London. The withdrawal of Leahy was seriously considered and he himself confessed that he was unlikely thereafter to have any useful influence with the Marshal or with other members of the government.[99] Welles even suggested to the President that Congress should extend the Monroe Doctrine to cover West Africa. The State Department, however, decided that its North African policy should continue if Weygand showed signs of resistance, and within days Murphy was reporting that the situation in North Africa was unchanged and that the supply programme should not be interrupted because of developments in Syria.[100]

The British government's line was a good deal more consistent. Events in Syria showed that there was little chance of resistance to Axis demands, and the Foreign Office did not believe that economic assistance to North Africa would effectively stimulate resistance. Any supplies provided would simply fall into the hands of the Germans and be employed by them against Britain and the United States. Only if Weygand declared himself unequivocally should anything be offered: 'It seems to us advantageous to make it clear to Weygand that he cannot get everything he wants merely by sitting on the fence until the Germans arrive.'[101]

This approach was not adopted in Washington. Welles told Halifax that 'to deny supplies to Weygand at this moment in the light of his solemn assurances that the position in North Africa had not changed could only have the effect of making him give up hope of help from other than Axis sources. A continuance of carefully regulated help on the other hand would plainly carry the implication of U.S. interest with the possibility of more concrete help should it later be requested.' In the same vein, Hull told Murphy in early June that he could see no objection to the resumption of the supply programme 'since Weygand had met his commitments honourably'.[102] The main outcome of the episode was to demonstrate to Vichy that it could collaborate with Germany without sacrificing American support, and indeed that such support might even be redoubled if Washington became sufficiently anxious. Renewed American aid became a bonus to collaboration with the Axis. The British Cabinet, having detained the relief ship *Sheherezade* in Bermuda at the State Department's request, now had no option but to release it again in order to meet the American desire to give Weygand 'some card to play against Darlan'. 'We must do what they tell us in these small ways', Churchill minuted. 'It is not a question of who is right or wrong.'[103] At every stage of the crisis, the American government had been willing to see what Langer was later to describe as 'at least some extenuating circumstances, some rays of hope' in the situation, and to accept the renewed verbal assurances of a man who confessed himself unable to see how Germany could be defeated as sufficient to justify the despatch to French North Africa of 13,000 tons of fuel, oil and petrol at the moment when the Vichy government was in fierce pursuit of a policy of collaboration going far beyond the terms of the Armistice. The lesson of the crisis must have been as plain in Vichy as it was in London to a despairing William Strang: 'The State Department never insist on anything where the French are concerned.'[104]

JUNE–DECEMBER 1941

Weygand's intervention in Vichy in early June had little effect in the long term upon Darlan's policy, while the resumption of the supply programme undermined the American government's credibility and reduced the future effectiveness of its threats. Nor did the German invasion of the Soviet Union on 22 June cause many second thoughts in Vichy. There, as in less defeatist quarters, the most likely outcome seemed to be a swift campaign and a speedy Russian defeat. French attempts to draw Germany into negotiation continued, and further progress towards collaboration was prevented not by American influence but by German indifference. An impression of French reticence nevertheless remains. The Syrian imbroglio had demonstrated the danger of granting concessions without a solid quid pro quo, and Darlan was insistent thereafter that political concessions should precede further measures of collaboration. Also, Darlan was too much of an opportunist – 'an astute and bloodless calculator' in Professor Funk's words – to commit himself irrevocably to the German cause.[105] A man so sensitive to the shift of political and strategic forces could hardly fail to have reconsidered the outcome of the war in the light of Germany's mounting difficulties in the east. Before the year was out, he had established tentative contact with both London and Washington.

These developments, however intriguing, were essentially side-bets, and Darlan's money remained on Germany at least until the Japanese attack on Pearl Harbour. British naval power in the Mediterranean was seriously hampering the supply of Rommel's troops in North Africa, and in July and August and again in November Germany sought transit facilities through Tunisia as well as direct deliveries of French war material held in North Africa. Weygand again travelled to Vichy in July to protest, but to no avail. Lorries, petrol, food, bedding and war material were handed over, including twenty heavy cannons, each with a thousand rounds of ammunition.[106] In July Vichy was obliged to submit to a 'joint-defence' pact with Japan. The last of these measures aroused considerable indignation in Washington, but not to the extent of bringing about a change of policy. 'Nothing had occurred', wrote Hull later, 'to change the basic points on which the President and I were resolved to maintain diplomatic ties with the Pétain Government.'[107] The North African supply programme also continued in principle, although disputes over shipping prevented the quotas being met. By 1 July only two tankers of petroleum products had reached North Africa and from then until October only one more tanker and four cargo vessels carrying mainly non-strategic goods had crossed the Atlantic. In themselves, these were of trifling importance, and the British government contented itself with carefully scrutinising the commodities in question and obstructing only those of strategic importance. The conclusion of the Official Historian of the blockade is that 'all the British efforts were directed towards increasing the balance of advantages to Anglo-American interests rather than ending the arrangement'.[108]

The Ministry of Economic Warfare's attitude to the blockade of Metropolitan France was unchanged, and evidence of the extent to which Germany was continuing to benefit from the massive quantities of supplies arriving in Marseilles strengthened their case.[109] One report – that of Mr Allen of the American Red Cross in France – estimated Germany's share of imports arriving in Marseilles to be as high as 95 per cent.[110] Although Eden regarded this situation as 'deplorable', he nevertheless asked the Cabinet in late July to consider the political implications of the severe food shortages which could be expected in Europe during the coming winter, and requested the right to plead occasionally for flexibility in the application of the blockade when this was expedient.[111] Dalton, however, with Churchill's support, argued forcefully that the case for maintaining the blockade remained overwhelming. There was no possibility of starvation if available supplies were fairly distributed and France was in any case better off than Belgium, Holland or Greece. Allen even reported that the blockade was widely accepted as just in France itself, and that the French were for the most part willing to pull in their belts in the Allied cause.[112]

Although the Foreign Office was prepared to be flexible over emergency supplies for Metropolitan France and over non-strategic commodities, it refused to include oil in the supply programme. Transfers of oil from North African stocks had already been made to the Axis forces in Libya and the British were also unconvinced that the economic stability of the area, 'from which the enemy is now gaining greater benefits than ourselves', should be maintained in this way.[113] There was equally no assurance that American supplies might not be used to carry out an expedition to recover Chad. On 7 September, therefore, the Prime Minister approved Cadogan's suggestion that the American proposal to despatch the tanker *Lorraine* with 7000 tons of fuel oil should be refused. On the same day, however, Hull informed the French government that the *Lorraine* would sail, and it was discovered that Murphy had made the same commitment to Weygand. However much the cavalier action of the State Department rankled, the British yet again felt they had no alternative but to comply with American wishes. 'We must submit, after stating our case', wrote Churchill on the 10th.[114]

THE DISMISSAL OF WEYGAND

No sooner had the American programme begun to inch forward, however, than it was brought to a halt once more by the most dramatic reversal which Washington had yet to suffer in its gamble to restrain the Vichy government. On 18 November, after a prolonged crisis, General Weygand was removed from his position as Delegate-General in North Africa.

Argument continues about the extent to which Weygand's dismissal was the result of a German ultimatum and the extent to which it was brought about by pressure from Darlan, either because Weygand was the most effective obstacle to his policy of collaboration, or, as has more recently been suggested, because Darlan feared that Weygand might precipitate a premature revolt in North Africa and thus sever the tentative links which the Admiral had already been trying to establish with American representatives in the area.[115] Since Darlan was regarded in both London and Washington as a German tool, the exact circumstances of his dismissal were of academic interest at the time. It was generally assumed that German pressure had brought it about, and this was naturally the sense in which Pétain explained it to Leahy on the 19th.[116] Whatever the truth of the situation, the news struck the State Department like a thunderbolt. The first prop upon which America's Vichy policy rested had been removed on 15 May when it became apparent that Pétain had not, after all, been fighting a lone hand against collaboration. Only Weygand's assurances about the unchanged condition of North Africa had provided a justification for its continuance. Now, at a stroke, the individual on whom so much hope had been pinned, and on whose personal honour so much reliance had been placed, had been removed.

For a time it indeed seemed that a drastic reappraisal of policy might take place. Leahy, who felt that Vichy, in the face of Axis threats, 'had shown all the courage and resistance of a jellyfish',[117] saw Pétain on the 19th and told him that his surrender to Axis demands would have 'definitely an adverse effect upon the traditional amity between our two peoples, that it would probably bring about an immediate suspension of the economic assistance that is being given to the French colonies, and that it might very probably cause America to make a complete readjustment of its attitude towards the Government of France'.[118] He called for his own recall for consultation and a complete review of policy.[119] The attitude in Washington was the same. A press statement was issued by Hull on the 20th to the effect that American policy towards France was being reviewed and that all plans for economic assistance to North Africa were suspended.[120]

This mood of despair was short-lived, however, and the State

Department was soon able to find new justifications for continuing its policy. A change of tactics, argued Hull after the war, 'might deliver Vichy to the Axis at the point when the Axis most desired collaboration'.[121] If the economic accord were abandoned, the American observers in North Africa would have to be withdrawn also. Even before hearing of the State Department's reconsideration of its policy, Murphy was arguing for its continuance with the ingenious statement that any drastic change of course now would reveal that Weygand had been dealing closely with the United States and would thus affect his future use. His removal reassured the Germans and thus reduced the pressure upon North Africa.[122] With the news of Pétain's forthcoming meeting with Goering, any possibility that Washington would maintain its hard line evaporated, and the question was finally resolved by reports on 5 December that Vichy had agreed to provide transport facilities to the Axis in Metropolitan France and bases in North Africa.[123] Leahy was consequently instructed to inform Pétain that the United States would consider the renewal of its supply programme if he would repeat his declaration that the dismissal of Weygand denoted no change in Vichy's policy towards its North African possessions. This he did on 12 December.[124]

In London, the strongest reaction to the news came from Churchill. With Hitler's Russian campaign becoming bogged down and Rommel hard pressed in Libya, he felt that 'all French Africa might open out to us . . . we must be ready to exploit success'. On the 20th he telegraphed Roosevelt:

It would be disastrous if Weygand were to be replaced by some pro–Hun officer just at the moment when we are likely to be in a position to influence events in North Africa both from the East and from home. I hope you will try your utmost to preserve Weygand in his command. If this cannot be achieved, some friendly figure from retirement, like General Georges, might be agreed upon. I have not seen Georges since the collapse, but I have reason to believe his heart is sound. I knew him very well. I am afraid, on the other hand, lest Hitler may demand to occupy Bizerta in view of the possible danger to Tripoli. It is now or never with the Vichy French, and their last chance of redemption.[125]

It is interesting to note this striking evidence of Churchill's renewed interest in a possible uprising in North Africa in late 1941. During the ARCADIA conference in December, he was to return insistently to the proposal for a final bid to draw Vichy once more into the struggle (see p. 138). Equally noteworthy is the extent to which his own growing deference to Washington led him to overestimate considerably the extent of American influence in Vichy. There was no prospect whatsoever that the United States would be able to preserve Weygand in his command, while the suggestion that it would be desirable to replace him with General Georges was quite preposterous.

The Foreign Office took a much less tragic view of the situation. As Mack commented on the 22nd, 'we never set much hopes on Weygand and American disappointment at his dismissal must be considerably greater than our own'.[126] The Joint Intelligence Sub-Committee similarly reported that the situation in North Africa had not radically altered, and expressed optimism about Weygand's successors, especially the anglophile General Alphonse Juin.[127] As in the previous March, the positions of the Foreign Office and the State Department seemed for a time almost to reverse, and to a certain extent one can appreciate the resentment which the State Department felt towards the British, whose reactions to successive crises in Vichy seemed so perverse. While maintaining a holier-than-thou attitude towards American dealings with Vichy and constantly interrupting the implementation of the policy by refusing the necessary navicerts, the British were nevertheless able to exert indirect pressure upon the Vichy government through the White House (as in the *Dunkerque* incident), and to benefit equally with the State Department from any information which American observers in North Africa were gathering and any political benefits which Leahy's presence in Vichy might secure. London's suggestion of undue deference to Vichy was no more galling than when, as in May and November 1941, it was the British who urged that American links with Vichy should be maintained and that the supply programme should proceed.

However illogical British policy may have seemed to an increasingly sensitive State Department, it was essentially consistent. London accepted American policy in Vichy and North Africa as an expedient which offered limited gains in return for equally limited concessions (all of which were in any case to be made by the Americans). It expected little, offered little, and was little disappointed when the results fell short of American expectations. 'I think it is most important that the United States should continue their relations with Vichy and their supplies to North Africa and any other contacts unostentatiously for the present', wrote Churchill on the 30th. 'It would be a great mistake to lose any contacts before we know the results of the battle of Libya and its reactions. There is always time to break but it is more difficult to renew

contacts.'[128] He used the same arguments to the Cabinet on 1 December
against the suggestion that Canadian and South African representation
in Vichy should be withdrawn.[129] The Foreign Office's opinion was the
same, although it had become sceptical that the State Department
would succeed in striking what it regarded as the right balance between
the need to maintain contact and the need to avoid appeasement. 'I
hope this does not mean', commented Mack on receiving the news that
Leahy was to remain in Vichy, 'that the Americans will go back to
being soft with Vichy or that they will try to be accommodating with
them.'[130]

AMERICA'S ENTRY INTO THE WAR

On 7 December the events in France were first eclipsed and then thrown
into yet bolder relief by the Japanese attack upon Pearl Harbour and
the consequent entry of the United States into the war. Even the most
convinced collaborationists were forced to admit that the war might
now end either in an Allied victory or in a compromise peace on a very
different basis from what had seemed likely twelve months before.
American relations with Vichy were bound to be conducted upon an
altogether different footing, while the supply programme, which had
been intended primarily to preserve the *status quo* in North Africa, was to
acquire the more urgent purpose of preparing the ground for invasion.
America's new status as a belligerent marked a watershed in its relations
with Vichy and a natural point at which American policy-makers at the
time, and their apologists later, arrived at some interim assessment of
the effectiveness of the policy.

Sumner Welles argued at the time that American policy had 'gained
fifteen valuable months' and the claim that Vichy's quasi-neutrality
had been secured by pressure from the White House formed the basis of
later arguments in its support.[131] Hull was convinced that a contrary
policy might have been disastrous:

Our policy toward Vichy had been firm throughout, and never
wavered from our basic principles. We had not once appeased. By
pressure, by protest, and occasionally by support, we had helped keep
Pétain in the stirrups and North Africa free. Throughout that time our
influence at Vichy was pre-eminent over that of any other nation, with
the possible – only the possible – exception of Germany. We were better
informed of developments at Vichy and in French North Africa than

any other nation. And we had done much toward laying the groundwork for our invasion of North Africa in the following year.[132]

This statement is without basis in fact in almost every particular. Since the American government had reacted to every sign of increased collaboration by Vichy with renewed assurances of good will and an even greater willingness to accept verbal guarantees which had previously been regarded as insufficient, it is difficult to avoid odious comparisons with British and French policy towards Germany and Italy before the war. Similarly, Pétain remained in the stirrups because it suited Germany that he should do so, while the suggestion that American influence in Vichy in any way equalled that of Germany is so absurd as to require no further comment. As Leahy confessed candidly in July 1941, 'it is impossible to guess what will happen in France tomorrow or the next day, and almost as difficult for me to point to any useful accomplishment that we have made since my arrival . . .'.[133] Pétain's and Darlan's actions and statements throughout 1941 bear witness to the Admiral's failure to convince the Vichy government of American strength and determination to defeat Hitler, while the dismissal of Weygand was urged by Darlan and accepted by Pétain in full knowledge of the likely American response.[134] The history of Vichy in 1941 is the history of that government's pursuit of collaboration with Germany, to which relations with the United States were entirely subordinate. The claim to have been well-informed of events in Vichy and North Africa is equally difficult to reconcile with the evident surprise and discomfiture with which the State Department reacted to each new development. 'We were operating pretty much in the dark', wrote Langer lamely in 1947. 'All we knew was that Vichy was a Pandora's Box and that we must be ready for anything.'[135] As events turned out, London's judgements of the situation in Vichy and North Africa were at least as accurate as those of Washington. In the months to come, however, it was American perceptions which shaped Allied policy towards Vichy, and American sources of information which determined Allied assessments of the political situation in North Africa upon which the military planners staked so much.

6   Britain and Vichy in 1942

BRITISH policy towards Vichy was an untidy compromise between expediency and principle. On the one hand, the government was constantly aware of the dangers of open conflict with Vichy, and was drawn by the alluring possibility that the French Empire and Fleet might be persuaded to rejoin the Allied cause. On the other hand, the Vichy regime was regarded with very genuine distaste by most British policy-makers and by the public at large. A feeling of contempt was widespread for those who had risen to power in the wake of their country's defeat and who, moreover, had tried to gain the favour of their conquerors by extending to them economic or military aid, and it was taken for granted that an Allied victory would bring about their removal. 'Particular punishment will be reserved for the Quislings and traitors who make themselves the tools of the enemy', Churchill promised the Canadian parliament in December 1941. 'They will be handed over to the judgement of their fellow countrymen.'[1] By the same token, it was natural to assume that the refugee governments in London would be restored as a matter of course in the vanguard of the advancing Allied armies. The French case, however, was quite different. The government had not fled abroad but had remained to sue for peace, while the Free French, who maintained the symbolic resistance of France, were, in Churchill's phrase, 'not the owners but the trustees of the title deeds of France'.[2] There was another, more practical, difference also. The liberation of Germany's neighbours would presumably take place in the final stages of the war, and the puppet governments installed by the Germans would be powerless to assist or to hamper the Allies. Vichy, on the other hand, possessed a colonial Empire and a Fleet which it could either place at the Allies' disposal or turn against them. By its action or inaction at the critical moment it could therefore hope to determine the treatment which it would be accorded by the victors at the end of the day.

In spite of their hostile attitude towards the Vichy regime, the British were aware of the advantages to be gained by the preservation of Vichy's neutrality or by her re-entry into the war, and accepted that these could be achieved only at a certain price. The Foreign Office had been willing to restrain de Gaulle in 1940 in return for guarantees about Vichy's continued neutrality, and Churchill also made it abundantly clear that decisive action by Vichy in North Africa would heal all wounds and restore the Alliance. In early 1941 the Foreign Office, at the invitation of the Chiefs of Staff, prepared reports which considered the political implications if France resumed the fight. The Foreign Office decided that if Weygand or Darlan were given full powers by Vichy, and authorised to act as the temporary government of France and the French Empire, the British government would recognise their authority, reaffirm the Alliance and send diplomatic representatives. If, on the other hand, it was authorised to act only as the temporary government of the *Empire*, it would be treated 'somewhat on the lines' of the Gaullist territories. Formal recognition would also be a problem if such an authority acted without Vichy's approval. The main difficulty, of course, was to reconcile such a body with de Gaulle. The initial assumption had been that if Weygand rallied, de Gaulle would put the resources of Free France under his command. Even in February 1941 the Foreign Office was taking comfort in the belief, already somewhat tenuous, that 'if we recognise a French Government, approved by Vichy or not, he would presumably place his sword at its disposal'. By June, however, the growing uncertainty of de Gaulle's willingness to compromise introduced a more cautious note. 'It is to be hoped that the two will join forces and become a single unit, and we should do everything possible to encourage a fusion at a very early date. But such steps as it will be useful for us to take are not susceptible of precise definition at this stage.'[3] What emerges most clearly from this report is that the Foreign Office was not at all concerned with constitutional niceties and wished only to keep its options open. Until the middle of 1941, there was little dissent in the British government from the view that Vichy could gain readmission to the Allied circle. The passage of time alone, however, and the public image of Vichy which twelve months of government propaganda and press comment had created, made such a policy increasingly difficult to contemplate. The turning point really came as a result of the aggressively anti-British policy of Admiral Darlan, and the bitter campaign in Syria. At the same time, de Gaulle had established an almost impregnable position, and would certainly not consent to any arrangement putting his movement under an authority derived from Vichy.

These issues became critical in 1942. However objectionable in principle an alliance with Vichy might appear, the entry of the United States into the war made the prospect seem not only more attractive but also more capable of achievement. It seemed reasonable to assume that Vichy, whose policy had been dictated until then by the conviction that Germany could not be defeated, would reassess the odds and tailor its policy accordingly. At the same time, the Allies could now consider assuming the initiative, and French North Africa, first proposed by Churchill at Christmas 1941, was eventually secured as the objective for the following year. Everything would depend upon the attitude of Vichy and its delegates in North Africa. If they resisted an Allied landing, they might give the Axis powers the opportunity to reinforce the area and involve the Allies in a protracted campaign which would long delay the liberation of Europe. If, on the other hand, they permitted Allied forces to establish themselves without opposition from Casablanca or Dakar to Tunis, and particularly if they despatched the Fleet to fight with the British and Americans, they would make a significant contribution to the war effort and one which might even give retrospective justification to the policy of *attentisme*. The British might find themselves once more the comrades-in-arms of men who had aided the Axis. Following their example, other governments or bodies which had co-operated with Germany would see the opportunity to edge their way back into the Allied camp. A balance would therefore have to be struck between the military advantages of a political compromise, and the need to preserve, even at a price in human life, the values which the war was ostensibly being fought to preserve.

It was the growing realisation of these issues which caused the Foreign Office to part company with the Prime Minister on the question of the degree of compromise which would be possible with the Vichy regime. It must be remembered not only that Churchill was responsible for the overall direction of the war and was consequently preoccupied with the pursuit of victory at the least cost in human life, but also that he was an opportunist by temperament, irresistibly drawn towards any scheme which promised great advantages at little cost. His concern to preserve good relations with the American President also inclined him to be tolerant of Washington's very different attitude towards the Vichy regime and the Free French movement. The upshot of this was that Churchill, although much given to scornful rhetoric at Vichy's expense, was reluctant to abandon all hope of Vichy and was convinced that Britain's survival and the entry of the United States into the war would eventually bring about a dramatic change in Vichy's policy. As far as Churchill was concerned, therefore, 'our consistent policy was to make the Vichy Government and its members feel that, so far as we were concerned, it was never too late to mend'.[4]

The Foreign Office took a quite different view of the problem and was deeply concerned by the political price which might have to be paid to secure short-term advantages on the battlefield. In particular, it argued that the future peace and stability of Europe could be assured only by the restoration of France as a Great Power and by the re-building of the Anglo-French Alliance, and that this argument held good whether one argued that the future threat to peace would come from Germany or the Soviet Union. As Eden broadcast on Bastille day 1942, 'For us the full restoration of France as a Great Power is not only a declared war aim and the fulfilment of a pledge made to a sister nation, but also a practical necessity, if post-war reconstruction is to be undertaken within the framework of that traditional civilization which is our common heritage.'[5]

But how could this be achieved? As in 1871, 'il y aurait toute une France à refaire'.[6] The problems of economic reconstruction would be daunting enough. Even more serious, however, was the very real danger that the bitter dissensions in French society would lead to civil war and to the continued eclipse of the country. France had welcomed Pétain because it was believed that he could protect France from the Germans. An Allied victory would discredit this claim and bring about a revulsion of feeling against Vichy. Looking ahead, Eden and the Foreign Office became convinced of the importance of the Free French movement for the future recovery of France and of the Anglo-French Alliance, and were impressed by the mounting evidence in 1942 that de Gaulle had gained acceptance in France as the leader of French resistance and that any attempt by the Allies to maintain the Vichy regime after the war, or to restore the old 'republic of pals', would provoke civil war.[7] This did not mean that the Foreign Office accepted de Gaulle's claims to represent France in any legal sense. As Eden wrote in July 1942, 'He cannot substantiate a claim to be regarded as France or as the Head of the Government of France. There is, in fact, no French authority today which can be regarded as generally representative of the French people.'[8] What it did mean was that the Foreign Office saw de Gaulle as the saviour of French national self-respect. Again, as Eden broadcast on Bastille day 1942, 'Thanks to General de Gaulle's decision to fight on, a decision which deprived the Bordeaux capitulation of all moral value,

France has never been absent from the battlefield.'⁹ De Gaulle was thus the means whereby the British were able to preserve the Alliance even when the *de facto* French government was aiding the common enemy. It was therefore vital, in the Foreign Office's view, that no arrangements which were made before the peace for the sake of military expediency should jeopardise de Gaulle's position or associate Britain with the agents of France's downfall.

These considerations were set forth in a remarkably perceptive analysis of the position of the Free French movement which Mr Parr sent to Eden in August 1941, and which met with widespread approval in the Foreign Office. De Gaulle's main anxiety, argued Parr, was that the authorities in North Africa,

semi-independently of Vichy, may gradually achieve a position in which they will be able to pretend that their policy has brought them to a point where they are morally aligned with the United States in hostility to Germany, and that, looking back on events since the Armistice, their policy has been justified by its material results. No doubt General Weygand and M. Boisson are by now aware that the Central Powers cannot win this war, and that their only hope of maintaining their reputations and their influence is to manoeuvre towards the position I have indicated. But, if it should prove practicable for them to achieve this, some similar way of escape might be open to the Government at Vichy. It might be possible that the fortune of war and their own adroitness would leave them so placed at the conclusion of hostilities that they could claim that their temporisings, however apparently open to criticism at the time, had spared France an ordeal which would have left her ravaged beyond recognition . . . . They could claim, too, that but for the disloyalty of the Free French the severity of the occupation might have been much less.

The implications of this for British policy in the long term were clear:

From the point of view of our own dealings with France after the war it would, I think, be unfortunate if the Vichy politicians were able at the last minute to scramble down on the right side of the fence, and were to succeed in justifying to French metropolitan opinion the shifts and intrigues and treacheries that have characterised their conduct of affairs. To do so would involve the deliberate and persistent fomentation of anti-British sentiment, and in this task they would be abetted by those elements which, while hostile to Germany, look forward to our victory with misgiving because of their attachment to political theories which that victory should permanently discredit. We would, furthermore, lose the support of the followers of General de Gaulle, who would have to decide between submission and exile. Our relations with France would deteriorate to their conditions of 40 years ago . . . .[10]

Nevertheless, however clear the realisation in London of the importance of preserving French self-respect and of the indispensable role which the Free French movement had to play in this, it was already apparent that it would be no easy task to maintain unswerving support for Free France. As de Gaulle himself put it, 'les bonnes intentions de M. Eden ne purent faire de l'alliance une rose sans épines'.[11]

A major difficulty was presented by the character of de Gaulle himself, by his increasing intransigence in defence of French rights, and by his mounting suspicions of British and American designs upon France. Relations with the British never recovered from the Syrian armistice, the terms of which had aroused all de Gaulle's suspicions of British designs in the Levant. At one stage he even threatened to withdraw his forces from British command.[12] Matters came to a head in late August 1941, with the publication in the Chicago *Daily News* of an interview in which he had given free rein to his anglophobia. Churchill told the Cabinet on 1 September that he found de Gaulle's behaviour 'disturbing', and that all departments should adopt in future a 'cautious and dilatory' attitude towards all requests made by the Free French.[13] On the 12th he confronted de Gaulle in Downing Street and took him to task. 'The Prime Minister said that he had witnessed with very great sorrow the deterioration of General de Gaulle's attitude towards His Majesty's Government. He now felt that he was no longer dealing with a friend.' After a difficult start, however, the meeting ended cordially enough and the order for departmental caution was rescinded.[14]

The underlying problem remained unsolved, however – the absolute dominance over the Free French of one man who envisaged France increasingly in terms of the Free French movement and the Free French movement in terms of himself. The formation of the Free French National Committee on 24 September 1941, which the British encouraged, was intended to clip de Gaulle's wings, but it did little to diminish his authority over his colleagues and nothing whatever to modify his own conception of his role.[15] Relations with the British remained poor throughout 1942. Churchill deplored the General's obstinate insistence upon French rights and came to regard him as more of a liability than an asset to the Allied cause. Persistent squabbling over the General's position in the National Committee, over the Muselier incident, over the situation in Syria and, above all, over the British occupation of Madagascar in mid-1942, kept relations in a state of permanent crisis, seriously prejudicing the Prime Minister against Free France at a time when he was increasingly apt to defer to the anti-Gaullist prejudices of the American government (see below, Appendix II, pp. 184–5).

The other major difficulty faced by the Foreign Office was the policy of the American government towards France. During 1941, American relations with de Gaulle had been frigid, but without serious incident. The feelings of mutual hostility, however, were apparent. De Gaulle resented the kudos which American support lent to Vichy and, as Parr pointed out, lived in constant apprehension lest Weygand or some other equivocal figure enjoying American patronage should succeed in edging his way back into the Allied camp. Nor did he shrink from bringing his views to the attention of the American government. In January 1942, for example, in a long memorandum to Hull, he argued that war was not a game of chess but a moral crusade, and American support for Vichy was having a dangerously demoralising effect upon French resistance. If the United States persisted in its policy of maintaining the neutrality of France, it would lose the confidence and friendship of the French people after the war and play into the hands of those elements who would exploit France's humiliation.[16]

The event which more than anything else had prompted de Gaulle to express so forcefully his dissatisfaction with American policy was the Free French liberation of the islands of St Pierre and Miquelon, off the Newfoundland coast, at Christmas 1941, an episode which was as much a symptom of the poor relations between Free France and the United States as it was a cause of their further decline. Langer has suggested that the dismissal of Weygand had brought about a reconsideration of policy in the State Department, and that a more sympathetic attitude towards Free France might have been adopted if de Gaulle had not resorted to such high-handed action.[17] In fact, there were few signs of any far-reaching changes in Washington at the end of the year. The violence with which the Secretary of State reacted to the incident was the clearest possible evidence of how far the State Department was from adopting a more moderate attitude towards de Gaulle and of how remote was the prospect of a more vigorous policy towards Vichy.

The possibility of a Gaullist liberation of the islands had been in the air since the previous June, when the Chiefs of Staff had been of the opinion that, although perhaps desirable politically, such an action would be of no value militarily. The Canadian government had been concerned at the reaction of the *Québecois*, while the American government had been worried by the possible infringement of the Monroe Doctrine and by the effect of such an expedition upon its relations with Vichy.[18] By the following September, however, the Chiefs of Staff had revised their opinion and decided that the radio transmitter on St Pierre constituted a threat to Allied convoys and that only the rallying of the islands to de Gaulle would provide the necessary security.[19] When the matter was considered in London in early December there was unanimous agreement that the matter had dragged on for too long and that the best course would have been for de Gaulle to occupy the islands 'without saying anything about it until it was done'. It was thought to be unlikely that the United States would object.[20] In fact, the contrary was the case. The American government was at that time renegotiating its agreement with Admiral Robert, Governor of the French West Indies, over the maintenance of the *status quo* in the western hemisphere, and the President expressed himself 'strongly opposed to any action by the Free French in connection with St. Pierre . . . in view of the unfavourable effect on the policy of Vichy'. The French National Committee was therefore informed that the British government could no longer give its support to the venture and Dejean, the Commissioner for Foreign Affairs, gave his assurance that no action would be taken.[21] After issuing this statement, however, de Gaulle became angered by the suggestion that the United States and Canada should establish their control over the transmitter while leaving the administration in the hands of Vichy, and on 18 December, without consulting the rest of the National Committee, he ordered Admiral Muselier to rally the islands 'without saying anything to the foreigners'.[22]

The expedition was carried out on Christmas morning without a shot being fired and on the following day the population voted overwhelmingly in favour of Free France.[23] The news came as a complete surprise to the British and American governments. But while the former were naturally willing to shrug the matter off, Hull reacted violently and issued a hasty statement condemning the action of the 'so-called Free French ships' and hinting at the restoration of Vichy's authority.[24] Hull's reaction was extreme and foolish, and the American public raised an outcry against the suggestion that the forces of democracy should be ousted to make way for a shabby compromise with Vichy.[25]

Adverse criticism succeeded only in increasing Hull's stubbornness. Churchill, then in Washington, was struck by his preoccupation with such a trifling matter while he and the President mapped out the future course of the war.[26] Most striking of all was Hull's complete miscalculation of the response of Vichy and Berlin. In a barely coherent memorandum to the President on 31 December, he suggested that the seizure of the islands had provided the Germans with the required pretext to occupy French North Africa, and also hinted that the British had spurred de Gaulle on.[27] In fact, there is no reason to doubt that Vichy would have accepted the loss philosophically if Hull's statement had not given them their cue.

The British deplored the fact that de Gaulle had acted in violation of his assurance, although they approved of the expedition in principle. Churchill wrote later that the matter did not affect the main discussions then in progress in Washington and that Roosevelt himself seemed to shrug it off.[28] At the time, however, he showed concern that the vital matters then under discussion might be affected, and sought a speedy compromise. In London, the Cabinet and the Foreign Office took a different view, arguing that it was unthinkable to remove de Gaulle by force and that any such solution would humiliate him for Vichy's benefit.[29] Eden pointed out that the State Department's attitude was creating the impression that the United States was afraid of Vichy, and was unmoved by the usual complaints that the United Kingdom had 'got the benefits' of America's policy without suffering the unpopularity, or by Hull's hysterical idea that the *coup* had 'jeopardised the whole delicate structure of Inter-American relations'.[30] As the issue dragged on into January, however, Churchill became increasingly impatient. 'However you dish it up he has got to take it', he cabled on 12 January. 'It is intolerable that the great movement of events should be obstructed and I shall certainly not intervene to save de Gaulle or other Free French from the consequences.'[31] Roosevelt was becoming equally insistent that 'two islands cannot be made an issue in the great effort to save the world'.[32] Although a compromise was eventually reached, the episode left a bitter legacy. Hull, in particular, regarded de Gaulle's action as a personal affront and seemed incapable thereafter of thinking objectively about the French problem.

During the early months of 1942, public support for the Free French movement grew steadily in the United States.[33] The State Department, however, remained morbidly suspicious of the Free French, suspected de Gaulle personally of Fascist tendencies (an accusation which could more reasonably have been pointed against Pétain) and argued that any degree of political recognition would alienate Vichy and at the same time be used by de Gaulle to bolster his claims to governmental status.[34] Another argument, put forward by Hull and Welles, and by Admiral Leahy on his return from Vichy in July, was that by supporting de Gaulle, the American government would effectively force a Gaullist dictatorship upon France.[35]

The most alarming manifestation of this attitude was the willingness of the State Department to engage in cordial discussions, not only with the Vichy government, but with the amorphous group of political trimmers who had gathered in the United States since the fall of France, and with various other discredited figures in retirement in the Un-occupied Zone. In May 1942 it came to light that steps had been taken to persuade Herriot and Jeanneney (Presidents respectively of the Chamber of Deputies and the Senate under the Third Republic) to leave France for the United States.[36] Even more serious were the discussions held by the State Department with people like Chautemps, Rougier and Alexis Léger. On 12 May 1942, Tixier, the Gaullist representative in Washington, wrote bitterly that the United States would deal just as cheerfully with Admiral Robert, who took his orders from Vichy, who took their orders from Germany, as they would with the governor of any Free French territory which was co-operating to the full with the Allies, while the French National Committee they preferred to ignore altogether. Taken in conjunction with Welles's recent meeting with Chautemps, this attitude indicated to Tixier that the United States government wished to deal separately with each part of the French Empire so that it could be dismembered more easily later on.[37] Dejean went further than this, and told de Gaulle in August that the State Department hoped to establish a sort of capitalistic democracy in France after the war by supporting Pétainist elements in Vichy and encouraging the establishment of a successor government to Vichy which would be heavily dependent upon the United States. Leahy was singled out as the main advocate of this approach. If the United States invaded Morocco, they would set up a local government independent of Fighting France, 'perhaps even with the silent blessing of Vichy'.[38]

These developments were the occasion of alarm and exasperation in London also. Although at this time the Foreign Office was reluctant to believe that the United States sought to perpetuate the Vichy regime into peacetime, the State Department's attitude left no room for complacency. 'We feel that tiresome though he is General de Gaulle possesses qualities which are not possessed by any other members of the Free French movement or by any of the Frenchmen in London or the United States who have hitherto held themselves aloof', wrote Mack on 12 May. Attempts by people like Chautemps and Rougier to form a 'middle movement' composed of time-servers who did not approve of de Gaulle, who felt that Pétain was 'doing his best' and who at the same time claimed to be supporters of the Allied cause, were particularly dangerous. 'I sincerely hope that the United States Government will give such a movement no encouragement', he concluded. 'Chautemps is the worst kind of French politician who holds a large responsibility for the surrender of Bordeaux.'[39]

The substance of Mack's arguments was conveyed in an *aide-mémoire* from Halifax to Welles on 14 May.[40] British policy, it was explained, was not to recognise the Free French movement as a government, but to broaden out the Free French National Committee by encouraging leaders of resistance within France, who would not be mere mouthpieces of de Gaulle, to adhere to it. Further exchanges between London and Washington in the following weeks brought about an apparent softening of the State Department's attitude, and on 29 June Eden was able to convey to de Gaulle on behalf of the American government a 'recognition' formula which, although guarded, was accepted by him with apparent satisfaction.[41] This improvement, however, turned out to be short-lived, and in August, the State Department had what Speaight called 'a bad relapse' over the question of Free French accession to the United Nations declaration.[42] The British met with no real success in 1942 in their attempt to lessen the anti-Gaullist feelings of the American government.

American belligerency turned the attention of the Foreign Office towards eventual victory and the problems of Anglo-French relations in peacetime, and led it to stress the long-term importance to Britain of maintaining support for the Free French movement. Upon the Prime Minister it had the opposite effect of reviving his enthusiasm for a fresh attempt to persuade Vichy to re-enter the war. Since the time of Weygand's dismissal, Churchill had been considering a final appeal to Vichy. 'It is now or never with the Vichy French and their last chance of redemption', he cabled Roosevelt in November 1941.[43] On 12 December he told the Cabinet that 'the time might shortly come when we should say to the Vichy French Government that if they would stand with us in maintaining the independence and integrity of North Africa, we would do our best to restore their Empire. But if they failed us at this point we would have nothing more to do with them.'[44] In a paper drawn up three days later on the way to the United States the Prime Minister expanded upon his theme. The main objective of the war effort in 1942, he argued, should be the occupation by Allied troops of the entire African coastline from Dakar to Turkey. The time was therefore ripe for a new diplomatic offensive.

We ought therefore to try hard to win over French North Africa, and now is the moment to use every inducement and form of pressure at our disposal upon the Government of Vichy and the French authorities in North Africa. The German setback in Russia, the British successes in Libya, the moral and military collapse of Italy, and above all the declarations of war exchanged between Germany and the United States must strongly affect the mind of France and the French Empire. Now is the time to offer to Vichy a blessing or a cursing. A blessing will consist in a promise by the United States and Great Britain to re-establish France as a Great Power with her territories undiminished. It should carry with it an offer of active aid by British and United States expeditionary forces, both from the Atlantic seaboard of Morocco and at convenient landing-points in Algeria and Tunis, as well as from General Auchinleck's forces advancing from the east. Ample supplies for the French and the loyal Moors should be made available. Vichy should be asked to send their fleet from Toulon to Oran and Bizerta and to bring France into the war again as a principal. . . .[45]

While the renewed possibility of action by Vichy encouraged the Prime Minister once more to let bygones be bygones, the difficulty of relations with de Gaulle also inclined him to adjust relations with the General accordingly. 'Our relations with General de Gaulle and the Free French movement will require to be reviewed', he wrote ominously. 'If Vichy were to act as we desire about French North Africa, the United States and Great Britain must labour to bring about a reconciliation between the Free French (de Gaullists) and those other Frenchmen who will have taken up arms against Germany.'[46]

Churchill's enthusiasm for a final call to arms was shared neither in London nor in Washington. Although he did not spell out what sort of 'cursing' he had in mind if Vichy failed to respond, it could only be the withdrawal of the promise to restore French greatness. The Foreign Office felt that it was quite the wrong time to attempt to force Vichy's hand and that in any case the withdrawal of the undertaking would bring about a crisis with de Gaulle. Why should France suffer for Vichy's sins? The right policy was to continue to exert pressure on Vichy through the United States, but not to issue violent threats.[47]

American belligerency did not in fact change the outlook of the Vichy government to any appreciable extent. Leahy reported that a momentary optimism at the time of Pearl Harbour was rapidly obliterated by America's heavy losses in the Pacific, while Mack conjectured, probably correctly, that Pétain thought the United States would be too preoccupied with the Far East to take any action in Europe in the foreseeable future.[48] Auchinleck's advance in December and January did not get as far as Wavell's the previous year, and Rommel's counter-attack in May brought him to within seventy miles of Alexandria. Despite German reverses in the east, Pétain remained convinced that France's policy should be one of continued *attentisme*. As for the Prime Minister's suggestion that Weygand might be despatched to Washington for staff talks, 'we have by now surely had enough experience of him to know that he is weak and, so far as this war is concerned, quite useless'.[49] In short, the Foreign Office realised that American belligerency had done nothing to rouse Vichy and that no purpose would be served by inviting their co-operation. The issue in Vichy during December and January was whether to break with the United States, not with Germany.[50]

In Washington, Churchill's plan was the first proposal which was put before the President when discussions began on 22 December, and it was agreed that plans would be drawn up for entering North Africa 'with or without invitation'.[51] The suggestion that Vichy should be presented with an ultimatum found no more favour in the State Department than it had in the Foreign Office, however. Instead of a call to arms, Roosevelt issued a message to Pétain on 20 January which called only for Vichy's resistance to an Axis attack on Unoccupied France or the French colonies. The President of the United States, Roosevelt warned Pétain, was 'just about the best friend that France has got', and wished to see France and the French Colonial Empire restored after the war. But any 'aid and comfort' which France gave to the Axis would harm the United States, which would not take it 'lying down'.[52] Pétain returned only the usual unsatisfactory assurances, including the ambiguous statement that there was no longer any question of Germany using French North African bases 'at the present time'. France would resist invasion from any quarter – Gaullist, German, British or American. Leahy concluded that Vichy would not even co-operate with the United States if Germany descended on North Africa.[53]

In London the news of this exchange was greeted with mounting impatience. 'The *status quo*, with which the President is content, does not help the war effort of the United Nations, and may do it harm', commented Mack on 2 February. The State Department was still willing to hold the scales between Britain and Vichy 'without showing any partiality for either'.[54] 'The trouble is that the United States Government do not seem to realise that Vichy is blackmailing them', noted Strang. 'What is particularly depressing is that the President seems to be as tolerant of Vichy as the State Department are: the latter are past all hope, I fear.'[55] For a time, however, a new note of vigour was apparent in American policy, and Welles told Halifax on 11 February that the United States was determined to pursue a stronger line.[56] Evidence which came to light in February that the Axis forces in Libya were again being provisioned from French sources prompted a swift threat that, if such assistance continued, Leahy would be withdrawn for consultation.[57] But this was as far as the State Department was prepared to go. The British Cabinet decided on the 16th to warn Vichy that ships engaged in supplying the Axis in Libya would be attacked without further warning, and that all ships in Tunisian waters were 'under suspicion'.[58] However, further exchanges between Vichy and Washington later in the month produced the necessary assurances, and the British fell in with the American wish that the drastic action contemplated should not be taken.[59]

The effect of America's entry into the war upon the attitude of Marshal Pétain was therefore disappointing, and nothing in the outward behaviour of the Vichy government gave cause for hope that it would adopt a more sympathetic attitude towards the Allied cause. Despite every discouragement, however, Churchill remained firmly of the opinion that, sooner or later, Vichy would have a change of heart. It was therefore vital that every channel of communication with Vichy should be kept open. In January 1942 he wrote: 'The Vichy contacts are extremely important at the present time in view of certain projects which are being considered. I certainly do not mind the United States strengthening their contacts with Vichy. On the contrary, it is on the influence of the United States with Vichy that I count for the decisive reactions in France.'[60] For the same reason, he had resisted throughout 1941 the suggestion that Canada and South Africa should withdraw their representatives from Vichy. 'We shall knock them about as much as may be necessary in the anomalous conditions prevailing while still preserving contacts which may be of value', he told Eden in May.[61] Similarly, while Eden told Mackenzie King during his visit to England in August that little was to be gained from Dupuy's contacts, Churchill spoke instead in encouraging terms of his need to have a window on Vichy.[62] Indeed, in view of the Foreign Office's low opinion of him and of King's own desire to still hostile criticism at home with a public demonstration of his disapproval of Vichy, it was only the British Prime Minister's continued support which kept Dupuy at his post. Even the dismissal of Weygand did not alter his stand. Smuts, convinced that a descent by the Germans upon French North Africa was imminent, cabled King that he intended to sever relations. King in his turn said he would continue to resist public pressure for a similar move only if Churchill would allow him to refer publicly to the views he had expressed in August.[63] Still Churchill hesitated, wishing to await the outcome of the Libyan battle, while Eden pressed for an end to an anomalous situation and for a demonstration of the unity of the Commonwealth in regard to the Vichy government. Dupuy's 'occasional pilgrimages' were, he argued, quite useless; on his last visit, Pétain had refused to see him, and his other contact, Huntziger, was dead. In Churchill's view, Eden was too eager to cut threads that might not be rejoined. 'Finland, Roumania, Hungary, and now Vichy.'[64] In the War Cabinet on 1 December it was Churchill's view which, as usual, prevailed.

In fact, there was little point in the continuation of Dominion representation in Vichy. The Foreign Office had long realised that formal diplomatic communications could achieve nothing in the prevailing circumstances. To be effective, Eden told the Cabinet in December 1941, 'contacts with the Vichy Government would have to be through unofficial sources'.[65] This was more than ever true when in April 1942 Darlan's long ascendancy was brought to an end by the return of Pierre Laval to office.

The British, as usually happened when Vichy seemed to act in conformity with Axis wishes, assumed that direct pressure had been brought to bear to reinstate Laval. Thus Eden told the Cabinet on 20 April that Laval's return was probably due in part to German anxiety about the internal situation in France or to a German desire to have wider access to French resources for their spring campaigns.[66] Darlan's continued control of the armed forces was seen as evidence that Pétain had 'stubbornly drawn the line' at a German demand that Laval should have absolute power. This was only partly true. The removal of Darlan

was brought about by his clear failure to establish satisfactory relations
with Berlin, and Pétain seems to have had in mind a new Cabinet of
traditionalist, clerical, neutralist friends, not one dominated by Laval
and his instruments.[67] However, news of the Marshal's secret meeting
with Laval in March leaked out and caused Washington to issue an
ultimatum stating that the return of Laval or any other figure 'who
would be identified as notoriously and completely with a policy of
abject servility to Germany' would oblige the United States 'to break off
the trustful relations which it presently maintains with the French
Government for the mutual good of the two countries'. When the
Germans heard of this ultimatum, the issue naturally became a test of
strength which the United States was bound to lose.[68]

Whatever the circumstances, with Laval in power there was little
that diplomatic representation could achieve. 'Laval has staked his life
on a German victory, and will do everything in his power to assist in
bringing it about', wrote Mack. 'We can hope for nothing good from
this government.'[69] This opinion was borne out by Laval's comments to
Leahy during their meeting on 27 April. 'He was ready to defend
France and the French Empire against all comers and he specifically
stated that if the British or the Americans should attempt to make a
landing either on the soil of Metropolitan France or on French
territory in North Africa, he would offer resistance to the best of his
ability.' A German victory or a negotiated peace would be better, Laval
thought, than a Soviet or a British victory, while if he possessed the
means to do so he would try to reconquer the territories which had
rallied to de Gaulle. Leahy concluded that Laval was 'committed fully
and may be expected to go as far as is practicable in the attempt to
collaborate with Germany'.[70]

The American government decided to withdraw Leahy 'for
consultation' – in effect permanently.[71] Having threatened to sever
relations if Laval returned they could hardly do less. Formal relations
were maintained, however, and Pinkney Tuck remained as Chargé
d'Affaires. The British government also withdrew its final objections to
the severance of contact by the Dominions. Smuts broke off relations on
23 April. In the case of Canada, however, Churchill still managed to
persuade the Cabinet to temporise 'until the position became clearer'.[72]
The United States government also asked the Canadians to maintain
contact 'with a view to salvaging whatever might be possible for the
advantage of the United Nations'.[73] This desperate optimism was short-
lived. Laval's speeches on taking office were so violently anti-British

that Eden felt it was indefensible to continue to urge King to maintain contact, an attitude to which Churchill finally assented. However, as a favour to Hull, Eden made a public statement of support for American links with Vichy on 8 May.[74]

Eden's increasing insistence that nothing was to be gained from contact with the Marshal, and that British support for de Gaulle should not be compromised by futile attempts to bring about a change of heart in Vichy, gave rise in the middle of 1942 to a remarkable exchange of views with Churchill, from which the Foreign Secretary emerged somewhat ruffled. On 1 June Eden presented to the Cabinet a memorandum on opinion in France, in which he concluded from recent reports that resistance in the Occupied Zone was synonymous with Gaullism, that General de Gaulle was the accepted leader of French resistance, and that the encouragement by the Allies of time-servers like Chautemps and Pierre Cot would have a disastrous effect in France.[75] Churchill countered this on 5 June with a long statement of his reasons for continuing to hold out hope of Vichy.

Whatever our feelings of well-placed scorn and distrust of the Vichy Government might be, we ought not to forget that it is the only Government which may perhaps give us what we want from France, namely, the Toulon Fleet and the entry into the French North African provinces. One has therefore to consider what, if any, are the chances of this. They do not seem to me entirely negligible. The Vichy Government under Darlan, Laval or perhaps Doriot must, of course, pay its way from week to week with its German masters. Their only alternative is the installation of a Gauleiter and complete occupation. From my own personal observation of what has happened, I do not feel that the Vichy Government have done anything more than was absolutely necessary to stave off this second alternative. They have borne Oran, Dakar, Syria, Madagascar, the British blockade and British air raids with the least possible show of anger. This attitude has been forced upon them by the sentiment against Germany of the vast majority of the French nation, both in Occupied and Unoccupied France, and by the French conviction that they must not sever the future of France from the United States.

The cardinal question not only for Vichy but for France is – who will win the war? At first there seemed no possibility of defeating Germany. But the campaigns in Russia, the entry of the United States, the enormous staying power of Great Britain, our evident growing preponderance in the air, have brought back hope to virile French hearts and affected ever-wider circles in France . . . .

I have always been ready to take rough action against Vichy, and have always been sure that Vichy would in one shape or another put up with it. I look forward to a time in the war, which I cannot fix but which may not be far off, when the great change of heart which has taken place in the French masses and the apparent certainty of an Allied victory will produce a sudden decisive change in the action of the Vichy Government.[76]

This extraordinary statement – the argument that Vichy had done no more than was absolutely necessary to keep out the Gauleiter could have come from the lips of Pétain himself – was not allowed to pass unchallenged. In a long draft, Eden took issue with Churchill's views, pointing out that there was nothing in the actions of Pétain, Darlan or Laval to suggest the remotest possibility of the change which the Prime Minister awaited.[77] Even if there were, Eden was firm in his opinion that the political repercussions of a *rapprochement* between Britain and Vichy would be disastrous, and on 10 June circulated to the Cabinet in support of this contention a report by a young Frenchman, then secretly in England, who had been Georges Mandel's Parliamentary Attaché. The report was emphatic that 'the Politicians of Resistance are absolutely hostile to the idea that Marshal Pétain can perform a second act of treachery and assist in the Victory'. As much as 85–90 per cent of the population in the Occupied Zone, and 70–5 per cent in the Unoccupied Zone, supported de Gaulle. Every day Frenchmen accepted death and imprisonment on his behalf. 'It is impossible to find in France the name of any other person for whom Frenchmen would agree to such sacrifices.' In following a policy of appeasement in regard to Marshal Pétain, the United States' government had maintained confusion in the minds of the people of France from which only the collaborators had derived benefit, since the United States had obtained no advantage from their attitude. 'In wartime those who fight must be united with simple ideas; by the maintenance of an equivocacy their ideas of their duty are removed.'[78] As Eden pointed out, the reliability of this report was somewhat questionable since its author had contacted the Free French in London before writing it. Most doubtful of all was the suggestion of widespread personal support for de Gaulle. A memorandum drawn up in September by Desmond Morton pointed out that *Gaullisme* was not necessarily the same as *de Gaullisme* and concluded that, while the majority of Frenchmen supported the General as a symbol of their desire to oust the Germans, few trusted him as a candidate for political leadership. On the other hand, no Frenchman, unless committed to an Axis victory, would approve of the abandonment of him or his movement, which if it took place would considerably alienate French loyalty to England.[79]

Churchill refused to shift his ground and took Eden to task in a long minute on 14 June.

For thirty-five years I have been a friend of France, and have always kept as closely in touch as possible with the French people. I therefore have a certain instinct about them on which I rely. It is very easy to make the kind of case you have set down out of all the shameful things the Vichy Government have done. But this does not make sufficient allowance for the unnatural conditions prevailing in a defeated country with a Government living on the sufferance of the enemy. It does not alter in any way my wish or extinguish my hope to have the French Fleet sail to Africa, and to get an invitation for British and American troops to enter French North Africa. Nor does it alter the fact that, at any rate for some time to come, Vichy is the only party that can offer these good gifts. At a certain stage it would not only be in their interests to offer them, but their lives may depend on it. President Roosevelt has the same feelings as I have about all this, and so, I believe, have the Chiefs of Staff. The position is so anomalous and monstrous that very clear-cut views, such as you are developing, do not altogether cover it. There is much more in British policy towards France than abusing Pétain and backing de Gaulle . . . .[80]

Churchill ended his minute with a warning that he would oppose Eden's paper in Cabinet and Eden, uncertain of support, withdrew it. He nevertheless put his views forward in a modified form the following month. He first made clear that he was not supporting de Gaulle in any governmental capacity. However, 'we have been largely responsible for building him up, and it is clearly impossible to drop him now'. Eden felt that his public statement on 8 May expressing British support for Washington's continued contacts with Vichy (which Hull had requested) was the furthest the British government could go, 'since any public support of the Vichy Government would have the effect of weakening resistance in France which we are pledged to assist and uphold'. Nothing in Vichy's policy held out any hope of bringing France back into the war. Pétain retained the loyalty of the generals, including Weygand, and there was no sign of a breakaway.

The picture is thus exceedingly confused, and the wisest policy, as I see it, is for us to continue our efforts to bring as much as possible of France and the French Empire back into the war at our side; to support all the forces of French resistance, wherever they may be, and whatever their allegiance, without binding ourselves exclusively to any; to continue to support General de Gaulle and at the same time to encourage him to strengthen his organisation by the enlistment of such representative Frenchmen as he can persuade to come over and join him. By following this policy we should at the same time be best serving the war effort and making provision for our post-war relationship with France.[81]

Churchill had told Eden in June that he did not think there were serious differences between them, but rather 'a shade of emphasis'. Eden's paper, too, had attempted to effect a compromise. The serious difference of opinion between the two men, however, could not be so easily charmed away by a form of words. Eden's paper did not formulate a policy at all; it simply expressed a series of pious hopes. What best served the war effort, as he knew, might well be a compromise with Vichy which would have disastrous effects upon Britain's post-war relations with France. Reliable observers continued to warn the Foreign Office in 1942 that any attempt to negotiate with members of the Vichy government would lead to civil war.[82] However, faced with Churchill's determination to keep open as many options as possible in his dealings with Vichy, and with his refusal to reject in advance the possibility of negotiation, the Foreign Secretary could only take refuge in the hope that the problem would not, after all, arise.

7 Operation 'Torch'

WHAT sharpened the Foreign Office's anxiety in 1942 about the sympathetic attitude of the Prime Minister and the American government towards Vichy was the increasing likelihood of action by the Allies to land an occupying force in North Africa before the end of the year, if necessary by force, but if possible with the acquiescence of the local authorities and the blessing of the Vichy government itself. The project was one which had long exerted a powerful attraction upon Churchill, and he employed all his considerable powers of persuasion in its support during his visit to Washington in December 1941. Six months were to elapse, however, before the final decision to proceed was reached. Although Roosevelt himself favoured the project, American military planners were almost unanimously hostile. Generals Marshall, Eisenhower and Clark were convinced that a direct assault upon the European mainland should be attempted, and the early months of 1942 were taken up with planning towards this end. Even as late as May, the American government was making qualified undertakings to Molotov that a second front would be established in Europe in 1942. When it became apparent that such a plan stood little chance of success, Marshall, supported by Admiral King, suggested a drastic change of strategy involving a decisive attack upon Japan in the Pacific. Roosevelt, however, was determined that Europe should be confirmed as the main theatre of war, and that American troops should see action before the end of the year. Faced with this situation, the American planners were left with the choice of sending heavy reinforcements to the Middle East or of launching the expedition to North Africa. They settled upon the latter, largely because it was an area in which American initiative had been asserted and because there would be no doubt as to the American character of the enterprise. The British Prime Minister and the Chiefs of Staff, who had favoured this strategy from the start, were delighted. 'Here is the true Second Front of 1942', enthused Churchill.[1] Final agreement was reached after further discussions in London in late July. The British conceded supreme command to the Americans, and it was also understood that the United States would exercise the initiative in political matters, in accordance with an agreement between Churchill and Roosevelt which had been concluded some time previously.[2]

A successful invasion of French North Africa promised a number of substantial benefits to the Allies. The supply route to Malta would be made safe, Rommel's armies would be threatened from the rear, and Axis forces in the Mediterranean finally destroyed. The blockade leak at Gibraltar could be stopped and valuable supplies diverted into Allied hands, especially if French West Africa adhered to the Allied cause, as it was expected to do.[3] These benefits seemed all the more attractive because of the very real possibility which seemed to exist that the French authorities in the area would offer slight, unco-ordinated resistance, or no resistance at all to an American force.

There are a number of explanations for this belief. In the widest sense, it owed much to the 'Lafayette tradition', which persuaded American policy-makers that the French people had the same sentimental regard for the United States as the American people had for France and that Vichy's resolve to defend the Empire *contre quiconque* would break down when it involved the shedding of American blood. More particularly, it was believed that American sympathy for the Vichy regime and for the sufferings of France, added to the concrete benefits which had accrued to North Africa under the supply programme, had created a widespread feeling of good will towards the United States. On the other hand, the American government believed that the British were violently unpopular because of the long tradition of anglophobia in the French colonial service, because of Oran, the blockade, British support of de Gaulle and condemnation of Vichy. Their part in the invasion, the Americans were advised, should be toned down as far as possible, while the participation of the Free French was ruled out from the start. The President insisted that de Gaulle should not be informed of the landings until after they had taken place.[4]

In reaching these conclusions, the American government relied upon the intelligence network which had been established in North Africa under the terms of the Murphy–Weygand agreement, and to a considerable extent upon the judgement of Murphy himself. In the event, this network proved to be singularly ineffective in operation and dangerously misleading in its conclusions about the degree of resistance which might be expected to an Allied invasion. Murphy committed the error of believing, as de Gaulle latter accused him, 'that France consisted of the people he dined with in town'.[5] Urbane, sophisticated, and of a conservative persuasion, Murphy mixed comfortably in the reactionary, *attentiste* circles of Algiers, believing too readily the professions of friendship and solidarity made to him. At the same time, his anglophobia made him a natural focus for anti-British elements who conveyed to him an exaggerated picture of the unpopularity of Britain in the region. The Vice-Consuls, Murphy's 'Twelve Disciples', were equally unreliable. None of them had any knowledge of Arabic or understanding of Moslem communities.[6] Far from 'watching events like a thousand hawks', as Hull later claimed, their supervision of the supply programme was lax and they conflicted badly with their counterparts in the American consular services.[7] Although their judgement that de Gaulle was violently unpopular in the French Officer corps was certainly correct, their reports gave rise to considerable false optimism in Washington about the possibility of an unopposed landing by American forces, convincing Roosevelt that 'a simultaneous landing by British and Americans would result in full resistance by all French in Africa, whereas an initial American landing without British ground forces offers a real chance that there would be no French resistance or only token resistance'.[8]

The British government was highly sceptical of such judgements and deeply suspicious of Murphy (see p. 101). There was also a feeling that American propaganda activities in North Africa were actually capitalising on British unpopularity by contrasting American generosity over supplies with British attempts to enforce the blockade. The Foreign Office believed that the Americans were too prone to overrate their popularity among the French and to exaggerate the disadvantage of having British forces at their side.[9] They had also underestimated the widespread demoralisation in North Africa. The reaction of the French Army to an American landing would be largely determined by the overall military situation at the time, and Eden concluded in June that 'we can expect no help from any of the French fighting services until it is clear that we are winning the war very rapidly'.[10] There would be at least token resistance to a landing, whether American or British, and the only way of ensuring success would be to employ overwhelming force.[11]

Churchill was in substantial agreement with this view. Although he told the Chiefs of Staff that he found it hard to imagine the French shooting down American troops – 'the whole of the past history of the two countries was against such an occurrence' – he repeatedly warned the President against assuming too complacently a French welcome.[12] 'We cannot count upon an invitation or a guarantee from Vichy', he stressed on 8 July. 'The stronger you are, the less resistance there would be and the more to overcome it.'[13] On 1 September he cabled again. 'I do not know what information you have of the mood and temper of Vichy and North Africa, but of course if you can get ashore at the necessary points without fighting or only token resistance that is best of all. We cannot tell what are the chances of this. . . . We could have stormed Dakar in September, 1940, if we had not been cluttered up with preliminary conciliatory processes. It is that hard experience that makes our military experts rely so much on the simplicity of force.'[14]

Another lesson of Dakar (and of Syria) which Churchill might have mentioned was that the French authorities would be much more likely to resist if the Free French were associated with the landings. The Americans insisted on the rigorous exclusion of the Gaullists from any participation in the venture and the British government accepted this view without demur; their own distrust of Free French security and their fear of provoking further resistance had led them to pursue exactly the same policy during the occupation of Madagascar. The Foreign Secretary, however, aware of the slight which de Gaulle would suffer, tried to sweeten the pill in various ways. In August he tried to persuade the Cabinet to bring de Gaulle into the planning of the administration of the liberated parts of France, but without success.[15] It was later agreed, however, that the administration of Madagascar would be handed over to him when the North African landings took place as a 'consolation prize'.[16] At the President's insistence, de Gaulle was not even informed of the landings until after they had taken place. The Foreign Office thought that the President's decision was silly, but did not press their objections.[17]

American optimism about the possibility of securing French North Africa against only token resistance rested not only upon a belief in American popularity and upon the effectiveness of the supply programme and the activities of the observers, but also upon the extensive clandestine contacts which had been maintained by Murphy with highly-placed political and military figures in North Africa since late 1941. In the aftermath of the landings, in November and December 1942, the American and British governments sought to still the outcry caused by the 'deal' with Darlan which secured the cessation of French resistance by stressing that it was a temporary expedient dictated by urgent military necessity. In his speech to the House of Commons on 10 December, Churchill made the further point that the political arrangements with Darlan were the work of the United States' government, which traditionally regarded north-west Africa as falling within its sphere of interest, and which had assumed responsibility for the command of the operation.[18] These disclaimers contain an element of truth. Although there exists a certain amount of circumstantial evidence to the contrary, it is probably true that Darlan's presence in Algiers on the night of the landings was fortuitous and that in this sense the political arrangements were a hasty improvisation. It is also true that the British played no direct part in the negotiations with him.

Nevertheless, however surprised the Allies were by Darlan's presence in Algiers, the principle of collaboration with Vichy or its agents in some form had been well established months before the attack was launched.[19] On every occasion on which the operation had been considered since December 1941 the desirability of securing the acquiescence and eventual co-operation of the North African authorities had been stressed, and all were naturally agreed that it would be preferable to avoid force if possible. Indeed, without a fairly swift capitulation, disaster might well overtake the whole expedition, as Churchill pointed out.[20] Clark put it with his usual brevity: 'the first battle we must win is the battle to have no battle with the French'.[21] Eisenhower, who carried the responsibility for accepting Darlan as a collaborator with the Allies in North Africa, was subjected to a good deal of criticism for his part in events, but argued quite truthfully in his own account that he had only been working within the guidelines which had been laid down by his superiors, and which obliged him to work with the established political leadership in the area.[22] Furthermore, although Darlan was of all the Vichy politicians except Laval the most notoriously identified with the policy of collaboration with Germany, the Allied governments had considered the possibility of working with him only three weeks before the attack was launched. Far from ruling out the prospect altogether on the grounds of principle, they had given it their qualified acceptance. Even Eden, who had been warning the Cabinet for months of the dangers of such dealings, failed to voice his objections clearly, let alone to reject them altogether.

However, although the two governments found common ground in their desire to reach agreement with whoever might deliver North Africa into their hands, they arrived at this position from quite different directions. The United States, having long maintained cordial relations with the Vichy government, was hardly likely to entertain sudden moral scruples over an agreement with its deputies. As for the long-term implications of their actions, it is difficult to decide on the available evidence whether American policy-makers were sincere in their belief that they could deal on a purely military level with the administration of the territories they liberated without prejudice to their political future, or whether they used this as a cloak to conceal their determination to perpetuate the Vichy regime into peacetime. The Free French were naturally convinced that the latter was the case, and interpreted American coldness in the period before the landing (which they knew to be in the offing) as a sign that Washington sought a free hand to re-establish Vichy in North Africa under Allied patronage.[23] If the Foreign Office shared these suspicions, they were rarely voiced in the period before TORCH. The tenacity with which Washington clung to its anti-Gaullist policy, however, led many in London to believe, in 1943 and 1944, that there was substance in the Free French argument (see below pp. 174-8). The British, on the other hand, although under no illusions about the dire complications which might arise from the political arrangements in North Africa, were unwilling to take a stand on a matter of principle. The short-term gains seemed so great that few dissented from the view held by Desmond Morton, although most would have put it less brutally. 'We shall have to hang some of our French "friends" alongside Darlan and Pucheu when the war is over', he wrote on Christmas Eve 1941. 'Meanwhile let us use them'.[24] Nor was there sign of any great determination in London to press de Gaulle's claims to a part in the North African administration. The Foreign Office decided to tell him when the landings were in progress that his relationship with the local North African administration was for him to settle. It was also agreed that if the French in North Africa joined the Allied side as a result of TORCH, 'the importance of de Gaulle and his movement will probably diminish and he may feel constrained to coalesce with the larger body of dissident Frenchmen in North Africa. This is a development which we should encourage.'[25]

CONTACTS WITH DARLAN

Darlan's first contacts with the Allies which suggested the possibility of future military co-operation were made in late 1941. Professor Funk has painted a convincing picture of the Admiral in the autumn of 1941, coolly reassessing the prospects of a German victory and conveying pointed hints to Leahy that his policy might be drastically changed by evidence of America's determination to defeat Germany.[26] Darlan was also careful to establish links with Murphy in North Africa through his friend Admiral Fenard, and to feed him with suggestions that his views on the outcome of the war had changed.[27]

American belligerency, and Leahy's apparent failure to grasp the significance of the hints which he had dropped, encouraged Darlan to make bolder approaches to the Allies. On 19 December Churchill, then *en route* to Washington, was informed that he had made a clandestine approach the previous month through a man with whom 'C' was in touch.[28] He had asked whether, if the war came to an end, the British would refuse to treat with a government of which he was a member. The Foreign Office proposed the following reply:

H. M. Government are prepared to work with any Frenchman who is prepared to work with them. Their attitude towards individual Frenchmen after the war will of necessity depend on attitude which Frenchmen concerned have adopted during the war, and whether they have done anything to assist our victory or whether on the contrary their attitude has been calculated to help Germans either actively or passively. Darlan can yet play his part in accelerating Allied victory which is certain by ordering French Fleet to sail for North and West African ports and instructing them to resist any German attacks.[29]

This was encouraging, but not unambiguous. Churchill's counter-proposal went significantly further:

At the present time the British, if victorious, would refuse to treat or meet at a peace conference any French Government which contained men who had actively hampered our effort to win the war. The war will certainly be won by Britain, the United States and Russia, but it is not won yet, and there may be time for an entirely new chapter to be written. (If the French Fleet at Toulon were to sail for North and West African ports and be prepared to resist German attacks, that would be an event of the first order. Whoever commanded or effected such a great stroke of policy and strategy would have made a decisive contribution to the Allied cause which carries with it the restoration of France as one of the leading powers in Europe. Such a service would entitle the author to an honourable place in the Allied ranks.) And the terrible difficulties in which we were all placed in the previous period would appear in their true light or fade away. The moment for such an action may be very near. . . . We should be prepared to discuss plans in detail with anyone who possessed the power and the will to take this invaluable step towards the salvation of France.[30]

The Chiefs of Staff gave their formal approval to this reply on the 22nd, and the bracketed portion of the message was consequently conveyed via 'C'. It is not clear from the record why the opening and closing sections were withheld, or upon whose authority. The effect of deleting the first sentence was obviously to render the message even more unequivocal in its encouragement of Darlan.[31] The American government received a similar enquiry and made a somewhat similar reply; Roosevelt told a plenary session of the ARCADIA conference that Darlan had been told that his presence at a conference would not be acceptable 'under present circumstances', but that if he brought the Fleet to North Africa, 'the situation would change'.[32] Darlan made no further approaches through these channels, (or at least none which have come to light), and his enquiries probably did not signify any immediate intention to act. American belligerency had certainly altered the long-term prospects of a German victory, but in the meantime France had still to live under the German yoke. Measures of collaboration with Germany, even at the military level, continued without interruption into 1942. Darlan had tried the Allied door, but was not yet ready to pass through it. Whatever his motives, however, Churchill's reply made quite plain the British government's willingness to deal with him. There was room on the bandwagon, even for Darlan.

THE NORTH AFRICAN CONSPIRACY

Although Darlan's *démarche* opened up intriguing possibilities to the Allies and also carried with it the prospect of securing the French Fleet, the project of drawing him into the Allied camp languished in the opening months of 1942. Darlan maintained contact with Murphy through Fenard and also used his son Alain as an intermediary. Through them he communicated to Murphy on several occasions his own and the Marshal's alleged belief in an ultimate Allied victory, and their determination to play for time until the opportunity for decisive action presented itself.[33] Washington, however, was at this time entirely preoccupied with the projected Channel crossing and, despite repeated appeals, Murphy received neither encouragement nor guidance from his superiors.[34]

While maintaining contact with Darlan, Murphy had also built up relations with the 'Group of Five', a conspiracy which had succeeded in establishing its control over the various resistance groups in Algiers and which had the added merit, in Murphy's eyes, of displaying impeccable right-wing credentials. At the end of April, the Group won a valuable adherent in the person of General Charles Mast, who had just been released from a German prison and subsequently appointed Chief of Staff of the XIX Army, based in Algiers. The movement still lacked a military leader with sufficient prestige to rally the North African Army and attract Allied support, however, and in the following weeks, steps were taken, apparently in co-operation with the *Deuxième Bureau*, to organise the escape from Koenigstein prison of General Henri Giraud, who had been captured during the Battle of France and who enjoyed the reputation of being a brave, dynamic soldier with an implacable hatred of Germany. In June, he had arrived in the Unoccupied Zone and made contact with the Group of Five through Jacques Lemaigre-Dubreuil, the Group's leader.[35]

The final decision for TORCH was reached in late July and Murphy was summoned to Washington in the middle of August to report on his contacts directly to the President. He then flew to London and conferred with Eisenhower on 16 September. The State Department was kept completely in the dark.[36] However, Murphy received no clear instructions as to whether he should continue his contacts with Darlan through Fenard or whether he should concentrate exclusively upon the Group of Five; he was authorised simply to work 'with those French nationals whom you consider reliable'.[37] Murphy's lack of clear guidelines was soon to create enormous problems for him. During August and September Darlan was becoming increasingly uneasy at the possibility of an American invasion of North Africa, and his fears were further sharpened by a report from Colonel Jean Chrétien, head of military security in North Africa, which revealed the existence of the Murphy–Group of Five conspiracy. He therefore despatched Chrétien to North Africa, where he met Murphy in 'an isolated spot' on 12 October, the day after Murphy's return.[38] Chrétien reported that a German descent upon North Africa was to be expected shortly, perhaps before 1 November, to forestall the Americans. He then indicated that Darlan would be willing to come to Africa and to bring with him the Toulon Fleet if he was made Commander in Chief of the French Armed Forces and given American military support.[39] Murphy immediately contacted Generals Marshall and Eisenhower with the request to be informed at once 'as to the limits I may go to in replying to Darlan's representative, who desires to know 1. Are we willing to cooperate with Darlan? 2. If so, will we be able to do so quickly and on a large scale here and/or in Europe?' His message ended with the recommendation 'that we encourage Darlan on the basis of securing his eventual cooperation with Giraud'.[40] Two days later Murphy also met Mast and the Group of Five, who informed him that the adherence of Giraud was now assured, but who emphatically refused to consider co-operating with Darlan.[41] Mast, however, assured Murphy that the confirmation of Giraud's command would assure an entry into North Africa 'practically without firing a shot', and requested that a high-level military mission be despatched forthwith to co-ordinate the American landings with action by the local resistance.[42]

The attitude of the Group of Five meant that the prospect of uniting them with Darlan was remote. Nevertheless, when Murphy's telegrams reached London on 17 October, Eisenhower and Clark refused to make a clear decision between Darlan and Giraud. They drafted a reply which agreed that, although the latter was to be recognised as 'our principal collaborator on the French side', and would be installed as Governor of French North Africa, he should be requested 'to make proper contact with Darlan and to accept him as Commander-in-Chief of military and/or naval forces in North Africa, or in some similar position that will be attractive to Darlan. In this way, the French Forces could co-operate immediately, under the general directive of the Allied Commander-in-Chief.'[43] This was hopelessly naïve. Even if the Group of Five had been willing to work with Darlan, Darlan knew the strength of his own position too well to accept the role of Giraud's deputy. In any event Eisenhower paused at the prospect of assuming responsibility for even so qualified an acceptance of collaboration with Darlan, and requested a high-level meeting with the British, which took place at Downing Street on the same afternoon.

Present at the meeting were Churchill, Attlee, Brooke, Eden (and Mack), Smuts, Pound, Eisenhower, Clark and Bedell Smith. There was little dissent from Eisenhower's formula. Eden suggested that Darlan's overtures might be the result of German attempts to find out what the Allied military plans were; as he told his colleagues before the meeting, 'it seemed too much like the way Germans would play their hand if they wanted to know our plans and delay them'.[44] However, his comments during the meeting were muted and he raised no clear objection in principle to the possible elevation of Darlan to the position of Commander-in-Chief of the French Forces in North Africa. Others were less reserved: Smuts commented that 'Darlan would be a big fish to land if it could be done'. Churchill, although reticent during the meeting, appears to have expressed great enthusiasm to Eisenhower afterwards. According to the latter's telegram to Marshall at the time, the Prime Minister 'several times reiterated his satisfaction at the attitude adopted by the Allied Command in handling this matter and states that he is perfectly willing to stand behind and back up whatever arrangements are made by Clark as my representative'.[45] In his memoirs, Eisenhower further quoted Churchill as saying at this time that 'if I could meet Darlan, much as I hate him, I would cheerfully crawl on my hands and knees for a mile if by doing so I could get him to bring that fleet of his into the circle of the Allied Forces'.[46] Thus, although Giraud's primacy had been reaffirmed, Darlan's participation had by no means been ruled out, and Eisenhower and Clark were fully justified in feeling that they had received prior approval at the highest possible level to an arrangement which might confer high office upon him.[47] It is true that Churchill and Eden had consented only to Darlan's holding a military post under Giraud's political leadership, and that Clark and Eisenhower later reversed these roles without consulting the British. This hardly seemed to matter on 17 October. As Professor Funk points out, the British could have said, 'for political reasons you will have no dealings with Admiral Darlan'. They did not.[48]

In the event, Darlan's possible participation was ruled out, not by the British, but by Clark who paid a daring visit to North Africa and met the Group of Five at a deserted farmhouse on the Algerian coast on 21–22 October.[49] Mast insisted that Darlan's co-operation should not be sought, since he could not be trusted. Clark was assured that Giraud would be able to rally the North African Army, and was consequently persuaded to abandon the idea of bringing him and Darlan together. Despite this extraordinary expedition, the Americans were very far from taking the Group of Five into their confidence. Murphy was only authorised to announce the date which had been fixed for the landings – 8 November – four days in advance, although he seems in the end to have divulged the date to Mast on 28 October.[50] During the final ten days all was confusion. The conspirators, angry that the Americans had not trusted them, nevertheless attempted hastily to activate the underground groups in time. However, since precise information on landing points had not been divulged, there was a limit to what could be done to neutralise resistance.[51] The political co-ordination of the expedition was in similar disarray. Roosevelt did not bother to keep Murphy informed, and he was therefore out of touch with the detailed planning of civil affairs, which took place in Eisenhower's headquarters in the weeks prior to the landings.[52] As a result, when faced with

Giraud's insistence that a simultaneous attack should be launched in southern France and that he should assume overall command, he had to mislead him to obtain his continued co-operation. Also, in order to satisfy the political demands of the Group of Five, he was obliged to make on his own initiative an undertaking to Giraud about America's intention to restore France which the President was later to find inconvenient.[53]

Although the British had conceded the initiative to the American government both in the military and political fields, the Foreign Office followed the final stages of the planning of TORCH quite closely. For reasons of his own, Roosevelt chose to bypass the State Department completely. The British therefore worked directly with Eisenhower on all military and political questions, the most important matters being settled by direct correspondence between the Prime Minister and the President. To retain contact with the Commander-in-Chief while the landings were in progress, and to represent the British point of view, Mack was appointed Political Liaison Officer to the American Forces in Europe and accompanied Eisenhower to Gibraltar before the landings. His position, however, was relatively weak and during the planning period he and Brigadier Mockler-Ferryman, head of TORCH Intelligence Section, found themselves 'outranked and outnumbered' by their American colleagues.[54]

There was a broad measure of agreement on most points, although the extent to which the British role was played down rankled, particularly with Eden.[55] Policy towards Vichy remained outwardly unchanged, the supply programme continuing without interruption despite the risk that the resources supplied might be used to repulse the landings.[56] 'Normal friction' was maintained in relations with Vichy.[57] The British were also agreed that the American commanders would have to work through the existing administration in North Africa, although the Foreign Office was understandably apprehensive about the possible outcome of these arrangements and feared that the Americans would hastily recognise an unrepresentative clique in North Africa as the rallying point for the whole of the French Empire.[58] The Foreign Office was unenthusiastic about American political preparations also, and felt that an overwhelming show of force was the best way to win speedy co-operation. There had been a ripple of interest in London the previous April when news of Giraud's escape was released, and Hankey had even suggested that he might make 'a splendid alternative' to de Gaulle as leader of the Free French movement.[59]

However, discussion of his possible usefulness died down when the General arrived in Vichy and affirmed his loyalty to Pétain, and the British did not establish direct contact with him at any time. This scepticism extended also to the Group of Five, and was reflected in the unanimous disapproval which met Roosevelt's directive to Murphy telling him to inform the conspirators in advance of the landings. This, Eden thought, was dangerous, 'even crazy'. 'I am sure there should be no warning before landing', he went on. 'Time enough to collect the Girauds, etc., after. They won't help before anyway.'[60] The Foreign Office had no time either for the suggestion that TORCH might have a decisive effect in Vichy, and the possibility that the government might flee to Algiers aroused alarm rather than enthusiasm. As Cadogan remarked, 'what do we do with Pétain and Laval in North Africa anyhow?'[61] There was equally little point in trying to win Pétain's approval, and the Foreign Office objected strongly to the fulsome message which Roosevelt proposed to address to the Marshal as the landings took place, which referred to him as 'my dear old friend', and as the 'Hero of Verdun'. This, thought Morton, was deplorable: 'I am convinced that anything like slop over Pétain will do more harm than good.' Eden was in full agreement and Churchill succeeded in having the message toned down.[62]

THE ALLIED LANDINGS

On 8 November the Allied Forces began to disembark on the North African shore from Casablanca to Algiers. The cover plans were completely successful in deceiving the Germans and the Vichy French, but hopes of only token opposition from the French proved to be groundless. Vigorous resistance was offered at many points, and particularly against Patton's Western Task Force at Casablanca, which was entirely American.[63] A rapid advance was made into Tunisia, but German reinforcements, whose landing was not resisted, succeeded in securing vital points and in delaying the Allied advance until the spring of 1943.

The military progress of the campaign, however, receded into the background, overshadowed by the extraordinary political events which accompanied it. On 5 November, after completing a tour of inspection of North Africa in October, Darlan returned to Algiers to visit his son who was seriously ill with poliomyelitis. He was still present when the

Allies landed. The Group of Five had activated the resistance groups and secured many key points, but Murphy was hampered by Giraud's failure to arrive (he was in Gibraltar, negotiating with Eisenhower) and decided to contact Juin, Commander of the Army in Algeria, who had not been told of the possibility of a landing and who had told Murphy only two days before that he would resist one if it took place.[64] Juin insisted that Darlan's presence rendered him powerless and Murphy therefore contacted Darlan and invited him to Juin's house. Cautious of Murphy's assurance that half a million men were being landed, Darlan played for time, placing Murphy under arrest, ordering resistance and appealing to Vichy for instructions. By noon, however, further resistance was clearly futile, and Darlan formally surrendered the city.[65]

As Commander-in-Chief of the French Forces, Darlan overrode any authority which Giraud, Mast or the Group of Five might have wielded in North Africa, and held undoubted mastery in Algiers. There was also the chance that he might be able to order the French Fleet out of Toulon. There was thus no question of 'dropping' him.[66] Unfortunately, while Murphy dealt with Darlan in Algiers, Eisenhower had been negotiating with Giraud in Gibraltar and had confirmed his position. When Clark arrived in Algiers on 9 November, therefore, he and Murphy decided to work towards a compromise which would enable the two men to work together. Their efforts in this direction were aided by the universal indifference with which Giraud's arrival in North Africa was greeted, and which rapidly persuaded him to abandon all political pretensions and seek only a military command; a decision which destroyed at a stroke. the Group of Five's chances of attaining political power.[67] There was no suggestion that Clark should avoid dealing with Darlan on grounds of principle, since the question had been thrashed out on 17 October. Clark's only concern was to find a sound instrument through which he could get the French to co-operate. 'I didn't care if that instrument were named Darlan, Giraud or Pétain himself.'[68]

Clark and Darlan eventually began to negotiate on the morning of 10 November. Fighting still continued in Oran and in Morocco and Clark insisted that Darlan should order a cease-fire before talks could proceed. Darlan argued that Pétain would repudiate him, but eventually gave way.[69] On the following day, the Germans crossed the demarcation line and Pétain named Noguès, not Darlan, his deputy in North Africa. Nevertheless Darlan was able to maintain his power by persuading his subordinates that he retained the Marshal's confidence. Clark was also impressed by his authority and his ability to command obedience and respect.[70] On 12 November Noguès arrived in Algiers and subsequently telegraphed to Vichy his recommendation that Darlan should be restored to command. On the following morning agreement was reached between Darlan, Juin, Noguès and Giraud to bring North Africa back into the war on the side of the Allies. Meanwhile the Vichy Cabinet had approved Noguès's recommendation and reinstated Darlan, in the hope that he would somehow preserve the neutrality of North Africa. Darlan was able to pass this off as an endorsement of his agreement that afternoon with Clark, and thus to give birth to the myth that Pétain approved his actions. These arrangements were confirmed by the Clark–Darlan agreement, which was signed on 22 November.[71]

REPERCUSSIONS

Since the British and American governments had both given their qualified acceptance before the landings of the idea of collaboration with Darlan, it is natural to question whether his presence in Algiers was entirely fortuitous. It was generally assumed in many quarters at the time, and particularly among the Free French, that his arrival had been co-ordinated with the American government, and it is significant of the Foreign Office's mistrust of American dealings with Vichy that this possibility was not ruled out in London either. 'I wouldn't put it past them', wrote Cadogan in his diary, and vowed that he would have 'a God-Almighty showdown' with them if it could be proved.[72] Strang wrote to Mack on 28 November to try to obtain a confirmation or denial of the rumour (which linked Pierre Dupuy with the alleged negotiations), but Mack's reply is not on record.[73] On balance, however, it seems unlikely that the Foreign Office's suspicions were well-founded. Dupuy was a notorious busybody who had sought every opportunity to become entangled in relations with Vichy. He had probably got wind of Darlan's tentative contacts with the Allies, no more. There is little more than circumstantial evidence to suggest that Darlan's presence was anything other than what Churchill called 'an odd and formidable coincidence', and the contrary argument, by Peter Tomkins, is based on pure conjecture.[74] Darlan's actions both before and after the landings are entirely consistent with the view that he did not expect an attack, at least not yet.[75] Even if Murphy is taken as an unreliable witness on this point, the very genuine delay and confusion on both sides in the days following the attack is difficult to explain if one assumes a prior agreement.

Another myth which persisted was that Pétain, although obliged outwardly to repudiate the actions of his Commander-in-Chief, was able to convey his approval to Darlan by using a secret naval code. This was believed by Clark at the time, and by Mack. It figured largely in Pétain's defence at his trial and in many post-war accounts.[76] Again, a certain amount of circumstantial evidence exists. Pétain's response to Roosevelt's message was stern and uncompromising, but his manner towards the American Chargé d'Affaires who delivered it was cordial.[77] More substantial evidence is provided by the series of telegrams which were conveyed to Darlan in naval code through Admiral Auphan, the Vichy Minister of the Navy, but even these will not withstand close scrutiny.[78] Nevertheless, when 'leaked' to the Americans and to senior French officers, they succeeded in creating the impression that Darlan retained the Marshal's confidence. The Admiral's hand was further strengthened on the 13th. Noguès arrived in Algiers on the 12th, determined that North Africa should maintain its neutrality and that Giraud should be eliminated. At 3 a.m. on the following morning, he cabled Vichy to confirm that Darlan was not a prisoner and that agreement 'in principle' had been reached with the Americans to maintain the military, political and administrative structure in North Africa, to preserve its neutrality, and to eliminate the dissident Giraud.[79] This was premature. Later in the morning Juin rallied to Giraud's support and destroyed Noguès's neutralist ideas for good. Unaware of this, the Vichy Cabinet approved his recommendations, but sought German approval before ratifying its decision. Auphan, aware that this would not be forthcoming, sent on his own initiative a telegram to Darlan: 'Accord intime du Maréchal et du Président Laval, mais avant de vous répondre, on consulte les autorités d'occupation.'[80] What Pétain had agreed to was the neutralisation of North Africa, the elimination of dissidence and the restoration of the *status quo*. Darlan, however, created the impression that Auphan's telegram gave the Marshal's approval to the exact opposite; the entry of French North Africa into the war on the Allied side under Giraud's command.[81] Pétain's subsequent action in depriving Darlan of all public office had little effect since it was assumed that he was now in German hands and could not voice his true thoughts. Thus, with consummate skill, Darlan preserved the 'apostolic succession', and the fiction of loyalty to Vichy, set at rest the troubled consciences of the Officer corps, and ranged North Africa against the Axis. As Churchill told the Commons a month later, 'if Admiral Darlan had to shoot Marshal Pétain he would no doubt do it in Marshal Pétain's name . . .'.[82]

Whether or not Darlan had arrived in Algiers by chance, and whether or not Pétain actually did approve of his actions, the fact remained that the American commanders had accepted as the supreme authority in North Africa a notorious political adventurer who had long been a leading advocate of a policy of collaboration, who was fiercely anti-British and who, with American approval, pointed to Vichy as the source of his authority. As William Bullitt pointed out, it was as though Jesus had called upon Judas and said, 'on this rock I found my Church'.[83] The liberating forces of the Allies, to whom the conquered millions of Europe looked for salvation, instead of sweeping away the time-servers and collaborators, had confirmed them in office. Under the patronage of the armies of the Allies, Vichy enjoyed a renaissance in North Africa.[84] For weeks after the landings, Vichy legislation, including the anti-Jewish laws, remained in force and fascist organisations flourished. Allied sympathisers and members of the resistance organisations, instead of being released from prison, actually continued to be arrested for their disloyalty to the Marshal, while in many powerful circles, the stigma of dissidence continued to cling to Giraud even after Darlan had endorsed him. As Churchill reported to Roosevelt a month after the landings, 'elements hostile to the United Nations are being consolidated within the administration and conditions are being created which will make North Africa a favourable resort to Axis troublemakers. . . . Not only have our enemies been thus encouraged but our friends have been correspondingly confused and cast down'.[85]

Few now doubted that American policy towards France aimed at the continuance of the Vichy regime into peacetime. In fulfilment of Parr's predictions in August 1941, numbers of discredited politicians saw the way open to them and began to arrive in Algiers, among them Marcel Peyrouton, promulgator of Vichy's anti-Semitic laws, Pierre Pucheu and Flandin. Piétri, Vichy ambassador in Spain, busied himself in December establishing contact between Noguès and Pétain, while Oliver de Sardan, Director of the Moroccan Phosphate Syndicate, was even in touch with Laval on his behalf.[86]

A violent outburst of public criticism accompanied the news of

Darlan's accession as head of the civil administration in North Africa. Both the British and the American press were outspoken in their condemnation, and none more so than Ed Murrow and Walter Lippmann, long-standing opponents of the Vichy policy.[87] Indignation was widespread in Britain, particularly within the Labour movement, and the Foreign Office received many letters of protest from the trade unions.[88] Despite a skilful speech by Eden on 26 November, criticism in Parliament was loud, and on the 27th the motion was put forward 'that this House is of the opinion that our relations with Admiral Darlan and his kind are inconsistent with the ideals for which we entered and are fighting this war'.[89] Even more alarming from the Foreign Office's point of view was the reaction which was to be expected from the Soviet government, from Allied governments in exile and from the Fighting French. For all of these, Allied relations with Darlan carried the most serious implications for the continuation of the Allied coalition and for the eventual peace settlement.

These wider dangers were set out in an anxious memorandum drawn up by Gladwyn Jebb of the Foreign Office's Economic and Reconstruction Department on 16 November.[90] British policy, Jebb argued, was based upon the closest possible collaboration in the post-war period between the Soviet Union, the United States, Great Britain and France, 'provided that the latter regains her independence and her greatness'. The willing co-operation of the smaller European states would also be required after the war 'to maintain Germany in subjection'. However, the Allies now appeared to be very nearly committed to recognising as the future government of France a body of men whose object for two and a half years or more had been to collaborate with Germany in order to preserve their personal wealth and to fight Communism. To the Soviet government, the North African arrangements could only indicate that Allied policy was based upon 'an Anglo-American-European quisling combination directed against the Soviet Union'. In fact, Jebb overstated the dangers of a rupture with the Soviet Union. His report was written when there still seemed to be a possibility that Darlan would become the head of a provisional government in North Africa and not just a local civil administration, and when this danger passed, the Soviet Union seemed willing enough to accept British assurances. Stalin later went out of his way to assure the President that, in his opinion, the policy which Eisenhower had adopted towards Darlan was perfectly correct.[91]

In other respects Jebb's warnings were much nearer the mark. What really mattered, he argued, was 'the general moral aspect'.

How can we possibly now represent to the submerged nations of Europe that we are fighting for a new and better system designed above all to liberate them from the ever-present fear of German aggression? What guarantee have they now got that we shall not, in the occupation of other countries, make terms with Mussert, Rost van Tönningen, King Albert, President Hacha, General Nedić and even with Quisling himself, provided only that these reptiles assert that they were really only guided by patriotic motives and were only prompted in their actions by their hatred of 'communism'? Shall we not even indeed convey the impression that our ultimate aim is to arrive at an arrangement with some good German General who may no doubt be just as anti-Communist as Admiral Darlan himself?[92]

This was indeed the crux of the matter. As Jebb anticipated, the European governments in exile became seriously alarmed by the North African situation in the following weeks.[93] The effect upon the resistance movements in Europe was equally demoralising, and Lord Selborne, Head of SOE, reported to Eden that the deal with Darlan 'had produced violent reactions on all our subterranean organisations in enemy occupied countries, particularly in France where it has had a blasting and withering effect'.[94]

Nowhere was the anger greater, however, than in the ranks of the Free French. A major crisis had been expected as a result of the American refusal to inform the Free French of the landings beforehand.[95] In the event, however, de Gaulle's initial reaction was much more satisfactory than the British had expected. Churchill and Eden met the General on 8 November, and informed him of the landings. The General answered that there must be a single centre of resistance, not a multiplicity of leaders from which only the Communists would benefit. However, Giraud was an excellent choice as leader. He had signed no Armistice and was without reproach. He, de Gaulle, did not matter; he was ready to put himself under 'any other chief who carried with him the mass of the French people'.[96] As the situation in Algiers developed, however, this unexpectedly satisfactory response gave way to violent anger. A proposal put forward on the 10th to send a Free French mission under Pleven to North Africa was dropped on the 14th when Darlan's position had crystallised. On the 12th, de Gaulle told Admiral Stark, Commander of the American Naval Forces in Europe, that Giraud had destroyed his position by the undertakings which he had made to Pétain the previous May, by refusing to contact the Free French and by accepting a military command from the American authorities.[97] As for Darlan, 'Je comprends que les États-Unis paient la trahison des traîtres si elle leur paraît profitable, mais elle ne doit pas être payée sur l'honneur de la France.'[98] On the 16th de Gaulle had another meeting with the Prime Minister and the Foreign Secretary and made plain that he would not be a party to any arrangement, however temporary, which gave authority to Darlan. No immediate military advantages could justify dealing with a traitor. He also insisted on issuing a communiqué that day publicly dissociating himself from the nego-tiations then taking place in North Africa with the representatives of Vichy.[99]

On 8 December de Gaulle and Catroux explained their position at length to Anthony Eden, in terms reminiscent of de Gaulle's message to Hull the previous January. War was not a game of chess, they argued, but a conflict of ideals. It was fought not by military forces alone but by people. The American President and his advisers were concerned only with gaining military advantages and seemed to have no conception of the wider political implications of what they were doing. In an appeal to British self-interest, the General pointed out that the Gaullists were the only party committed to the Alliance with Britain. If the Vichy regime were able to establish itself in France after the war as a result of American sponsorship, the outcome would be disastrous. The United States would withdraw from involvement in Europe and the Soviet Union, as Molotov had warned, would switch its support from the Free French to the Communists. De Gaulle concluded that the interests of Great Britain and of Fighting France were indissolubly engaged, and that the Prime Minister should assume the 'moral leadership of Europe' which Roosevelt was rapidly losing, by dissociating himself publicly from American policy.[100]

THE FOREIGN OFFICE AND THE 'DEAL WITH DARLAN'

While de Gaulle argued in terms of moral abstractions, the British and American leaders, whose forces were engaged in the campaign, were naturally more preoccupied with securing the most rapid military success at the least cost in human life. Eisenhower and Cunningham argued that, with barely adequate forces and long lines of com-munication over hostile terrain, the acceptance of Darlan was the only possible means of ensuring the safety of the Allied forces. The American

President gave his unqualified support to this position, arguing that the means justified the ends in a *reductio ad absurdum* of the appeal to expediency which had long been the standard defence of America's Vichy policy. He had dealt with Darlan because Darlan had given him Algiers, and he would deal with Laval, if Laval would give him Paris.[101] Churchill's position was more ambiguous, and was well summarised by his cable to Eisenhower on 14 November: 'Anything for the battle but the politics will have to be sorted out later.'[102] Although conscious of both the political and the military dimensions of the problem, his own natural opportunism and his customary deference to the wishes of the President led him to feel that, in the final analysis, the arrangements with Darlan were justified. 'I must say I think he is a poor creature with a jaundiced outlook and disorganised loyalties', he told the House of Commons on 10 December, 'who in all this tremendous African episode, West and East alike, can find no point to excite his interest except the arrangements made between General Eisenhower and Admiral Darlan.'[103]

The Foreign Office's attitude to the deal with Darlan took some time to crystallise. During the first few days after the landings, there was a feeling that it would be wrong to question the actions of the Commander-in-Chief while the battle was at a critical stage. This was all the more natural in view of the fact that TORCH was the first major Anglo-American venture and was under American control. Even later, the Foreign Office had great difficulty in knowing what was going on in Algiers, and felt enormous frustration at its inability to bring its influence to bear. At the root of the problem was the failure to establish effective liaison with the American commanders. Mack found it difficult to reconcile his status as British Political Liaison Officer at Eisenhower's headquarters with his position on the Commander-in-Chief's Staff and as a result failed to press the Foreign Office's views.[104] In any case, while the crucial negotiations were taking place in Algiers, Mack remained with Eisenhower in Gibraltar. The Foreign Office was aware that there was little that Mack could have done to alter the course of events, especially since Murphy and Clark could point to the Prime Minister's attitude on 17 October in support of their actions. They became exasperated, however, firstly by Mack's silence and later by the extraordinary extent to which he had come to endorse the American position. On 29 November he was reporting that the success of the Tunisian campaign was the most important consideration, that the French people themselves must take care of their future and that de

Gaulle should consider uniting himself with the North African administration.[105] There was thus nobody in North Africa during the critical period who could represent with authority the views of the Foreign Office.

Very little information filtered through to London during the first few days after the landings about the events in progress in Algiers. The Foreign Office was aware of Darlan's presence, but the earliest reports available, on the 10th, indicated only that he had been taken into custody and later that he had been in conference with Clark and Giraud.[106] There was no suggestion that he might be given a political appointment. The Foreign Office's main aim was therefore to implement its long-standing policy of encouraging a coalition of the forces of resistance in London and Algiers. De Gaulle's request that he should be allowed to make contact with Giraud was readily agreed to; it was regarded as undesirable that he should be left 'running after the bandwagon in a manner unjust to him and embarrassing to His Majesty's Government, who have recently renewed through the lips of the Prime Minister their refusal to discard him in favour of a temporarily more glittering candidate'.[107]

On the following day, 11 November, however, the text of Darlan's order calling for a cease-fire in the name of the Marshal and for the preservation of North Africa's neutrality was received in London and the fear began to take root that the American commanders would reinstate the Vichy regime in Algiers. 'They have maintained relations with them up to now', wrote one official, 'and I think they are inclined to be impressed with the names they know.' Furthermore, Murphy had always been pro-Vichy and was now at Eisenhower's right hand.[108] On the same day, Churchill cabled Roosevelt on the importance of unifying 'all Frenchmen who regard Germany as the foe'. 'You will, I am sure, realise that HMG are under quite solemn and definite undertakings to de Gaulle and his movement. We must see that they have a fair deal', he stressed. 'It seems to me that you and I ought to avoid at all costs the creation of rival French *émigré* Governments, each favoured by one of us.'[109] Roosevelt's reply left little room for complacency. Although willing to allow a Gaullist representative to fly to Algiers, the President seemed not to grasp the serious political issues at stake in the 'cat fight' then in progress in Algiers, and adopted a tone of lofty condescension. 'The principal thought to be driven home to all three of these prima donnas [Darlan, Giraud and de Gaulle] is that the situation is today solely in the military field, and that any decision by any of them, or by all of them, is subject to review and approval by Eisenhower.'[110]

On the same day, Eisenhower reported that Darlan and Giraud had reached a tentative agreement whereby the former would assume the political and the latter the military authority in North Africa, and also that Darlan had ordered the Toulon Fleet to sail to North African ports.[111] At Cadogan's prompting, Eden despatched a telegram to Mack that night asking if there was any question of accepting Darlan as head or member of any French administration set up in North Africa. If he could really deliver the Toulon Fleet, or Tunis, into Allied hands, he would have established a claim to 'a seat on the bandwagon', but 'if he cannot render this service his inclusion in a French administration, even if Giraud agrees, would cause more trouble than it would be worth'. Eden's telegram also served as the basis for a message to Halifax urging him to warn the President of the dangers of including Darlan in the North African administration and of the effect such a move would have upon the Free French.[112]

Despite their misgivings, both Churchill and Eden, in varying degrees, seemed willing to accept Darlan as a collaborator in some capacity, provided that he could 'deliver the goods' in the form of the Toulon Fleet or entry into Tunis. What alarmed them was not the principle of collaboration but the danger that the Americans would pay too high a price to secure it. The strongest objections to the Darlan negotiations came from Cadogan. 'An awful tangle in North Africa,' he wrote on 14 November, 'Eisenhower and Cunningham have made agreement with Darlan, Giraud, Noguès, Juin. *What* a party! A [Eden] and PM still seem to take this lightly. PM has telegraphed Eisenhower "Anything for the battle. Politics will have to be sorted out later." That's all right, but will they be? The Americans and naval officers in Algiers are letting us in for a *pot* of trouble. We shall do no good till we've killed Darlan.'[113] For the time being, however, such objections were overridden by the urgency of the military situation. On the evening of the 14th Eisenhower justified his actions in negotiating with Darlan in a long telegram to the Combined Chiefs of Staff. Sentiment in North Africa, he explained, did not agree even remotely with 'some of [the] prior calculations', and the expectation that the landings would be unopposed had turned out to be unfounded. The name of Marshal Pétain was something to conjure with, and everyone from the highest to the lowest attempted to create the impression that he lived and acted under the shadow of the Marshal's figure. 'The civil governors, military leaders and naval commanders will agree on only one man as having an obvious right to assume the Marshal's mantle in North Africa. That man is Darlan.' Giraud was considered to be guilty of at least a touch of treachery in urging non-resistance to the American landings, and had agreed to accept a military command under Darlan.[114] Furthermore only Darlan could command the obedience of Noguès and Estéva, upon whom the pacification of Morocco and the rapid conquest of Tunisia depended. There was also the possibility that he would be able to win the adherence of the Fleet at Toulon and of Governor-General Boisson of West Africa. Eisenhower insisted that anyone who was not on the spot would fail to appreciate the 'complex currents of feeling and of prejudice that influence the situation', but that ten minutes at his headquarters would be sufficient to dispel any doubts which prevailed about the soundness of the moves which had been made.[115]

Put in such terms, the Commander-in-Chief's arguments were unanswerable, and the British felt they had no alternative but to accept the situation. 'We cannot say that our doubts or anxieties are removed by what is proposed or that the solution will be permanent or healthy', Churchill cabled Roosevelt on the following day. 'Nevertheless in view of the dominating importance of speed and of the fact that the Allied Commander-in-Chief's opinion is so strongly and ably expressed and that it is endorsed by our officers, including Admiral Cunningham, who were with him on the spot, we feel we have no choice but to accept General Eisenhower's arguments.'[116] Although the Foreign Office was thus obliged to accept that some sort of arrangement with Darlan was inevitable, it attempted to salvage what it could from the situation. The most important aim was to ensure that Darlan should not be admitted to a position of permanent political power, and in this it achieved a certain amount of success. On the 16th, Eden pressed Churchill in the Cabinet on the importance of telling the President 'that we thought it would be disastrous if we were to make any permanent arrangement with Admiral Darlan', but the Prime Minister was reluctant to convey this message and the decision was deferred.[117] On the following day, however, he gave way and pressed the President once again, tactfully but firmly.

I ought to let you know that very deep currents of feeling are stirred by the arrangement with Darlan. The more I reflect on it the more convinced I become that it can only be a temporary expedient, justifiable solely by the stress of battle. We must not overlook the serious political injury which may be done to our çause, not only in France but throughout Europe, by the feeling that we are ready to make terms with the local Quislings. Darlan has an odious record. It is he who has inculcated in the French Navy its malignant disposition by promoting his creatures to command. It is but yesterday that French sailors were sent to their death against your line of battle off Casablanca, and now, for the sake of power and office, Darlan plays the turncoat. A permanent arrangement with Darlan or the formation of a Darlan Government in French North Africa would not be understood by the great masses of ordinary people, whose simple loyalties are our strength.[118]

One phrase, deleted from the Prime Minister's telegram but figuring in another communication, put the case in a nutshell. 'We are fighting for international decency and Darlan is the antithesis of this.'[119]

Roosevelt, under pressure himself from a hostile public, issued a strong statement on the same day which, while endorsing the actions of the Commander-in-Chief, nevertheless stated categorically that 'in view of the history of the past two years, no permanent arrangement should be made with Admiral Darlan'. The President went on to stress that nobody in the Army was authorised to discuss the future government of France or the French Empire, that there was no intention to reconstitute the Vichy government in France or any French territory and that the future French government would be established 'not by any individual in Metropolitan France or overseas, but by the French people themselves after they have been set free by the victory of the United Nations'. Borrowing a phrase from the Prime Minister's telegram, Roosevelt insisted that the arrangement with Darlan was 'a temporary expedient, justified solely by the stress of battle'.[120]

As far as it went, this statement was completely satisfactory, especially in its rejection of the principle of the 'Vichy succession' upon which Darlan based his claim to authority, and in its stress upon the temporary nature of the arrangements. However, it was very far from being a complete solution. The oblique promise that Darlan would be dispensed with at some future time when his usefulness was exhausted did not resolve the moral dilemma which faced the Allied governments; it simply made them seem more cynical than ever. As Harold Nicolson wrote to his sons, 'I do not see how one can maintain one's credit if one announces to the world that one has employed a trickster in order to trick his followers, and that one will discard him once it is clear that the trick has come off.'[121] Nor was this aspect lost on Darlan and his followers. Smuts, who passed through Algiers on 20 November, reported that the President's statement had had an unsettling effect upon the French leaders and warned that it would be dangerous to go further along the same lines. Noguès had already threatened to resign. 'From the point of view of securing French co-operation and stabilising [the] situation nothing could be worse than [the] impression that we were merely using leaders to discard them as soon as they have served our purpose.'[122] These views were supported by Cunningham and Eisenhower, who had already warned of the danger that precipitate action might upset the delicate equilibrium which had been established in North Africa.[123] The head of the Political Warfare Executive in Algiers was also to report later that although the President's speech had given some consolation to ardent supporters of the Allies 'who had felt sadly let down by this shabby but inevitable compromise', it had come as a bombshell to the wealthy, grasping *colons* whose passive co-operation was essential to the maintenance of order.[124] Two weeks later Darlan addressed a letter to Clark in which he described himself as 'only a lemon which the Americans will drop as soon as they have squeezed it dry'.[125]

The major problem, however, was not to maintain Darlan's continued collaboration with the Allies but to ensure that the President's declared policy would be carried out. Darlan was aware that, although he had rendered a great service to the Allies in bringing about the cessation of resistance, 'each gift that he brings . . . diminishes his utility, since he has that much less to bring. His acts as head of Pétain's governing apparatus hang like an albatross round his neck. He cannot get it off.'[126] Aware of his vulnerability, Darlan could be expected to employ all his considerable political skill to make himself indispensable to the Allies. At the same time the Foreign Office was determined that he should be removed from office as soon as the military situation permitted, although it was hazy about how this would be brought about. As Cadogan commented, 'while from our point of view the most satisfactory arrangement might be to use Darlan until we had possession of Tunis and then push him down a well . . . General Eisenhower might not be prepared to carry out such a policy'.[127] The only possibility, it was felt, was to apply the maximum pressure to Darlan to force him to repeal obnoxious legislation and to introduce democratic measures. In this way it was hoped to make his situation 'uncomfortable', and to render it easier to unseat him later when the opportunity arose.[128]

The Foreign Office was aware, however, that it was confronted by a formidable adversary who far outclassed those with whom he was dealing in political skill. Sherwood wrote later that the Foreign Office derived 'a certain private satisfaction from the embarrassment of the United States Government throughout the Darlan affair', and there is a notable degree of *schadenfreude* in the Foreign Office's minuting and in Cadogan's diary. 'When it comes to drafting protocols, General Eisenhower is out of his depth', wrote Cadogan on 21 November, and added as an afterthought 'and Darlan is hardly paddling'.[129] For all his dislike of the political arrangements with the Admiral, Cadogan could not entirely suppress his professional's admiration for Darlan's skill. 'Fact is, Darlan has bluffed and diddled US and UK', he wrote in his diary on the 21st, and on the following day: 'Darlan has made rings round Eisenhower and old mother Cunningham. What a man!'[130]

Eden and Cadogan were particularly dismayed by the negotiations which led up to the signing of the Darlan–Clark agreement on 22 November. Roosevelt was careful to avoid endorsing any form of diplomatic document which would imply that Darlan was a national plenipotentiary, but he was prepared to accept Eisenhower's draft agreement as it stood. Eden, on the other hand, while agreeing that the best course would be for Eisenhower to issue a statement and for Darlan to adhere to it, felt that the Commander-in-Chief had given away in negotiation more than was necessary to secure the Admiral's co-operation.[131] During the evening of the 20th he attempted to win Churchill over to his point of view, but without success. 'I cannot get W. [Winston] to see the damage Darlan may do to the Allied cause if we don't watch it', he remarked in his diary.[132] On the following day the Cabinet accepted Churchill's view that Eisenhower should not be troubled with detailed amendments and agreement was finally reached the following day.[133]

Eisenhower had argued in support of the proposed 'protocol' that Darlan's appointment as 'High Commissioner' in North Africa did not bind the Allies to him in perpetuity and Churchill also took the view, in urging its acceptance to the Cabinet, that it was a transaction in the field rather than a diplomatic document.[134] Such niceties, however, hardly affected the reality of Darlan's growing power. In spite of the President's statement, Darlan broadcast on 20 November praising Pétain's policy since the Armistice and claiming to be the real interpreter of his thoughts. There could be no doubt that Darlan's authority rested upon his position as the inheritor of the *pouvoir légitime*, and that he was obeyed in North Africa as the deputy of Pétain and as the representative of the Vichy government. As Eden said, 'his administration is in effect a Vichy regime'.[135] With consummate skill, he exploited his position to the full. Prevented from assuming governmental powers, he nevertheless allowed Algiers radio to say that he had, which came to much the same thing.[136] Although his position was weakened by the scuttling of the Fleet at Toulon on 26 November, he was able to demonstrate his continuing usefulness by securing the obedience to his orders of Governor-General Boisson of West Africa. At the end of November his position seemed to have become more secure than ever.

Eden had clashed vigorously with Churchill over the terms of the Eisenhower protocol and on the 26th he set out his position at length in a personal minute to the Prime Minister. Admiral Darlan, he pointed out, was cleverly exploiting the vagueness of the President's declaration to consolidate his position in North Africa. He had made it clear, for example, that he interpreted 'temporary' to mean 'until the liberation of France is complete', and 'we can be sure he will use all his skill and resource and power of decision to fortify himself in his present position'. He had also made it clear that he regarded himself as holding authority in the Marshal's name. Even on military grounds, the situation was dangerous. 'We are dealing with turncoats and blackmailers and until the French administration and armed forces are in better hands, it would not be safe to arm them with modern weapons.' But above all, there was the moral aspect:

Our appeal to the French people, whose resistance is steadily stiffening, is now stultified. In Europe as a whole, the 'filthy race of quislings,' as you once so aptly called them, will take heart since they now have reason to think that if only they happen to be in authority when the forces of the United Nations arrive, they will be treated as being the Government of the country.

Eden concluded that 'if we do not eliminate Darlan *as soon as the military situation permits* we shall be committing a political error which may have grave consequences not only for our good name in Europe but for the resistance of the oppressed people for whom we are fighting'.[137]

Churchill continued to resist Eden's pressure for a fresh exchange of views with the President for some days, but in the end gave way and approved a strongly worded telegram to Halifax:

In spite of the President's statement that political arrangement with Darlan was temporary, Darlan appears to be digging himself in more and more firmly. His administration is in effect a Vichy regime, and it appears that some of our best friends, like Generals Béthouard and Mast, are still without active employment.

It therefore seems to us now a matter of urgency that the United States Government and His Majesty's Government should send political representatives of high authority to Algiers. Political developments in North Africa cannot fail to have far-reaching effects in Europe and in the world at large, of which General Eisenhower can hardly be expected to be conscious.

It would also be the function of these representatives to try to secure such changes in the regime in North Africa as would facilitate an agreement between the North African administration and de Gaulle and thus unite the French Empire once again.[138]

These arguments made little headway in Washington. The State Department had shown some signs of sympathy for the Foreign Office's position, but remained completely eclipsed.[139] The most powerful influence upon Roosevelt at this time was none other than Admiral Leahy, whose views on Vichy were well known and who was urging the continued support of Darlan.[140] The President remained firm in his insistence that policies adopted for the sake of military expediency would not in any way prejudge the political issues at stake. At a lunch with Lord Halifax on 8 December, he opposed any early action to eliminate Darlan from the scene and would go no further than to suggest that his power might be reduced by the creation of an Inter-Allied Commission for French North Africa, of which Darlan would be only one member. Halifax replied that this would not succeed in stilling criticism, especially in the occupied countries, while Roosevelt demonstrated his continuing immunity to public feeling by talking of concluding further 'deals' during the liberation of Europe, for example in Czechoslovakia.[141] The Foreign Office's real purpose in suggesting the appointment of high-level political advisers in Algiers was to force the President to remove Murphy from involvement with Darlan, but this plan was scotched by Roosevelt's decision to elevate Murphy instead. The prospect that the principal architect of the Darlan deal would continue to represent the United States in North Africa obviously destroyed any possibility of a vigorous effort to oust the Admiral from power. Indeed Murphy seemed content to continue to deal with Darlan in every capacity except that of head of the French government, and behaved on occasions, according to one (admittedly hostile) witness 'rather as if he were Darlan's Chef de Cabinet than as representative of the President of the United States of America'.[142] The appointment of Harold Macmillan as Minister Resident in Algiers, although it failed to provoke the appointment of a more acceptable substitute for Murphy, showed that the British were determined to have their views strongly represented in future, but there was every sign at the year's end that the creation of an acceptable authority to represent French interests in North Africa was as distant as it had even been.[143]

THE MURDER OF ADMIRAL DARLAN

By the middle of December the situation in Algiers had reached an apparent impasse. There was no indication of a change in the attitude of the United States, and a strong message from Churchill to the President on the situation in North Africa was without effect.[144] There were signs, however, that public indignation was beginning to subside. Parliamentary criticism was largely stilled by Churchill's masterly explanation of British policy to the Secret Session of the House of Commons on 10 December. Opinion in the House changed 'palpably and decisively', and this in turn had its effect upon feeling in the country.[145] The Foreign Office, too, appears to have come to accept more or less philosophically the view put forward by Mack that the removal of Darlan would have to be a gradual process and, moreover, that it would have to be effected by Frenchmen themselves.[146] At the same time, although de Gaulle maintained his unbending attitude towards Darlan personally, he was careful to stress that no other obstacle stood in the way of the unification of French resistance. Members of de Gaulle's entourage, especially Catroux, began to make tentative contact with the North African administration in mid-December, and on the 19th François d'Astier de la Vigerie, whose brother was a member of the Group of Five, arrived in Algiers on an unofficial mission to explore the ground. These developments were welcomed by the Foreign Office, which saw in them the possibility of an eventual *rapprochement* between the Free French National Committee and the North African administration.[147]

How the situation might have developed in the ensuing weeks and months, and with what effects upon France's future, will never be known. On Christmas Eve Darlan was shot down in his office by a young Royalist, Bonnier de la Chapelle, and died within the hour. The 'apostolic succession' of Vichy was thus brutally severed, and the single obstacle to the unification of French resistance removed. Although

Giraud was immediately installed as head of the civil administration in Darlan's place, in a matter of months de Gaulle had established his unquestioned authority over the entire French Empire.

The news of Darlan's death was greeted with unanimous quiet satisfaction. Hull described the murder as 'an odious and cowardly act', but Darlan had been cordially detested in Washington (Roosevelt on one occasion described him as a 'stinking skunk') and the denunciation carried little conviction.[148] De Gaulle's condemnation of the assassination as 'a detestable crime' was equally insincere, and the general feeling in Fighting French circles was, understandably, 'that is one the fewer'.[149] Darlan's passing was greeted in London with the same grim satisfaction, although the Foreign Office's immediate reactions to the news remain unknown.[150] Cadogan commented cautiously in his diary that 'if order is maintained in N. Africa this may be a blessing'.[151] In fact, early fears that his death might lead to civil disorder proved to be groundless, and the news was greeted with widespread public indifference.[152] The Admiral had enjoyed little personal popularity even among those who accepted his authority, and his removal enabled many to effect relatively painlessly their further transition from a position of loyalty to Vichy to one of open dissidence.

The assassin's bullet was the neatest possible solution to a troublesome dilemma. As Churchill wrote, it 'relieved the Allies of their embarrassment at working with him, and at the same time left them with all the advantages he had been able to bestow during the vital hours of the Allied landings'.[153] Clark was equally candid. 'Darlan's death was, to me, an act of providence. . . . He had served his purpose, and his death solved what could have been the very difficult problem of what to do with him in the future.'[154] Indeed, the murder of the Admiral was so obviously in the interest of so many people that its likelihood was being freely discussed for some time before it actually happened. 'No one expects Darlan to be allowed to end his days in peace', reported Mack on 29 November. 'There are too many people who want his blood.'[155]

The circumstances surrounding Darlan's murder, like those in the case of President Kennedy, were sufficiently suspicious for it to be natural to question whether a wider conspiracy existed. In each case the assassin was himself speedily despatched by somebody who had close connections with groups known to be bitterly hostile to the victim. In the case in question, de la Chapelle was court-martialled and shot on Boxing Day, under Giraud's orders, confidently expecting to the last the intervention of powerful friends on his behalf. This would not appear too suspicious if it were not for the fact that Giraud had been brought to North Africa at the instigation of the Group of Five, with whom the assassin had numerous contacts. A wealth of circumstantial evidence links the former members of the conspiracy with the killing of Darlan, and suggests the existence of a plot to eliminate him and to replace him with the Comte de Paris, the pretender to the French throne. It is known, for example, that Henri d'Astier de la Vigerie was active in this plan, and that he was instrumental in bringing the Comte to Algiers on 10 December. It is also known that a plan existed to demand Darlan's resignation on the 18th, but that this was abandoned for lack of support from Eisenhower. It may be that this setback encouraged the Royalists to more drastic action. D'Astier and the Abbé Cordier, a priest who knew de la Chapelle well, were arrested but later released for lack of evidence and given the *Croix de Guerre* by Giraud – who had originally ordered their detention. Despite this, however, no authoritative study exists and the question remains open.[156] It may simply be that de la Chapelle mixed in circles where Darlan's removal was under discussion, and took his cue accordingly. Disappointed hopes and the continued persecution of pro-Allied sympathisers had brought feelings to a dangerous pitch in many circles by late December.[157]

The Gaullists were, of course, the other party who stood to gain most from Darlan's death, and it is tempting to see a connection between the visit of General François de la Vigerie to Algiers and the death of Darlan five days later. Even though the visit was unofficial, however, it seems unlikely that de Gaulle would have invited conjecture by despatching so prominent a representative for such a task. D'Astier's mission was in all probability what it purported to be – an exploratory visit and prelude to negotiation. Although insistent that Darlan himself was an insurmountable obstacle to any agreement, de Gaulle seemed increasingly willing to bide his time and work towards a negotiated solution, and d'Astier's meeting with Darlan, Giraud, Fenard and Bergeret was, it would appear, a positive step in this direction.[158] Nor was the hope that Darlan would step down altogether remote. Murphy later claimed that he had offered to do so whenever he became more of a liability than an asset to the Allied cause, and the tone of his letter to Churchill on 4 December certainly gives the impression of a man worn down by weeks of anxiety and tension.[159] Perhaps universal vilification had affected even Darlan.

Much the same can be said for the possibility of British involvement in the murder. No evidence exists in the Foreign Office archives and although many files are withdrawn during this period, one would not expect to find political assassination figuring as a serious subject of discussion. Numerous references do exist to the need to 'eliminate' or 'get rid of' Darlan, but these remarks, which read so alarmingly in retrospect, suggest by their very flippancy a lack of complicity in the crime.[160] All are consistent, on the contrary, with the policy of manoeuvring Darlan from power gradually. There remains the possibility that the Secret Service was involved on its own initiative, and in this connection it is interesting to find the Prime Minister requesting the Foreign Secretary to investigate 'certain disquieting, but probably mendacious reports which had been received concerning SOE activities in North Africa, including the allegation that the British were responsible for the assassination of Darlan'.[161] This being said, however, there is no evidence on the available British record that the government was involved.

8   Aftermath

WHILE Vichy enjoyed a brief renaissance in North Africa under Allied patronage, in France the last remnants of power were plucked from the government's grasp. On 11 November Hitler put into effect Operation ATTILA, the total occupation of France, a move which the British government had predicted but which it regarded with indifference, since it was of little strategic significance.[1] The only danger was that the occupying forces might succeed in gaining control of the warships in Toulon harbour. The Germans at first made an agreement with Admirals Laborde and Marquis which left the port unoccupied, but on 27 November attempted a *coup de main*. The Fleet therefore scuttled itself, 'a melancholy conclusion to an armada about which there had been so many hopes, fears and premonitions'.[2] Vichy's writ ceased to run in the Colonial Empire also. Gaullist and British action had already accounted for large tracts of West Africa, Oceania, Syria and St Pierre and Miquelon. Madagascar surrendered to the British on 6 November. Tunisia was conquered in early 1943. Darlan rendered his last service to the Allied cause in late November 1942 by securing the adherence of Boisson, Governor-General of West Africa. Djibuti passed over on 28 December, the French West Indies the following July.

It is tempting, therefore, to draw a line and say, with Churchill, 'so much for Vichy'.[3] Certainly the government had lost the resources with which to conduct a foreign policy as well as the authority which it would have needed to play a role during the liberation of France. After ATTILA, the British adopted the position that France was without a government.[4] However, because of the American government's continued hostility towards de Gaulle and its apparent willingness to contemplate a successor regime to Vichy as the post-war government of France, 'Vichy' remained a live issue in the context of Anglo-American relations for two years after the government of that name had lost its last vestige of independence.

In the period before TORCH, de Gaulle's behaviour had been so disturbing that even the Foreign Office had hoped for a time to see a strong authority emerge in North Africa with which he would be obliged to coalesce (see above, p. 143).[5] In the event, however, de Gaulle's position had been strengthened, not weakened, by the events of November and December 1942, and the Foreign Office saw no prospect that acceptable rivals would thereafter come forward. Cadogan declared as late as May 1944 that if the Americans could come up with an alternative to de Gaulle (apart from Vichy) he would consider it, but this gave nothing away. No body of men who had failed to step forward before 1943 could challenge the integrity of the Gaullist position.[6] Giraud was widely regarded as an American puppet and commanded no personal following. Instead of being an obstacle to de Gaulle, he became a springboard to his yet greater authority.[7] The politicians of the Third Republic were largely discredited. Some, like Reynaud, Mandel and Blum, were in German prisons. Others, like Lebrun, whose resurrection was briefly considered by Eden as a means of removing Darlan, were in discreet retirement.[8] None could form a rallying point for France. For a time, in 1941, there had been some support in the Foreign Office for the idea of a Royalist restoration. However, this suggestion found little favour with Churchill or Eden, and in August 1942 the Comte de Paris destroyed what little credit he enjoyed in London by travelling to Vichy in an attempt to persuade Pétain to nominate him as his successor. His cause was further tainted in December by his association with the former supporters of Giraud whose ambitions for political power had been thwarted by the Darlan–Clark agreement, by his absurd attempt to replace Darlan, and by the involvement of his followers in the latter's assassination. His suggestion in January 1943 that de Gaulle should become his Commander-in-Chief was dismissed by Eden as 'laughable' and no further attention was paid to him.[9]

After Darlan's assassination, Eden and Cadogan remained unwavering in their support of de Gaulle and argued that British policy should aim to create, as soon as possible, a strong central authority which would represent French interests, assume control of civil affairs in France in the wake of the Allied forces and supervise the restoration of French democracy. Although it was necessary to defer to American prejudices to the extent of withholding formal recognition of the Committee of National Liberation until after it was installed in Paris, and although the Foreign Office argued somewhat disingenuously that it did not back de Gaulle 'for any position of primacy', there was no doubt in London or Washington that this policy would place de Gaulle in an unassailable position. Mack was candid enough to admit in

December 1943 that, as far as he was concerned, the Committee of National Liberation was the government of France.[10]

The American government, on the other hand, refused to modify its policy of reserve and seemed more determined than ever to prevent de Gaulle's accession to power. The President and the State Department argued with some justification that, however much the British might disclaim this intention, their policy of establishing a strong 'caretaker' authority led by de Gaulle would put him in a position from which he could not later be removed. The only way to avoid 'forcing' de Gaulle upon France was to deal with local authorities in the French Empire on an *ad hoc* basis and to resist the formation of a single body. While the British worked for the unification of the Fighting French with the Giraudist administration in Algiers, the United States government was therefore content that they should remain separate.[11] They were also willing to contemplate a prolonged period of military rule by the Allies in liberated France, while the Foreign Office argued that civilian government should be restored with all possible speed and that power should devolve naturally upon reliable elements under the supervision of officers appointed by the Committee of National Liberation and attached to the Allied Forces.[12]

Both London and Washington defended their respective positions with the argument that theirs was the best course to ensure the restoration of French democracy. Such scruples, however, only thinly concealed their pursuit of differing national interests. The British wanted a strong and friendly France, and the Gaullist movement was the only party which had reaffirmed its intention of rebuilding the Anglo-French Alliance. Fears of a Gaullist dictatorship in France were largely offset by the anxiety that the Communists might take over instead, an anxiety which de Gaulle was aware of and which he exploited.[13] American observers who had backed the 'Vichy Gamble' tended to see in this policy a veiled attempt to 'run' France after the war, but the British were under no illusions on this score.[14] American policy was equally aimed at the installation in Paris of a government which would be amenable to Washington's wishes, and it is this which provides the key to continued American hostility towards de Gaulle.

While the British could claim that their interests were identical with those of France, the American President had in mind a post-war settlement which would ratify France's demotion from the status of a Great Power. Roosevelt envisaged a world system within which smaller states might proliferate and in which colonial ties would be loosened, with the 'Big Four' acting as policemen. Within this scheme of things, France would not only be denied front-rank status, but would be obliged to suffer various indignities, such as disarmament or the creation from her territory of a Flemish buffer state. On a number of occasions the President also spoke of the need to prevent France regaining control of Indo-China and of the desirability of placing various strategic points in the French Empire under the control of the United Nations. When Eden pointed out to him that the French would be likely to object, the President replied that France would no doubt require assistance after the war, 'for which consideration might be the placing of certain parts of her territory at the disposal of the United Nations', and to Welles's reminder that the United States government had gone on record as being in favour of the restoration of French possessions, he replied that 'in the ironing out of things after the war this kind of position could be rectified'. Roosevelt clearly considered that France had been defeated and was not entitled to full Allied status.[15] It was equally apparent that only a French government which had accepted defeat would be likely to acquiesce; certainly not the Gaullist movement, whose contention was that France had never left the battlefield and therefore merited full Allied treatment.

The Foreign Office had always been somewhat perplexed by American prejudices against de Gaulle. Even if one accepted all the arguments of expediency advanced in support of the policy of cordiality towards Vichy, and even making allowance for Roosevelt's and Hull's personal dislike of the General, the degree of hostility aroused, for example, by the St Pierre and Miquelon episode, was difficult to explain in such terms alone.[16] The President's conjecturings about France's future seemed to provide the answer. Before TORCH, the Foreign Office had been reluctant to heed the warnings of the Gaullists that the aim of American policy was to establish in France a successor regime to Vichy which would open its colonies to American commercial exploitation, admit international supervision of those parts of its Empire which fell within areas of American strategic concern, and accept the role of an American client state. Roosevelt's attitude during the Darlan episode, however, made this conclusion seem inescapable. The Foreign Office began to suspect that the insistence upon the military character of the North African occupation and the desire to resist the formation of a central French authority were not means of deflecting criticism about the deal with Darlan or of holding the ring clear for the restoration of French democracy, but were intended to keep France weakened and divided. As Eden wrote later, 'it seemed to me that Roosevelt wanted to hold the strings of France's future in his own hands so that he could decide that country's fate'.[17] The disquieting behaviour of American personnel in West Africa and the exclusion of the British from participation in American negotiations with Boisson left little room for further doubt.[18] The choice of Giraud also took on a new significance. As one official wrote with admirable clarity, 'their whole policy culminating in the Darlan experiment only makes sense on the assumption that they have believed it possible to create a sort of American party in France to form the basis for a future Government. A central administration headed by Giraud might have appeared consistent with this aim but not a fusionist Giraud–de Gaulle administration.'[19]

These developments were the occasion of a good deal of exasperation in the Foreign Office in 1943 and 1944, especially in view of the Prime Minister's increasing preoccupation with the need to maintain what he saw as his special relationship with Roosevelt, and his consequent readiness to offer up de Gaulle on the altar of Anglo-American relations.[20] Both Eden and Cadogan, with their essentially European outlook, fought long and hard to counteract the President's influence upon Churchill. Roosevelt's plans for France could be expected to have a disastrous effect upon the future of Europe, and Eden was insistent that British policy should not be dictated by Washington.[21] As Cadogan also expressed it in May 1944: 'We are nearly 3,000 miles closer to this unhappy continent than is President Roosevelt. We take the first brunt of all the knocks. We – or at least I – believe that without a rejuvenated and friendly France the front line is going to be extremely uncomfortable in the years of "peace".'[22]

It was against this background that the suspicion began to take root in the Foreign Office in 1943 that the American government contemplated the survival of Vichy into the post-war period, and it was this suspicion in turn which made the question of civil administration during the liberation of France so vital. As was to be expected, the increasing certainty of Allied victory and the growing fear of Gaullist purges brought about a steady movement of former collaborators and of those who had remained uncommitted into the Allied camp. Some, like Flandin and Peyrouton, were encouraged by America's policy towards Vichy to believe that a future existed for them in Algiers. Much more sinister were the activities of the powerful group of interests represented by such men as Lemaigre-Dubreuil and Rigault, who had backed

Giraud in 1942 and whose ambitions for political power had been thwarted by the Darlan episode. Even after his death, the increasing power of Gaullist sympathisers in the North African administration made it impossible for them to maintain their positions, and in April 1943 Lemaigre-Dubreuil and Rigault escaped to Portugal with the help of Robert Murphy.[23]

Evidence exists that Roosevelt established contact in late 1943 and 1944 with such groups with a view to preventing de Gaulle's accession to power. In late 1943 an American journalist contacted Piétri, the Vichy ambassador in Madrid, with a message for Laval to the effect that Roosevelt was fearful of the situation which would arise in France if de Gaulle took charge and that he wished to discuss the situation outside normal diplomatic channels. Laval reported this conversation to Abetz and made no reply.[24] The following June, Lemaigre-Dubreuil and Rigault approached Piétri with the similar message that 'Washington greatly fears a dictatorship by General de Gaulle, whom the British are backing up to the hilt. It must be stopped by the force of legality. . . . It is imperative that the Marshal hands over his powers to [Parliament] in such a way that, when the time comes, the Algiers Committee will be confronted by a *fait accompli* and a ready-formed Provisional Government.' Laval again informed Abetz, who sent an SS representative to talk with Lemaigre-Dubreuil and Rigault, but the contacts were eventually broken off by Ribbentrop in July.[25]

It is uncertain how far these contacts were genuinely inspired by Roosevelt himself and how far they were the initiative of the intermediaries themselves, or of sympathisers within the American government who shared Hitler's illusion of an eleventh-hour peace in the west (involving Vichy's survival) to hold back the Soviet Union. At the very least, the President's continued refusal to commit the United States to the acceptance of the Free French National Committee as the civil authority in liberated France kept hope alive in collaborationist circles and encouraged intrigue. Similarly although the present writer has had access to neither the American nor the German sources, it is significant that the persistent rumours of contact between Vichy and Washington were not lightly dismissed in London.

Rumours that the President was in touch with Vichy with a view to securing the handover of France during the liberation were in wide circulation in late 1943, and the Foreign Office began to feel that it should 'have it out' with the State Department. Although the sources of the Foreign Office's information were not regarded as completely reliable, Speaight remarked that 'we have our own reasons for suspecting that there may be some smoke behind this fire'.[26] These reports were all the more disquieting in view of the powerful influence of Admiral Leahy, whose views on France were well known and who enjoyed easy access to the President.[27] The Foreign Office harboured deep suspicions of Leahy and believed that a link existed between him and Vichy through Allen Dulles, head of the OSS in Switzerland, whom he used to pass 'encouraging messages'. It was not known how far the President was aware of this.[28] There was certainly no doubt about the Admiral's position on the Vichy–de Gaulle issue. In February 1944 he advised the President that the most reliable person to rally France to the Allies when the invasion was launched was Marshal Pétain. As Cadogan remarked, 'it's simply Alice in Wonderland'.[29]

These rumours became sufficiently widespread in March 1944 to prompt the State Department to issue a statement to the effect that the American government had no intention of dealing with Vichy except for the purpose of abolishing it.[30] The continued reluctance of the President to agree to a directive to Eisenhower which obliged him to work with de Gaulle rather than simply permitting him to do so, however, kept alive in the Foreign Office the fear that there would be another pact with the Devil. Had not the President once said that he would deal with Laval, if Laval would give him Paris? 'I must assume that he is not hankering after Vichy,' wrote Cadogan in May 1944, 'though I can't convince myself altogether from the belief that he is.'[31] Even in June 1944 Cadogan found Roosevelt so 'odd' on the French question that 'I think he must have made a secret agreement with Pétain and/or Laval!' Duff Cooper made a similar observation in his diary only a week later.[32] In the event, the matter was settled by Eisenhower himself, who had been convinced since the beginning of 1944 that the handing over of civil administration in France to the National Committee should proceed with all speed, and who put this policy into effect without question. Pétain's pathetic attempt to preserve the principle of legitimacy by handing over his powers to de Gaulle was naturally rebuffed, and another attempt by a former Vichy minister to contact the Allied forces in September 1944 was ignored.[33] De Gaulle moved naturally into his inheritance and the French Committee of National Liberation was recognised by the United States, in July as the 'temporary de facto authority' in France, and on 23 October 1944 as the Provisional Government.

It seems superfluous to add that the British naturally refused to have

anything to do with any of the various groups working to prevent de
Gaulle installing himself in Paris. On 15 June 1944 the Cabinet
considered a memorandum by Eden which described the formation of a
new group, the 'Comité National des Corps Élus de la République',
which opposed both Vichy and de Gaulle and aimed to restore
democracy and build closer ties with England. The movement claimed
to control an army or resistance of 45,000 men and to count Wendel and
Schneider, the armaments manufacturers, and various politicians of the
centre among its members. Eden dismissed it as only 'the latest attempt
by the "Comité des Forges" and suchlike elements who have hitherto
been collaborationist to re-insure in advance of the Allied victory'. It
was known that these elements had been planning for some time to
secure United States support for a modified Vichy government which
would retain Pétain but get rid of Laval. SHAEF was therefore
informed that the Comité's delegation would not be received.[34]

The firm British refusal to treat with Vichy in 1943 or 1944, or to
contemplate its painless transition into peacetime, need come as no
surprise. There was little purpose in dealing with a government which
lay wholly within the enemy's power and which no longer retained the
authority or power to affect the outcome of the war. From 1940 to 1942,
however, the distinctive feature of British policy towards Vichy had
been its apparent lack of consistency and its refusal to adopt a firm line.
'I have not yet been able to discover here the basis of a constructive
diplomatic policy in relation to the Vichy Government', reported the
American ambassador in London in April 1941.[35] As the Foreign Office
itself confessed when explaining its policy to the State Department in
early 1941, the pursuit of its various objectives in its dealings with Vichy
involved inconsistencies between principle and practice (see above, pp.
98–9). The British government was willing to reach an accommodation with a regime which it had roundly condemned as the
enemy's handmaiden in return for an immediate military advantage.

Such a statement is perhaps not very instructive. The interplay of
principle and expediency is an enduring theme in most foreign policies
and it would be naïve to expect consistency. Attitudes and perceptions
shift and personnel change. Priorities are constantly reassessed. Chance,
doubt and misinformation play their part. When studying British
foreign policy, in particular, one must also take account of the Foreign
Office's rooted aversion to the theoretical approach and its long
tradition of cautious pragmatism. It is difficult to discern a clear pattern

in Britain's policy towards Vichy, or even to make, in regard to that policy, a single statement which does not require endless qualification. British responses ran the whole gamut from violent hostility to extreme cordiality and often seemed illogical or self-defeating even to those, like Admiral Somerville, Sir Samuel Hoare and David Eccles, whose job it was to put them into effect. One searches in vain for consistency in the minutes, writings and speeches of those who shaped policy. The most extreme example was Churchill himself, and it is startling to find with what absolute conviction he pressed forward in June 1942 almost exactly the same viewpoint which he had condemned with equal fluency when advanced by the Foreign Office in 1940 (see above, p. 74 and pp. 134–7).

There are several explanations for the diffuse and fragmentary character of British policy and the apparently confused responses of British policy-makers. Most important of all is the fact that Britain was engaged throughout the period in question in a struggle for national survival to which all other considerations were naturally subordinate. This is a simple but fundamental point. Vichy was at no stage of the war the most important issue facing the British government, and responses had to be measured against the changing pattern of the conflict as a whole. In 1940 and 1941, with national survival imminently threatened, the British were on the whole content to maintain a rough equilibrium in relations with Vichy. In 1942, with eventual victory assured, Vichy's renewed participation in the war on the Allied side promised a short-cut to victory. Whatever the situation, there were always persuasive reasons to play for time and avoid a break. At the same time, Vichy's relatively low priority widened the gap between the planning of policy and its implementation. The economic blockade could not be enforced because of the shortage of ships. Offers of military support to Weygand could not be made good because the demands of other theatres were always more pressing. Neither coercion nor persuasion could be made effective without resources, and these were usually deployed elsewhere.

Another major difficulty was the lack of reliable information about the intentions of the Vichy government. Pétain himself was thought to favour a policy of neutrality, but the extent of his control over the actions of his ministers was unknown. In this respect, American policy was based upon the assumption that a constant struggle was being waged in Vichy between the forces of neutrality represented by Pétain and Weygand and the forces of collaboration represented by Laval and

Darlan. Its aim was therefore to strengthen the hand of the former by emphasising the benefits of continued neutrality and to a lesser extent by threatening their withdrawal. Such a theory bore little relation to the facts. In particular, it underestimated the opportunism which formed the basis of Pétain's policy and overestimated the effect of the American presence. Only one question really affected Vichy: who would win the war? And Pétain did not accept the possibility of an outright Allied victory until it had almost taken place. Churchill understood this and always made self-interest the basis of his exhortations to Vichy. Roosevelt's appeals to honour or to the traditional friendship of the French and American peoples were largely without effect. Nevertheless, the American theory did provide a framework for policy, and the 'Vichy Gamble', however misguided, at least displayed a consistency of purpose which was altogether lacking in London. The British never made up their minds whether threats or cajolery would have most effect upon Vichy. On the whole, Churchill's view held sway; the British could 'knock the French about' without too much danger of pushing Vichy into Germany's arms. The mild response of Vichy to Dakar and Syria lends support to the essential soundness of this judgement. Beyond this, however, there was little agreement. Would Vichy respond to being led gently along, as Halifax thought, or would such a policy simply enable France to sit out the war in relative comfort, 'browsing on chocolates', as Eden suspected?

These questions were often raised in 1940 and early 1941 without any firm answer being given. After that the matter became somewhat academic, since the American government had assumed the initiative in handling Vichy. The British could therefore mould their policy accordingly, calling upon the United States to use its moderating influence when drastic action was called for, as in Syria and Madagascar. Indeed, apart from military action of this kind, the British hardly had any dealings with Vichy after the breakdown of the Madrid negotiations and the refusal of Weygand to raise the standard in North Africa. Influence was brought to bear at one remove, usually through the State Department. Again, because of this situation, the British were able to leave Washington to deal with Vichy, and to confine their own actions to a series of *ad hoc* corrective measures as the situation seemed to demand. The Foreign Office did not like American policy, suspecting its effectiveness, its soundness in principle, and even the motives which inspired it. But one wonders how far British policy might have been modified if the American government had not provided a safety net, and how far Hull was justified in his complaint that the British benefited from American policy even while they hampered its execution.

These considerations – the need to subordinate Vichy policy to the supreme task of defeating the enemy, the doubts about the intentions of Pétain and his ministers, or about the most effective means of bringing pressure to bear, and the need to take account of American initiatives – explain much of the apparent lack of purpose in British policy. The basic reason for this, however, is that Vichy did confront the British with a genuine moral dilemma. Shifts and compromises and backstairs 'deals' with regimes tainted by their association with the enemy are difficult to reconcile with the ideals which modern wars are fought to uphold and in whose name whole populations are mobilised. De Gaulle understood this perfectly. 'La guerre est une chose morale. Pour que des hommes fassent la guerre, il est nécessaire qu'ils se croient moralement obligés de la faire et qu'en la faisant ils soient moralement soutenus.'[36] Churchill's fierce reaction to the French Armistice equally demonstrated his instinctive grasp of this. The violent revulsion of feeling which took place in London in June 1940 against the Pétain government was in large measure an outpouring of long-restrained feelings of resentment and betrayal. But it was at the same time a sound response, and Churchill was surely right in sensing that an attitude of complete understanding and forgiveness towards France would have been impossible to reconcile with a determination to continue the war. Compromise with Vichy would have led inexorably to compromise with Hitler. On the other hand, it is natural, when faced with a powerful adversary, to avoid provoking a confrontation with even hostile 'neutrals', even though such a policy might be distasteful and invite charges of appeasement.

These were not questions which could easily be resolved and the attitudes of most ministers and officials underwent drastic and sometimes frequent changes. Attitudes became more clearly defined in 1942, but remained essentially ambivalent. Churchill, his natural opportunism sharpened by his deference towards Roosevelt and his difficulties with de Gaulle, refused to tie Britain's colours to the General's mast and made it clear in his exchanges with Eden in June that he would not be bound by Cabinet decisions which limited his freedom of action. The Darlan 'deal' had its origins as much in this decision not to decide as it did in Washington's more straightforward preference for the Vichy regime. Eden proved in the last analysis unwilling to pursue his objections even to the extent of opposing the

Prime Minister in Cabinet. Between 1940 and 1942, the positions of the Prime Minister and the Foreign Office almost reversed. It was Churchill who denounced the Vichy regime as a sham in July 1940, maintaining British support for de Gaulle through the autumn of that year in the face of Foreign Office hostility. By 1942 it was the Foreign Office, albeit under different leadership, which was pressing de Gaulle's claims against a hostile Downing Street. That it should have argued so forcefully for the support of de Gaulle as the surest means of preserving the Anglo-French Alliance is surely, in retrospect, the sharpest irony of all.

Appendixes:

Note: for abbreviations, see Notes and References, p. 200

I THE INVASION OF SYRIA, 1941

THE British and Free French invasion of Syria in June 1941 was the most violent measure which the British government took against Vichy French territory until the launching of Operation TORCH in 1942. Nevertheless, although the terms of the Armistice concluded in July were to be the occasion of considerable bitterness between the British and the Free French (who had been altogether excluded), both the British and the Vichy governments were to a large extent willing to see the conflict localised. Darlan insisted upon vigorous resistance by the forces of General Dentz in order to demonstrate to the Germans his resolve to defend the French Empire, but he refused German offers of military support. The British, in their turn, although determined to take vigorous action, were heavily committed in other theatres and were willing to offer generous terms in order to bring about the cessation of resistance. Relations between Britain and Vichy, which were in any case non-existent in mid-1941, were hardly affected by the campaign, although British distrust of Darlan was naturally deepened. For this reason, the campaign has not been dealt with in the text.

A dispassionate account of the affair can be found in Woodward, *British Foreign Policy*, vol. I, pp. 560–70. The terms of the Anglo-French Armistice are in ibid., pp. 587–8. A good account of the effect upon Britain's relations with Free France is in Morton, 'Free French', pp. 451–6, and the military angle is covered in C. Buckley, *Five Ventures* – official history (1954) pp. 49–135. G. Warner, *Iraq and Syria* (1974) suffers to some extent from not being based on the original British sources, but is balanced and contains a useful bibliography. A useful account can also be found in Hytier, *French Foreign Policy*, pp. 275–85. Paxton, *Vichy France*, pp. 109–31, places the Syrian imbroglio within the context of Darlan's efforts to reach a broad settlement with Germany. See also

Churchill, *Grand Alliance*, pp. 287–97. The deliberations of the Cabinet can be found in CAB 65/18, those of the Chiefs of Staff in CAB 79/9–12 and CAB 80/18, and those of the Defence Committee in CAB 69/2. The Foreign Office was little involved, but see also FO 371/28476/28348/28350.

II THE OCCUPATION OF MADAGASCAR, 1942

THE entry of Japan into the war in December 1941 gave rise in London to the fear that the Japanese would attempt to establish naval bases on the island of Madagascar. The Free French drew up a plan for the island's capture in February 1942, but it called for British naval and air support and Churchill, with Dakar and Syria in mind, refused to consider a 'mixed' expedition. A sufficient force was eventually assembled and captured the main port, Diego Suarez, in May. Churchill, concerned at the danger of tying up forces, then favoured a discreet *modus vivendi* with the Vichy authorities who remained in control of the rest of the island, and he was supported in this by the Chiefs of Staff. The Foreign Office, however, encouraged by the mild reaction of the Vichy government, and supported by General Smuts, argued that the Vichy Governor-General, Annet, would only play for time, and that the island should be completely occupied. Further operations took place in September, and the final surrender was received on 5 November. As with British action in Syria the previous year, the expedition was a source of friction between Britain and Free France, but had little impact upon relations with the Vichy government.

The Madagascar episode has attracted little attention, and no completely satisfactory account exists. Churchill's version, which fails to convey his enthusiasm for a *modus vivendi* between the two campaigns, is in *Hinge of Fate*, pp. 197–212. The 'full explanation of our policy' which Churchill quotes on p. 208 is in fact an edited version of the complete text of a telegram which can be found in full in CAB 66/25-WP (42) 242 (8.6.42). Brooke opposed the project throughout: Bryant, *Turn of the Tide*, pp. 365–6, 428. Official accounts of the campaign, and of the British administration of the island, can be found in Buckley, *Five Ventures*, pp. 167–208, and Lord Rennell of Rodd, *British Military Administration of Occupied Territories in Africa* – official history (1948) pp. 208–41. De Gaulle's views can be found in *L'Appel*, pp. 204–7, 580–3,

591–2, 594–7, 604–5. Cabinet and Chiefs of Staff discussions are widely dispersed in CAB 79 (17, 18, 21, 22, 57), CAB 80 (24–36), CAB 65 (26–32) and CAB 66 (25–7). The story can best be followed in FO 371/31897 and 31907 and PREM 3/265/1–11.

Chronological Table

1939	3 September	Britain and France declare war on Germany
1940	20 March	Replacement of Daladier by Paul Reynaud as French Premier.
	28 March	Joint declaration by Britain and France rejecting possibility of a separate armistice or peace except by mutual consent
	10 May	Churchill replaces Chamberlain as Prime Minister
		German invasion of the west begins
	18 May	Marshal Pétain joins the French government
	25 May	French Cabinet first discusses possibility of armistice. Disengagement of BEF begins
	27–28 May	Collapse of Belgian resistance. Beginning of Dunkirk evacuation. British Cabinet considers 'British Strategy in a Certain Eventuality' and rejects Halifax peace proposal
	26 May–4 June	Evacuation of British and French forces from Dunkirk
	5 June	Resumption of German offensive: Italy declares war
	9 June	Pétain demands an armistice
	10 June	French government leaves Paris
	11 June	Anglo-French Supreme War Council meeting at Briare
	12 June	General Weygand orders a general retreat
	13 June	Anglo-French meeting at Tours; Churchill refuses to release France from its undertaking not to negotiate a separate armistice
	14 June	French government retreats to Bordeaux
	15 June	Chautemps proposal accepted by French Cabinet

16 June	British government grants conditional release from March agreement; offers perpetual union of Britain and France. Fall of Reynaud. Pétain forms a government and requests armistice terms. Baudouin becomes Foreign Minister
17–18 June	General de Gaulle flies to London; makes first broadcast appealing for continued resistance
22 June	British ambassador leaves Bordeaux
23 June	British government takes note of the formation of the French National Committee
24 June	Franco-German Armistice signed
25 June	Britain declares France to be 'territory in the occupation of or under the control of the enemy'.
26–27 June	Mission of Duff Cooper and Lord Gort to Rabat
28 June	De Gaulle recognised as leader of 'all Free Frenchmen who rally to him in support of the Allied cause'
3 July	Operation CATAPULT
8 July	France breaks off diplomatic relations with Britain
10 July	Senate and Chamber of Deputies vote full powers to Marshal Pétain
25 July	British Cabinet agrees to try and establish Vichy successor regime in French North Africa
13 August	Cabinet approves Operation MENACE
26–28 August	Chad and French Equatorial Africa rally to Free France
6 September	Weygand appointed Delegate-General of Vichy government in North Africa
23–24 September	Operation MENACE
September – November	Cabinet discussions lead to the decision to approach individuals in the Vichy government
22–28 October	Mission of Professor Rougier to London

24 October	Hitler and Pétain meet at Montoire
25 October	Resignation of Baudouin; Pierre Laval becomes Minister of Foreign Affairs
6 November	Rougier and Weygand meet in Algiers
13 November	Pierre Dupuy leaves for Vichy
24 November–	
7 December	Dupuy's first visit to Vichy; meets Pétain, Darlan, Huntziger, Chevalier
27 November	Britain invites Vichy to economic discussions
6 December	War Cabinet refuses to allow relief measures in Metropolitan France
13 December	Laval dismissed from office and arrested; Pierre Flandin becomes Minister of Foreign Affairs
21 December	Robert Murphy meets Weygand in Dakar
23 December	Anthony Eden replaces Lord Halifax as Foreign Secretary; Halifax becomes ambassador to USA
24 December	Churchill proposes offer of military support to French authorities in North Africa
31 December	Roosevelt proposes programme of relief for Unoccupied France
1941 3 January	War Cabinet gives conditional agreement to American relief programme
5 January	Admiral Leahy arrives in Vichy as US ambassador
9 February	Admiral Darlan replaces Flandin as Minister of Foreign Affairs
13 February	Germans order Vichy to break off economic discussions with Britain
10 March	Darlan ratifies Murphy–Weygand agreement for provisioning of French North Africa
April	Chartier, French Consul-General, expelled from Britain
11 May	Darlan meets Hitler and declares resolve to enter war against Britain
June	Mission of Colonel Groussard to London
8 June	Invasion of Syria by British and Free French Forces

	22 June	Germany invades the Soviet Union
	14 July	Syrian Armistice
	24 September	Formation of Free French National Committee
	18 November	Dismissal of Weygand from post as Delegate-General in North Africa
	7 December	Japanese attack on Pearl Harbour
	11 December	Germany and Italy declare war on the United States
	12 December	Pétain assures United States that his policy is unchanged by Weygand's dismissal; American supply programme resumed
	24 December	Liberation of St Pierre and Miquelon by Gaullist forces
	December, n.d.	First approaches by Darlan to Britain and USA through secret channels
1942	January–July	Anglo-American discussions on Allied strategy in 1942–43. 'Group of Five' conspiracy in North Africa contacts Murphy
	14 April	Laval replaces Darlan as Minister of Foreign Affairs. USA withdraws its ambassador 'for consultation'
	17 April	Escape of General Giraud from German prison
	5 May	British invasion of Madagascar
	June–July	Churchill and Eden exchange views on policy towards Vichy
	22 June	Laval states publicly that he desires a German victory
	24 July	Decision to occupy French North Africa reached by Britain and United States (Operation TORCH)
	4 September– 5 October	Robert Murphy recalled to Washington and London for consultations
	12 October	Murphy–Chrétien meeting near Algiers – Darlan's collaboration with Allies proposed
	15 October	Group of Five reject possibility of collaboration with Darlan

	17 October	Downing Street meeting gives qualified acceptance of Darlan as military collaborator in North Africa
	21–22 October	General Clark meets the Group of Five at Cherchell
	23–30 October	Darlan tours North Africa
	4 November	Group of Five informed of date of Allied landings
	5 November	Surrender of Vichy forces in Madagascar. Darlan returns to North Africa
	6 November	Giraud picked up from South of France by British submarine
	7–8 November	Allied landings in North Africa
	10 November	Darlan orders cease-fire in North Africa
	11 November	Pétain disavows Darlan and appoints Noguès his representative in North Africa; Germans launch Operation ATTILA, the occupation of the Free Zone
	13 November	French military leaders in North Africa agree to re-enter war on Allied side
	22 November	Clark–Darlan agreement signed
	23 November	French West Africa rallies to Allies
	27 November	House of Commons motion condemning 'deal with Darlan'
		French Fleet at Toulon is scuttled; Germany disarms the French 'Armistice Army'
	10 December	Churchill's speech to the House of Commons on the Darlan affair
	24 December	Assassination of Darlan. Giraud succeeds to position of High Commissioner in French North Africa
1943	4 June	Creation of French Committee of National Liberation under joint presidency of de Gaulle and Giraud
	August	Anglo-American recognition of French Committee of National Liberation as the body administering French overseas territories
	November	Resignation of Giraud
1944	June	Allied landings in Normandy

| 23 October | Recognition of FCNL as Provisional Government of France by Britain and USA |

Bibliography and List of Sources

This is divided into two main sections:

    i   Unpublished Sources: 1 Public Record Office, London
                                      2 Papers, Diaries and Theses
   ii Published Sources: 1 Collections of Documents, Reports
                                      2 Official Histories
                                      3 Works
                                      4 Articles and Essays

I   UNPUBLISHED SOURCES

1. Public Record Office, London

Admiralty Records – ADM

Cabinet Office Records:
   Minutes of War Cabinet meetings – CAB 65
   Memoranda submitted to the War Cabinet – CAB 66 and CAB 67
   Meetings of the Defence Committee (Operations) – CAB 69
   Minutes of the Chiefs of Staff Committee meetings – CAB 79
   Memoranda drawn up by the Chiefs of Staff – CAB 80

Foreign Office Records:
   Foreign Office Correspondence, General Series – FO 371
   Foreign Office Private Papers – FO 800

Prime Minister's Office:
   Papers – PREM 3 and PREM 4

Transcripts, translations and extracts of Crown copyright material in the Public Record Office appear by permission of the Controller of Her Majesty's Stationery Office.

2. Papers, Diaries and Theses

CUNNINGHAM, LORD: The Papers of Viscount Cunningham of Hynd-hope (British Museum). See also work cited in section II, 3 below.

DALTON, HUGH: The Diary of Hugh Dalton (London School of Economics and Political Science).

HALIFAX, LORD: The Diary of Lord Halifax (The Halifax Library). See also under Birkenhead in section II, 3 below.

THOMAS, R.: 'The Vichy Dilemma in British Foreign Policy, 1940–1942' (D. Phil. thesis, Sussex University, 1976). This contains a fuller listing of sources and more extensive treatment of the subject than has been possible in this book.

II PUBLISHED SOURCES

1. Collections of Documents, Reports

La Délégation Française auprès de la Commission Allemande d'Armistice: Recueil de Documents publié par le Gouvernement Français, 4 vols (Paris, 1947–57)

Despatch to His Majesty's Ambassador in Paris regarding the Relations between His Majesty's Government in the United Kingdom and the Vichy Government in the Autumn of 1940, Cmd. 6662 (HMSO, London, 1945)

DGFP: Documents on German Foreign Policy, 1918–1945, ser. D, *1937–1945* (Washington, D.C., various dates)

EADE, CHARLES (ed.), *The War Speeches of the Rt Hon. Winston S. Churchill*, 3 vols (London, 1965)

Les Événements survenus en France de 1933 à 1945: rapport de M. Charles Serre, député au nom de la commission d'enquête parlementaire, 2 vols; *Témoignages et documents recueillis par la commission d'enquête parlementaire: annexes*, 9 vols (Paris, no date)

FRUS: Foreign Relations of the United States: Diplomatic Papers, 1940–1942 (Washington, D.C., various dates)

PÉTAIN, MARÉCHAL PHILIPPE, *Paroles aux Français: messages et écrits, 1939–1941*, intro. by G. L. Jaray (Lyon, 1941)

Le Procès du Maréchal Pétain: Compte rendu in extenso des audiences transmis par le secrétariat de la haute cour de justice (Paris, 1945). A transcript can also be found in FO 371/49145.

2. Official Histories (published by HMSO)

BUCKLEY, CHRISTOPHER, *Five Ventures: Iraq, Syria, Persia, Madagascar, Dodecanese* (London, 1954)

BUTLER, J. R. M., *Grand Strategy*, vol. II (London, 1957)

ELLIS, L. F., *The War in France and Flanders, 1939–1940* (London, 1953)

FOOT, M. R. D., *SOE in France* (London, 1968)

HOWARD, MICHAEL, *Grand Strategy*, vol. IV (London, 1969)

MEDLICOTT, W. N., *The Economic Blockade*, 2 vols (London, 1959)

PLAYFAIR, I. S. O., *The Mediterranean and the Middle East*, vol. I (London, 1954)

RENNELL of RODD, LORD, *British Military Administration of Occupied Territories in Africa during the Years 1941–1947* (London, 1948)

ROSKILL, STEPHEN W., *The War at Sea, 1939–1945*, 2 vols (London, 1954; 1956). See also work cited in section II, 3 below

WOODWARD, Sir E. LLEWELLYN, *British Foreign Policy in the Second World War*, vol. I and vol. II (London, 1970; 1971)

3. Works

ABETZ, OTTO, *Histoire d'une politique Franco-Allemande, 1930–1950: mémoires d'un ambassadeur* (Paris, 1953)

ABOULKER, MARCEL, *Alger et ses complots* (Paris, 1945)

ADAM, COLIN FORBES, *Life of Lord Lloyd* (London, 1948)

ARON, ROBERT, *The Vichy Regime, 1940–1944*, trans. Humphrey Hare (London, 1958)

BANKWITZ, PHILIP C. F., *Maxime Weygand and Civil–Military Relations in Modern France* (Cambridge, Mass., 1967)

BAUDOUIN, PAUL, *The Private Diaries of Paul Baudouin*, trans. Sir Charles Petrie (London, 1948)

BEAUFRE, Gen. ANDRÉ, *The Fall of France*, trans. Desmond Flower (London, 1967)

BELL, P. M. H., *A Certain Eventuality: Britain and the Fall of France* (Farnborough, 1974)

BIRKENHEAD, EARL of, *The Life of Lord Halifax* (London, 1965)

BLOCH, MARC, *Strange Defeat* (New York, 1968)

BOND, BRIAN, *France and Belgium, 1939–1940* (London, 1975)

BOURBON, PRINCE XAVIER de, *Les Accords secrets Franco-Anglais de décembre 1940* (Paris, 1949). See also works cited in section II, 4 below

BOUTHILLIER, YVES, *Le Drame de Vichy*, vol. I, *Face à l'ennemi, face à l'allié* (Paris, 1950)

BRYANT, ARTHUR, *The Turn of the Tide, 1939–1943: A Study Based on the Diaries and Autobiographical Notes of Field Marshal the Viscount Alanbrooke, K. G., O. M.* (London, 1957)

BULLITT, ORVILLE H. (ed.), *For the President: Personal and Secret: Correspondence between Franklin D. Roosevelt and William C. Bullitt* (Boston, Mass., 1972; London, 1972)

BUTCHER, HARRY C., *My Three Years with Eisenhower: The Personal Diary of Harry C. Butcher, USNR, Naval Aide to General Eisenhower, 1942 to 1945* (New York, 1946; London, 1946)

CADOGAN, SIR ALEXANDER: David Dilks (ed.), *The Diaries of Sir Alexander Cadogan, 1938–1945* (London, 1971)

CARCOPINO, JÉROME, *Souvenirs de sept ans, 1937–1944* (Paris, 1953)

CATROUX, GEN. G., *Dans la bataille de la Méditerranée: Egypte-Levant, Afrique du Nord, 1940–1944* (Paris, 1949)

CHAPMAN, GUY, *Why France Collapsed* (London, 1968)

CHARLES-ROUX, FRANÇOIS, *Cinq Mois tragiques aux affaires étrangères, 21 mai–1 novembre 1940* (Paris, 1949)

CHAUTEMPS, CAMILLE, *Cahiers secrets de l'armistice, 1939–1940* (Paris, 1963)

CHURCHILL, WINSTON S., *The Second World War*, vol. II, *Their Finest Hour*; vol. III, *The Grand Alliance*; vol. IV, *The Hinge of Fate* (London, 1949; 1950; 1951)

CIANO, COUNT GALEAZZO: Malcolm Muggeridge (ed.), *The Ciano Diaries, 1939–1943* (London, 1947)

CLARK, Gen. MARK W., *Calculated Risk* (New York, 1951; London, 1951)

COOPER, DUFF (Lord Norwich), *Old Men Forget* (London, 1953)

CRUSOÉ [Jacques Lemaigre-Dubreuil], *Vicissitudes d'une victoire* (Paris, 1946)

CUNNINGHAM, VISCOUNT, *A Sailor's Odyssey: The Autobiography of Admiral of the Fleet Viscount Cunningham of Hyndhope, K. T., G. C. B., O. M., D. S. O.* (London, 1951). See also papers cited in section 1, 2 above.

DARLAN, ALAIN, *L'Amiral Darlan parle . . .* (Paris, 1952)

DHERS, PIERRE, *Regards nouveaux sur les années quarante* (Paris, 1958)

DILKS, DAVID (ed.): see under Cadogan

DU MOULIN DE LABARTHÈTE, HENRI, *Le Temps des illusions: souvenirs, juillet 1940–avril 1942* (Paris, 1946)

EDEN, SIR ANTHONY (Earl of Avon), *The Eden Memoirs*, vol. III, *The Reckoning* (London, 1965)

EISENHOWER, GEN. DWIGHT D., *Crusade in Europe* (New York, 1948)

FERNET, VICE-ADM., *Aux Côtés du Maréchal Pétain* (Paris, 1953)

FREEDMAN, MAX (ed.), *Roosevelt and Frankfurter: Their Correspondence, 1928–1945* (New York, 1968; London, 1967)

FUNK, ARTHUR L., *The Politics of Torch: The Allied Landings and the Algiers Putsch, 1942* (Lawrence, Kansas, 1974)

GAULLE, GEN. CHARLES DE, *Mémoires de Guerre*, vol. I, *L'Appel, 1940–1942* (Paris, 1954)

GLADWYN, LORD (Sir H. C. Gladwyn Jebb), *Memoirs of Lord Gladwyn* (London, 1972)

GODFROY, VICE-ADM., *L'Aventure de la force X à Alexandrie* (Paris, 1953)

GROUSSARD, COL. GEORGES A., *Service secret, 1940–1945* (Paris, 1954)

HALIFAX, VISCOUNT, *Fullness of Days* (London, 1957). See also papers cited in section 1, 2 above.

HARVEY, JOHN (ed.), *The Diplomatic Diaries of Oliver Harvey, 1937–1940* (London, 1970)

HOARE, SIR SAMUEL (Viscount Templewood), *Ambassador on Special Mission* (London, 1946)

HORNE, ALISTAIR, *To Lose a Battle: France 1940* (London, 1959)

HUDDLESTON, SISLEY, *Pétain–Patriot or Traitor?* (London, 1951)

HULL, CORDELL, *The Memoirs of Cordell Hull*, 2 vols (New York, 1948; London, 1948)

HYTIER, ADRIENNE DORIS, *Two Years of French Foreign Policy: Vichy 1940–1942* (Geneva, 1958)

ISRAEL, FRED L.: see under Long

KAMMERER, ALBERT, *La Passion de la flotte française: de Mers-el-Kébir à Toulon* (Paris, 1951)

LANGER, WILLIAM L., *Our Vichy Gamble* (Hamden, Conn., 1965)

LEAHY, WILLIAM D., *I Was There* (New York, 1950; London, 1950)

LEBRUN, ALBERT, *Témoignage* (Paris, 1945)

LONG, BRECKENRIDGE, *The War Diaries of Breckenridge Long: Selections from the Years 1939–1944*, sel. and ed. Fred L. Israel (Lincoln, Nebraska, 1966)

LYTTELTON, OLIVER (Viscount Chandos), *The Memoirs of Lord Chandos* (London, 1962)

MARDER, ARTHUR J., *From the Dardanelles to Oran: Studies of the Royal Navy in War and Peace, 1915–1940* (London and New York, 1974)

——, *Operation Menace: The Dakar Expedition and the Dudley North Affair* (London and New York, 1976)

MAST, GEN. CHARLES, *Histoire d'une Rébellion: Alger, 8 novembre 1942* (Paris, 1969)

MURPHY, ROBERT, *Diplomat among Warriors* (London, 1964)

NICOLSON, NIGEL (ed.), *Harold Nicolson, Diaries and Letters*, vol. II, *1939–1945* (London, 1967)

NÖEL, LÉON, *Le Diktat de Réthondes et l'armistice Franco-Italian de juin 1940* (Paris, 1954)

OSGOOD, SAMUEL M., *French Royalism under the Third and Fourth Republics* (The Hague, 1960)

PASSY, COL., *Souvenirs*, vol. II, *Deuxième Bureau à Londres* (Monte Carlo, 1947)

PAXTON, ROBERT O., *Parades and Politics at Vichy: The French Officer Corps under Marshal Pétain* (Princeton, N. J., 1966)

——, *Vichy France: Old Guard and New Order, 1940–1944* (New York, 1972; London, 1972)

PENDAR, KENNETH, *Adventure in Diplomacy: Our French Dilemma* (New York, 1945)

PERTINAX [ANDRÉ GÉRAUD], *The Gravediggers of France: Gamelin, Daladier, Reynaud, Pétain and Laval* (New York, 1968)

PIÉTRI, FRANÇOIS, *Mes Années d'Espagne, 1940–1948* (Paris, 1954)

REYNAUD, PAUL, *Au Coeur de la Mêlée, 1930–1945* (Paris, 1951)

ROSKILL, STEPHEN W., *Churchill and the Admirals* (London, 1977). See also work cited in section II, 2 above

ROUGIER, LOUIS, *Les Accords Pétain–Churchill: histoire d'une mission secrète* (Montreal, 1945)

——, *Les Accords secrets Franco-Britanniques de l'automne 1940: histoire et imposture* (Paris, 1954)

SAINSBURY, KEITH, *The North African Landings 1942* (London, 1976)

SCHMITT, GEN. GEORGES, *Les Accords secrets Franco-Britanniques de novembre-décembre 1940: histoire ou mystification* (Paris, 1957)

SHERWOOD, ROBERT E., *The White House Papers of Harry L. Hopkins: An Intimate History*, 2 vols (New York, 1948, 1949; London, 1948, 1949)

SHIRER, WILLIAM L., *The Collapse of the Third Republic: An Enquiry into the Fall of France in 1940* (New York, 1969; London, 1970; paperback 1972)

SMITH, R. HARRIS, *OSS: The Secret History of America's First Central Intelligence Agency* (Berkeley, Calif., 1972)

SOUSTELLE, JACQUES, *Envers et contre tout*, vol. II, *De Londres à Alger* (Paris, 1950)

SPEARS, SIR EDWARD, *Assignment to Catastrophe*, vol. I, *Prelude to Dunkirk*,

July 1939–May 1940, vol. II, *The Fall of France, June 1940* (London, 1954)

——, *Two Men Who Saved France: Pétain and de Gaulle* (London, 1966)

THOMSON, DAVID, *Two Frenchmen: Pierre Laval and Charles de Gaulle* (London, 1951)

TOMKINS, PETER, *The Murder of Admiral Darlan* (London, 1965)

TOURNOUX, J. R., *Pétain and de Gaulle*, trans. Oliver Coburn (London, 1966)

TRUCHET, ANDRÉ, *L'Armistice de 1940 et l'Afrique du Nord* (Paris, 1955)

TUTE, WARREN, *The Deadly Stroke* (London, 1973)

VAN HECKE, GEN. A. S., *Les Chantiers de la jeunesse au secours de la France* (Paris, 1971)

VARILLON, PIERRE, *Le Sabordage de la flotte* (Paris, 1954)

WAITES, NEVILLE (ed.), *Troubled Neighbours: Franco-British Relations in the Twentieth Century* (London, 1971)

WARNER, GEOFFREY, *Pierre Laval and the Eclipse of France* (London, 1968)

——, *Iraq and Syria, 1941* (London, 1974)

WEYGAND, GEN. MAXIME, *Mémoires*: vol. III, *Rappelé au service* (Paris, 1950)

WHEELER-BENNETT, SIR JOHN, *Life of King George VI* (London, 1958)

WILLIAMS, JOHN, *The Guns of Dakar* (London, 1975)

4. Articles and Essays

BELOFF, MAX, 'The Anglo-French Union Project of June 1940', in *Mélanges Pierre Renouvin: études d'histoire des relations internationales* (Paris, 1966)

BOURBON, PRINCE XAVIER DE, 'Révélations sur les accords secrets Halifax–Chevalier de décembre 1940', *Le Figaro* (7 Apr 1953)

——, 'Les Accords Franco-Britanniques de 1940', *Revue des Deux Mondes* (1 July 1954)

CAIRNS, JOHN C., 'Great Britain and the Fall of France: A Study in Allied Disunity', *J. of Modern History*, XXVII 4 (Dec 1955)

——, 'Perplexities of a "Nation of Shopkeepers" in Search of a Suitable France', *American Historical Review*, LXXIX 3 (June 1974)

CHEVALIER, JACQUES, 'Un Témoignage direct sur deux points d'histoire', *Écrits de Paris* (July 1953)

FUNK, ARTHUR L., 'Negotiating the "Deal with Darlan"', *J. of Contemporary History*, VIII 2 (Apr 1973)

JOHNSON, DOUGLAS, 'Britain and France in 1940', *Trans. of the Royal Historical Society*, 5th ser., XXII (1972)

MARIN, LOUIS, 'Contributions à l'étude des prodromes de l'armistice', *Revue d'histoire de la deuxième guerre mondiale*, III (June 1951)

MELKA, ROBERT L., 'Darlan between Britain and Germany', 1940–1941', *J. of Contemporary History*, VIII 2 (Apr 1973)

MORTON, DESMOND, 'The Free French Movement', in Arnold and Veronica Toynbee (eds), *Survey of International Affairs, 1939–1946*, vol. IV, *Hitler's Europe* (Oxford, 1954)

NÖEL, LÉON, 'Le Projet d'union Franco-Britannique de juin 1940', *Revue d'histoire de la deuxième guerre mondiale*, XXI (Jan 1956)

SAINSBURY, KEITH, 'The Second Wartime Alliance', in Waites (ed.), *Troubled Neighbours* (see section II, 3 above)

STOLFI, R. H. S., 'Equipment for Victory in France in 1940', *History*, LV (Feb 1940)

WATSON, D. R., 'The Making of the Treaty of Versailles', in Waites (ed.), *Troubled Neighbours* (see section II, 3 above)

WRIGHT, GORDON, 'Ambassador Bullitt and the Fall of France', *World Politics*, X, No. 1 (Oct 1957)

Notes and References

All works cited are given fuller listing in the Bibliography and List of Sources (pp. 192–9). In the case of writers with more than one work cited, references subsequent to the first citation have a 'short title' after the writer's name. In all other cases the writer's name only is given after the first citation.

ABBREVIATIONS

ADM   Admiralty Papers, London
CAB   Cabinet Office Papers, London
DFCAA   La Délégation Française auprès de la Commission Allemande d'Armistice
DGFP   Documents on German Foreign Policy 1918–1945 (Washington D.C.)
FO   Foreign Office Papers, London
FRUS   Foreign Relations of the United States: Diplomatic Papers, 1940–1942
          (Washington D.C.)
Hansard   Hansard Parliamentary Debates, 5th series
PREM   Prime Minister's Office Papers, London

I FROM VERSAILLES TO RÉTHONDES: ANGLO-FRENCH RELATIONS, 1919–40

1. D. R. Watson, 'The Making of the Treaty of Versailles', in N. Waites (ed.), *Troubled Neighbours* (1971) p. 67.

2. B. Bond, *France and Belgium, 1939–1940* (1975) pp. 13–16.

3. J. C. Cairns, 'Perplexities of a "Nation of Shopkeepers" in Search of a Suitable France', *Am. Hist. Rev.*, LXXIX, 3 (1974) 729.

4. See FO/24293 *passim*; D. Johnson, 'Britain and France in 1940', *Trans. of the Roy. Hist. Soc.*, XXII (1972) 142–6; J. C. Cairns, 'Great Britain and the Fall of France: A Study in Allied Disunity', *J. of Mod. Hist.*, XXVII, 4 (1955) 397; and G. Wright, 'Ambassador Bullitt and the Fall of France', *World Politics*, X, 1 (1957) 76.

5. P. M. H. Bell, *A Certain Eventuality: Britain and the Fall of France* (1974) p. 6.

6. Ibid.

7. CAB 65/2–WM (39) 107 (7.12.39). See also ibid. –WM (39) 109.

8. Ibid. –WM (39) 120 (20.12.39); FO 371/24297–C941/9/17.

9. FO 371/24298–C4359/9/17.

10. FO 371/24297–C2986/9/17.

11. CAB 65/6–WM (40) 74 (21.3.40). See also J. Harvey (ed.), *The Diplomatic Diaries of Oliver Harvey, 1937–1940* (1970) p. 341 – hereafter cited as Harvey.

12. 'Pertinax' [André Géraud], *The Gravediggers of France* (1968) pp. 172–3.

13. The full text can be found in CAB 99/3–SWC (40) 6 (28.3.40), and in PREM 3/173/2, p. 13.

14. See L. F. Ellis, *The War in France and Flanders, 1939–1940* – official history (1953); Bond; G. Chapman, *Why France Collapsed* (1968); A. Horne, *To Lose a Battle* (1969); and W. Shirer, *The Collapse of the Third Republic* (1969; paperback 1972).

15. A. Bryant, *The Turn of the Tide, 1939–1943* (1957) pp. 71–3; Sir E. Spears, *Assignment to Catastrophe*, vol. 1, *Prelude to Dunkirk, July 1939–May 1940* (1954) p. 203.

16. R. H. S. Stolfi, 'Equipment for Victory in France in 1940', *History*, LV (1970) 1–20; Shirer, pp. 695–706.

17. 'Pertinax', pp. 11–19.

18. Cairns, 'Britain and Fall of France', pp. 365–7.

19. M. Bloch, *Strange Defeat* (1968) pp. 27–8; Bryant, p. 120; A. Beaufre, *The Fall of France* (1967) pp. 18–23; CAB 65/7–WM (40) 151 (1.6.40). On Billotte, see also Bond, pp. 110–11. Ironside's views are noted in D. Dilks (ed.), *The Diaries of Sir Alexander Cadogan, 1938–1945* (1971) p. 287 – hereafter cited as Cadogan.

20. Cairns, 'Britain and Fall of France', p. 398.

21. Bell, pp. 31–52.

22. Bond, pp. 114–31; Bryant, pp. 113–14; Shirer, pp. 826–30.

23. P. Baudouin, *The Private Diaries of Paul Baudouin*, trans. Sir Charles Petrie (1948) pp. 56, 76. His 'diaries' were in fact extensively revised after the war and must be treated with extreme caution. The original manuscript was destroyed in circumstances described by Baudouin after the war to the Parliamentary Commission of Enquiry: *Les Événements survenus en France de 1935 à 1945: Témoignages*, VII 2041–3 – hereafter cited as *Événements . . . Témoignages*.

24. Ellis, pp. 173–4; Shirer, pp. 842–4; Bond, pp. 135–41; W. S. Churchill, *The Second World War*, vol. II, *Their Finest Hour* (1949) pp. 74–6; M. Weygand, *Mémoires*, vol. III, *Rappelé au service* (1950) p. 126; Cairns, 'Britain and Fall of France', 373–5.

25. Churchill, *Finest Hour*, pp. 96–100; P. Reynaud, *Au Coeur de la mêlée, 1930–1945* (1951) pp. 694–7; Spears, *Prelude*, pp. 294–317; Bond, pp. 172–80.

26. CAB 65/13–WM (40) 128 [CA] (18.5.40); CAB 66/7–WP (40) 168 (25.5.40); ibid. –WP (40) 169 (26.5.40). The designation [CA], or Confidential Annexe, indicates that the minutes of the meeting were of particular secrecy and were therefore retained on the Cabinet Secretary's Standard File. See also J. R. M. Butler, *Grand Strategy* – official history, vol. II, *September, 1939–June, 1941* (1957) pp. 209–17; Bell, pp. 31–54.

27. CAB 65/13–WM (40) 139, 140 and 142 [CAs] (26–8.5.40); Bell, pp. 39–48; Harvey, p. 372: entry for 29 May 1940.

28. Baudouin, p. 73.

29. Bullitt to Cordell Hull: *FRUS*, vol. I (1940) pp. 238–9.

30. Baudouin, p. 89.

31. Churchill, *Finest Hour*, p. 139; Cadogan, p. 293: entry for 1 June 1940 ('French . . . evidently worse than useless! Dreadful! I should like to be quit of them.')

32. Campbell to Cadogan: FO 371/24383–C7074/5/18.

33. CAB 80/11–COS (40) 391 (26.5.40); Hankey to Halifax, 27 May 1940: FO 371/24383–C7074/5/18.

34. CAB 65/13–WM (40) 140 [CA] (26.5.40); Cadogan, p. 290.

35. CAB 99/3–SWC (40) 13 (31.5.40); ibid., –SWC (40) 14 (11.6.40); CAB 65/7–WM (40) 163 (12.6.40); Reynaud, pp. 740–57; Churchill, *Finest Hour*, pp. 135–41; Weygand, pp. 200–6; Spears, *Assignment to Catastrophe*, vol. II, *The Fall of France* (1954) pp. 138–71.

36. Reynaud, pp. 759–62; Weygand, pp. 209–14; Baudouin, pp. 98–101; C. Chautemps, *Cahiers secrets de l'armistice, 1939–1940* (1963) pp. 118–30.

37. Sources for this crucial meeting: FO 371/24310–C7263/65/17; FO 371/36094–Z8495/8008/17; PREM 4/22/2; CAB 65/7–WM (40) 165 (13.6.40); Churchill, *Finest Hour*, pp. 158–62; Cadogan, p. 298; Spears, *Fall of France*, pp. 199–220. The British ambassador's version is in Sir Ronald Campbell's final despatch in CAB 67/9 – hereafter cited as Campbell. An accurate and dispassionate summary of the British records is in E. L. Woodward, *British Foreign Policy in the Second World War* – official history, vol. I (1970) pp. 256–9. On the French side, see Reynaud, pp. 769–74; Baudouin, pp. 101–6; C. de Gaulle, *Mémoires de Guerre*, vol. I, *L'Appel, 1940–1942* (1954) p. 57.

38. Baudouin, p. 102.

39. Ibid., p. 109.

40. Churchill, *Finest Hour*, p. 162; Weygand, p. 215; Shirer, p. 769.

41. Campbell to Foreign Office, No. 406 DIPP, 15 June 1940, FO 371/24310–C7263/65/17.

42. Weygand, pp. 223–4, 227–8; see also P. C. F. Bankwitz, *Maxime Weygand and Civil–Military Relations in Modern France* (1967).

43. For this meeting, see Chautemps, pp. 154–64; Reynaud, pp. 803–13; Baudouin, pp. 112–14; Y. Bouthillier, *Le Drame de Vichy*, vol. 1, *Face à l'ennemi, face à l'allié* (1950) pp. 77–8; A. Lebrun, *Témoignage* (1945) p. 81; L. Marin, 'Contribution à l'étude des prodromes de l'armistice', *Rev. d'hist. de la deuxième guerre mondiale*, III (1951). See also the testimony of Reynaud (pp. 61–5), Lebrun (p. 155) and Blum (pp. 235–6) in *Le Procès du Maréchal Pétain* (1945), and Spears, *Fall of France*, pp. 270–3, quoting Mandel.

44. See Campbell, Annexe I, where the text is given in full; FO 371/24310–C7263/65/17; Woodward, I, pp. 272–3; Harvey, p. 390.

45. All of which are in FO 371/24310–C7263/65/17. See also Woodward, I, pp. 272–4.

46. CAB 65/13–WM (40) 168 [CA] (16.6.40).

47. FO 371/24310–C7263/65/17; PREM 3/174/4, at p. 33; Woodward, I, p. 275.

48. FO 371/24310–C7263/65/17.

49. Spears, *Fall of France*, p. 282.

50. Ibid., pp. 282–6; Reynaud, pp. 823–6; FO 371/24310–C7263/65/17.

51. Telegrams 371 and 374; FO 371/24310–C7263/65/17 and FO 371/24311–C7294/65/17.

52. CAB 65/7–WM (40) 169 (16.6.40); Woodward, I, pp. 277–80.

53. A full text of the proposal is in FO 371/24311–C7294/65/17; PREM 3/176; Campbell, Annexe II; Woodward, I, p. 280; Churchill, *Finest Hour*, pp. 183–4. See also M. Beloff, 'The Anglo-French Union Project of June 1940', in *Mélanges Pierre Renouvin* (1966) pp. 199–219; L. Noël, 'Le Projet d'union Franco-Britannique de juin 1940', *Rev. d'hist. de la deuxième guerre mondiale*, XXI (Jan 1956) 22–37; and Bell, pp. 72–6.

54. H. Dalton, unpublished diary: entry of 28 June, 1940, quoting Spears's account.

55. Campbell, p. 167; Spears, *Fall of France*, p. 293; Reynaud, pp. 825–7; *Événements . . . Témoignages*, IX, p. 2851; Bell, pp. 75–6.

56. Spears, *Fall of France*, p. 294; FO 371/24311–C7293/65/17. Churchill's rueful comment on this episode is in *Finest Hour*, p. 185.

57. Reynaud, pp. 830–8. But see Chautemps, pp. 118–30 and Marin, pp. 14–21.

58. Baudouin, p. 117. Like so much else in Baudouin's 'diary', this has the flavour of a later addition. It remains a sound judgement, however.

59. Ibid., p. 118; another post-war addition.

60. *DGFP*, ser. D, vol. IX (1957) p. 590; and L. Noël, *Le Diktat de Réthondes et l'armistice Franco-Italien de juin 1940* (1954) p. 26.

61. Campbell, p. 168. Shortly before this meeting, Darlan had assured Campbell that 'as long as I can issue orders to it, you have nothing to fear': FO 371/24310–C7294/65/17.

62. Campbell, p. 168; Spears, *Fall of France*, p. 318.

63. See telegrams 379 and 380 DIPP, sent at 11 a.m. and 1 p.m. respectively, in FO 371/24311–C7294/65/17 and –C7301/65/17.

64. F. Charles-Roux, *Cinq mois tragiques aux affaires étrangères, 21 mai – 1 novembre 1940* (1949) p. 57. He gave them to Baudouin that afternoon. See Baudouin, pp. 122–3; and *Événements . . . Témoignages*, VII, pp. 2077–80. See also Campbell to Foreign Office No. 444 DIPP, sent at 11.45 p.m. on 17 June; FO 371/24311–C7301/65/17.

65. Baudouin, pp. 122–4.

66. Charles-Roux, p. 59; Campbell, p. 169.

67. See, for example, the conflicting testimonies of Weygand and Baudouin in *Événements . . . Témoignages*, VI, p. 1566 and VII, p. 2081.

68. Campbell thought him 'voluble, specious and unreliable'. Campbell, p. 175. Harvey (p. 377) described him as 'the real villain of the piece'.

69. PREM 3/468, pp. 135–8; Cadogan's minute of 19 June 1940 in FO 371/24311–C7352/65/17.

70. FO 371/24311–C7301/65/17; Woodward, I, p. 296.

71. Alexander's report is in PREM 3/186A/7, pp. 515–18.

72. PREM 3/174/4, pp. 5–9. C. F. Adam, *Life of Lord Lloyd* (1948) pp. 299–300; Harvey, p. 396.

73. Adam, p. 299.

74. A. Darlan, *L'Amiral Darlan parle* . . . (1952) p. 68.

75. Baudouin, p. 129; Chautemps, pp. 193–4; FO 371/24311–C7352/65/17.

76. G. Warner, *Pierre Laval and the Eclipse of France* (1968) p. 179.

77. *DGFP*, ser. D, vol. IX, pp. 622, 629.

78. Shirer, pp. 839–40; Warner, *Pierre Laval*, pp. 180–1.

2 ARMISTICE

1. M. Muggeridge (ed.), *The Ciano Diaries 1939–1940* (1947) p. 67 – hereafter cited as Ciano.

2. See the 'History of the Armistice and Armistice Commission' written by Professor Stewart of the Foreign Relations Press Service in 1942 in FO 371/32173–Z9255/9235/17.

3. Notably Weygand, pp. 273–87.

4. Churchill, *Finest Hour*, p. 196, and his telegram to Sir Samuel Hoare, ambassador in Madrid, on 19 October 1940, in FO 371/24334–C11099/7327/17. See also A. Truchet, *L'Armistice de 1940 et l'Afrique du nord* (1955).

5. *DGFP*, ser. D, vol. IX, pp. 608–11.

6. CAB 66/9–WP (40) 224 (27.6.40).

7. Campbell, p. 172.

8. Baudouin, pp. 133–4.

9. Campbell, p. 172.

10. *DGFP*, ser. D, vol. IX, p. 665.

11. CAB 66/13–WP (40) 421 (15.10.40).

12. Ibid., –WP (40) 448 (14.11.40).

13. Baudouin, p. 207.

14. De Gaulle, *L'Appel*, p. 303.

15. Woodward, I, pp. 356, 401.

16. See, for example, *DFCAA*, vol. I, pp. 389–90 and Baudouin, p. 248.

17. *DFCAA*, vol. I, pp. 252–62; *DGFP*, ser. D, vol. X, p. 300.

18. Weygand, pp. 273–94.

19. FO 371/28243–Z204/22/17.

20. Warner, *Pierre Laval*, pp. 215–18; A. Hytier, *Two Years of French Foreign Policy: Vichy 1940–1942* (1958) pp. 108–15.

21. CAB 65/104–WM (40) 290 (18.11.40). See also Halifax's minute of 6 December 1940 in FO 371/24304–C13606/9/17, and Laval's remark in R. Murphy, *Diplomat among Warriors* (1964) p. 83.

22. Campbell to Foreign Office, No. 432 DIPP, 16.6.40, FO 371/24311–C7294/65/17.

23. Chautemps, p. 210.

24. Hytier, pp. 127–8.

25. See Hitler's directive of August 1940, in *DGFP*, ser. D, vol. X, p. 468.

26. Ibid., pp. 438–9.

27. Baudouin, p. 216.

28. Weygand, p. 266.

29. Warner, *Pierre Laval*, p. 210; S. Osgood, *French Royalism under the Third and Fourth Republics* (1960) p. v. A useful summary of French attitudes in June 1940 is given in R. Paxton, *Vichy France: Old Guard and New Order, 1940–1944* (1972) pp. 3–50.

30. See the despatch written by William C. Bullitt, the American ambassador, in O. Bullitt (ed.), *For the President: Personal and Secret* (1972).

3   PICKING UP THE PIECES: BRITAIN'S RESPONSE TO THE ARMISTICE

1. Bryant, p. 160.
2. Viscount Halifax, *Fullness of Days* (1957) p. 163. See also Halifax's diary entry for 8 February 1941.
3. Dalton, diary for 22 February 1941, reporting Desmond Morton.
4. Cadogan, p. 290; the Earl of Birkenhead, *Life of Lord Halifax* (1965) p. 459.
5. Cadogan, pp. 293, 304.
6. CAB 65/13–WM (40) 140 [CA] (26.5.40).
7. Cadogan, diary for 2 June 1940, p. 293, misquoting Shakespeare; J. Wheeler-Bennett, *Life of King George VI* (1958) p. 460.
8. Viscount Cunningham of Hyndhope, *A Sailor's Odyssey* (1951) p. 238; see also Walter Lowan's letter to Cunningham on 4 July 1940, in the Cunningham Papers, 525.62/764A, and A. Eden, *The Reckoning* (1965) p. 113.
9. Bell, p. 124. An excellent survey of public opinion can be found in ibid., pp. 109–32.
10. Dalton, diary for 14 June 1940; Churchill, *Finest Hour*, p. 138.
11. Bryant, p. 181; Dalton, diary for 28 June 1940.
12. CAB 69/1–DO (40) 10 (25.6.40).
13. Dalton, diary for 25 June 1940; Hankey to Halifax, 22 June 1940, in FO 800/312, and 11 July 1940, in PREM 3/186A/7, p. 523.
14. Dalton, diary for 17 June 1940.
15. FO 371/24348–C7375/7362/17.
16. CAB 65/7–WM (40) 179 (24.6.40).
17. PREM 3/174/2.
18. CAB 65/7–WM (40) 178 (24.6.40).
19. CAB 65/7–WM (40) 181 (25.6.40); CAB 66/9–WP (40) 221 (24.6.40).
20. CAB 66/11–WP (40) 362 (4.9.40).
21. The definitive study of Operation C A T A P U L T is now A. Marder, *From the Dardanelles to Oran* (1974) pp. 179–288. See also Bell, pp. 137–64; W. Tute, *The Deadly Stroke* (1973).
22. PREM 3/188/2, pp. 3–8.
23. Ibid.
24. Hansard, 5th ser., CCCLXII, cols 304–5.
25. *Événements . . . Rapport*, II, pp. 442–66; I. Playfair, *The Mediterranean and the Middle East* – official history (1954) vol. I, p. 462.
26. Marder, *Oran*, pp. 226–7.
27. CAB 65/14–WM (40) 190 [CA] (1.7.40).
28. Butler, p. 221; Playfair, pp. 131, 138–9.
29. Campbell, p. 175; CAB 66/9–WP (40) 226 (28.6.40).
30. CAB 65/13–WM (40) 180 [CA] (24.6.40); Marder, *Oran*, pp. 203–4.
31. CAB 80/14–COS (40) 505 (JP) (29.6.40). The Naval Staff advised against action on the 24th; Butler, p. 222.
32. CAB 65/13–WM (40) 184 [CA] (30.6.40).
33. CAB 80/14–COS (40) 510 (30.6.40); Butler, p. 222; Marder, *Oran*, pp. 224–6.
34. S. Roskill, *The War at Sea 1939–1945* – official history (1954) vol. I, pp. 240–1.

35. The story of Admiral Godfroy's 'Force X' is unfortunately too complex to examine here. British sources are scattered through PREM 3/179/3–7, and there are brief accounts in Woodward, vol. II, pp. 308–19, and S. Roskill, *Churchill and the Admirals* (1977) pp. 150–7. See also Vice–Amiral Godfroy, *L'Aventure de la force X à Alexandrie 1940–1943* (1953) and Cunningham, pp. 242–55.

36. The Cabinet's instructions to Somerville are in CAB 65/8, PREM 3/179/1, and ADM 1/10321. See also Playfair, pp. 134–5.

37. Playfair, p. 132; Roskill, *War at Sea*, p. 243.

38. *Événements* . . . *Témoignages*, VI, pp. 1904, 1909 (testimony of Gensoul).

39. Weygand, p. 335; *Événements* . . . *Témoignages*, VIII, p. 2535 (testimony of Bouthillier); ibid., VI, p. 1899 (testimony of Gensoul).

40. This, with all the other messages exchanged by Force H and the Admiralty on 3 July, is in PREM 3/179/1.

41. *The Times*, 5 July 1940; but see Churchill, *Finest Hour*, p. 211.

42. Ciano, p. 274.

43. C. Hull, *The Memoirs of Cordell Hull* (1948) vol. I, p. 798. See also Roosevelt's remark to the French ambassador, Saint-Quentin, quoted by Charles-Roux,*Cinq Mois*, p. 130, and the *New York Times* of 5 July 1940, quoted by Hytier, p. 65.

44. CAB 80/14–COS (40) 529 (JP).

45. Bullitt, pp. 481–7.

46. Baudouin, p. 161.

47. Cadogan, p. 311; Hansard, 5th ser., CCCLXII, col. 1049.

48. Marder, *Oran*, pp. 275–88; Playfair, pp. 137–8.

49. CAB 66/8–WP (40) 207 (15.6.40); Butler, p. 229.

50. FO 371/24311–C7278/65/17.

51. Ibid., –C7343/7327/17; CAB 65/7–WM (40) 182 (25.6.40); PREM 3/178/5, *passim*.

52. CAB 65/7–WM (40) 180 (24.6.40).

53. See Cooper's report to the Cabinet on 28 June in CAB 66/9–WP (40) 226 and CAB 65/7–WM (40) 185 (28.6.40), and D. Cooper, *Old Men Forget* (1953) pp. 282–4.

54. CAB 66/9–WP (40) 226.

55. CAB 80/14–COS (40) 508 (Draft) (1.7.40).

56. K. Sainsbury, 'The Second Wartime Alliance', in Waites, p. 236.

57. Dalton, diary for 24 June 1940.

58. CAB 65/7–WM (40) 185 (28.6.40); Bell, p. 179.

59. CAB 65/7–WM (40) 171 (18.6.40). The full text of the appeal is in de Gaulle, *L'Appel*, pp. 267–8, and in English in Sir E. Spears, *Two Men Who Saved France: Pétain and de Gaulle* (1966) pp. 132–4.

60. Cadogan, diary for 19 June 1940, p. 304. The draft of de Gaulle's proposed statement is in FO 371/24349–C7389/7389/17.

61. Minute by Halifax, FO 371/24349–C7389/7389/17.

62. CAB 65/7–WM (40) 176 (22.6.40).

63. FO 371/24349–C7389/7389/17; CAB 65/7–WM (40) 178 (24.6.40).

64. Full text in PREM 3/174/2.

65. See, for example, Churchill's speech to the House of Commons on 25 June 1940: Hansard, 5th ser., CCCLXII, cols 301–5.

66. CAB 65/7–WM (40) 186 (28.6.40); PREM 3/186A/7, p. 538.

4 VICHY FRANCE, DE GAULLE FRANCE, WEYGAND FRANCE

1. FO 371/28351–Z10733/92/17; minute by Mack, 23 November 1941.

2. Labour members of the Government proposed the establishment of a left-wing

alternative to Vichy under Léon Blum, but this idea had little hope of success and did not get far. See Dalton, diary for 23 July 1940, and Attlee's comments in CAB 65/14–WM (40) 212 [CA] (25.7.40).

3.   Johnson, p. 157.

4.   CAB 65/15–WM (40) 265 [CA] (3.10.40); Churchill's personal minute to Eden (No. M.562/1) of 19 May 1941.

5.   The phrase was Sir Ronald Campbell's: CAB 66/13–WP (40) 437 (12.11.40).

6.   FO 371/24304–C13606/9/17, minute by Halifax, 6 December 1940; FO 371/28312–Z447/54/17, minute by Eden, 26 January 1941.

7.   CAB 66/15–WP (41) 48 (3.3.41); see also the Foreign Office's telegram to Halifax of 11 January 1941, in FO 371/28372–Z296/132/17; the memorandum explaining British policy to the State Department dated 24 January 1941, in FO 371/28375–Z1098/132/17; and Mack's minute of 27 February 1941, in FO 371/28376–Z1373/132/17.

8.   FO 371/28234–Z16/16/17.

9.   Many graphic accounts exist of conditions in Vichy. See, for example, Charles-Roux, pp. 113–15; H. du Moulin de Labarthète, Le Temps des Illusions (1946) p. 15, and W. Leahy, I Was There (1950), pp. 24–5.

10.   Événements . . . Témoignages, VIII, p. 2504 (testimony of Bouthillier).

11.   Ibid., VII, p. 2127 (testimony of Baudouin). See also Vice-Amiral Fernet, Aux Côtés du Maréchal Pétain (1953), J. Tournoux, Pétain and de Gaulle, trans O. Coburn (1966), p. 30, and Événements . . . Témoignages, VI, p. 1616 (testimony of Weygand).

12.   As one associate cynically remarked, 'Au bout de vingt minutes, on "l'avait" toujours.' Événements . . . Témoignages, V, p. 1415 (testimony of Jacques Bardoux).

13.   Leahy, p. 57.

14.   The phrase is from S. Huddleston, Pétain–Patriot or Traitor? (1951) p. 12.

15.   This revealing expression was Pétain's own. See the facsimile of his letter to Weygand on 9 November 1940 in Weygand, Appendix x.

16.   Sent variously through his stepson in Madrid (FO 371/24302–C9873/9/17), Salazar (ibid., C9857/9/17), General Smuts, the State Department and the Turkish government (ibid., C10647/9/17), and even the American Legation in Sofia (FO 371/24303–C11135/9/17).

17.   FO 371/24303–C11135/9/17, minute by Hankey, 22 October 1940.

18.   FO 371/24302–C9873/9/17; ibid., –C9679/9/17, minute by Cadogan, 8 October 1940.

19.   FO 371/24301–C7652/9/17.

20.   Ibid., –C7700/9/17; CAB 65/8–WM (40) 196 (7.7.40). Halifax told the House of Lords on 24 July, with justification, that every effort had been made to prevent the severance of relations: FO 371/24301–C8234/9/17.

21.   FO 371/24301–C7700/9/17; Hytier, p. 76.

22.   CAB 65/8–WM (40) 200 (11.7.40); FO 371/24301–C7700/9/17E.

23.   FO 371/24302–C10510/9/17.

24.   FO 371/24301–C7652/9/17.

25.   Ibid.

26.   CAB 66/10–WM (40) 288 (27.7.40); CAB 65/8–WM (40) 214 (29.7.40).

27.   FO 371/24301–C7829/9/17.

28.   FO 371/24302–C8834/9/17; Mack's comment on Baudouin's speech on 15 August in FO 371/24296–C8734/9/17; the note on Halifax's meeting on 26 August with the Canadian High Commissioner in FO 800/312, p. 129.

29.   Baudouin, pp. 209–25.

30.   FO 371/24302–C9390/9/17. Hoare's tribute to de la Baume can be found in Viscount Templewood, Ambassador on Special Mission (1946) pp. 83, 87, 90. See aslo Charles-Roux, p. 354.

31.   FO 371/24302–C9390/9/17.

32. The definitive study of MENACE is now A. Marder, *Operation Menace* (1976). See also J. Williams, *The Guns of Dakar* (1976). Churchill's account is in *Finest Hour*, pp. 419–37, that of Spears in *Two Men*. See also de Gaulle, *L'Appel*, pp. 96–108, and Bell, pp. 201–12. Official studies made at the time can be found in PREM 3/276.

33. CAB 80/16–COS (40) 601 (JP) (4.8.40).

34. PREM 3/276, pp. 266–7; Churchill, *Finest Hour*, pp. 419–20; Marder, *Menace*, pp. 15–16.

35. Cadogan, p. 329; Butler, pp. 313–14; Marder, *Menace*, pp. 16–17. Cabinet approval was given on the 5th: CAB 65/14–WM (40) 219.

36. PREM 3/276, pp. 264–5: Minute by COS to Churchill, 5 August 1940.

37. Ibid., p. 247: COS (40) 252, Annexe II (7.8.40).

38. Churchill, *Finest Hour*, p. 421.

39. Ibid., pp. 421–2; PREM 3/276, pp. 242–5; Marder, *Menace*, pp. 18–22. Sir John Slessor later wrote that Churchill had exerted severe, even improper pressure upon the reluctant Joint Planners, 'even to the extent of coming in to us in Committee and bullying us'. Marder, *Menace*, p. 25.

40. CAB 65/14–WM (40) 225 [CA].

41. Churchill, *Finest Hour*, p. 422.

42. CAB 80/16–COS (40) 643 (19.8.40); PREM 3/276, p. 230; Marder, *Menace*, pp. 33–7.

43. CAB 80/17–COS (40) 697 (2.9.40), minute by Morton dated 30 August.

44. PREM 3/276, pp. 195–6, 160–1.

45. Ibid., pp. 26–7; Marder, *Menace*, p. 90; Churchill, *Finest Hour*, pp. 429–30. 'I warned against the possible result of another Oran. But everyone in favour.' Cadogan, diary for 17 September 1940, p. 327.

46. Accounts can be found in Marder, *Menace*, pp. 104–57, Williams, pp. 105–63, and PREM 3/276.

47. PREM 3/276, p. 179.

48. See, for example, CAB 80/19–COS (40) 792 (30.9.40), PREM 3/276, p. 214, and Marder, *Menace*, pp. 46–50.

49. Marder, *Menace*, p. 26.

50. CAB 65/15–WM (40) 258 [CA] (25.9.40).

51. Cadogan, diary for 31 October 1940, p. 333.

52. CAB 66/11–WP (40) 362 (4.9.40).

53. CAB 66/12–WP (40) 396 (30.9.40). These arguments were repeated in ibid., –WP (40) 418 (13.10.40). See also Mack's summary of the Admiralty view in FO 371/24302–C10490/9/17.

54. CAB 65/9–WM (40) 260 (27.9.40); CAB 65/15–WM (40) 263 [CA] (1.10.40); CAB 66/12–WP (40) 392 (27.9.40).

55. Bell, pp. 225–7.

56. CAB 80/19–COS (40) 788 (29.9.40).

57. CAB 66/13–WP (40) 421 (15.10.40). See also Churchill's personal minute D105 of 31 October 1940, in PREM 3/186A/7, p. 497, and his minute to the First Lord of the Admiralty on the same day in PREM 3/186A/1.

58. CAB 65/17–WM (41) 1 (1.1.41).

59. CAB 66/15–WP (41) 48 (3.3.41); Paxton, *Vichy France* p. 89; FO 371/28346–Z178/92/17.

60. FO 371/28342–Z966/87/17, Minute by Strang, 15 February 1941. See also ibid., Z87/87/17, CAB 65/17–WM (41) 11 (29.1.41), and the minutes by Barclay and Mack of 9 and 10 January 1941, in FO 371/28346–Z178/92/17.

61. The Rougier case is stated in L. Rougier, *Les Accords Pétain–Churchill: histoire d'une mission secrète* (1945), *Les Accords secrets Franco-Britanniques de l'automne 1940: histoire et imposture* (1954) and an article in *Le Figaro* of 13 February 1953. A memorandum on the

mission which Rougier drew up and sent to Roosevelt in December 1940 is to be found in M. Freedman (ed.), *Roosevelt and Frankfurter: Their Correspondence 1928–1945* (1967) pp. 568–73. (Freedman does not reveal the author's name but it is beyond question Rougier.) The British version of the mission was published as a *Despatch to His Majesty's Ambassador in Paris Regarding Relations between His Majesty's Government in the United Kingdom and the Vichy Government in the Autumn of 1940* (Cmd. 6662, 1945). See also General G. Schmitt, *Les Accords secrets Franco-Britanniques de novembre–décembre 1940: histoire ou mystification* (1957). The story can be followed in the British records in FO 371/24314/24361/36042/49139/ 49141/49142/49145 and in PREM 3/390. A detailed account based on these records is given in R. Thomas, 'The Vichy Dilemma in British Foreign Policy' – unpublished D. Phil. thesis (1976).

62. FO 371/24303–C11429/12183/9/17; FO 371/24361–C13251/11442/17; Cadogan, pp. 334, 337.

63. FO 800/312, p. 152; Cadogan, p. 337.

64. FO 371/24361–C13251/11442/17, minute by Strang, 12 December 1940.

65. FO 371/28234–Z727/16/17, Annexe 1. The source of this information was not, however, reliable.

66. The message is in CAB 65/9–WM (40) 277 and in FO 371/28346–Z446/92/17. See also Cadogan, pp. 332–3. Pétain's reply is in FO 371/24303–C11949/9/17. Roosevelt's much harsher message and Pétain's much milder reply to it can be found in *FRUS*, vol. II (1940) pp. 475, 591–2.

67. Cadogan, p. 342.

68. CAB 66/14–WP (40) 486 (19.12.40); ibid., –WP (40) 488 (22.12.40).

69. FO 371/24306–C11499/45/17.

70. CAB 65/14–WM (40) 281 [CA] (1.11.40).

71. CAB 65/16–WM (40) 285 [CA] (8.11.40).

72. See Dalton's letter to Alexander on 10 November 1940, in PREM 4/95, p. 8; CAB 65/10–WM (40) 290 (18.11.40); Churchill, *Finest Hour*, pp. 455–6.

73. CAB 66/13–WP (40) 437 (12.11.40); see also ibid., –WP (40) 442 (13.11.40).

74. Ibid., WP (40) 448 (14.11.40); Churchill, *Finest Hour*, pp. 466–7.

75. See the minutes by Cadogan and Churchill on 12 and 15 December 1940, in FO 800/312, pp. 156–60, the editor's note in Cadogan, pp. 339–40, and Bell, p. 257.

76. FO 800/399–Fr/41/1, Cadogan's minute of 21 January 1941 and Churchill's note of agreement.

77. Most of the material on Dupuy's first visit, including his reports to Mackenzie King and Eden on his return, can be found in FO 371/28234/28235/24296. On the French side, we have the evidence of Chevalier at the Pétain trial and his later account, 'Un Témoignage direct sur deux points d'histoire', *Écrits de Paris* (July 1953) pp. 83–7. Using Chevalier's papers, Prince X. de Bourbon produced three accounts: *Les Accords Franco-Anglais de décembre 1940* (1949), 'Révélations sur les accords secrets Halifax–Chevalier de décembre 1940', *Le Figaro* (7 April 1953), and 'Les Accords Franco-Britanniques de 1940', *Rev. des Deux Mondes* (1 July 1954). Essential reading is again Schmitt, pp. 98–109.

78. CAB 65/10–WM (40) 287 (12.11.40); ibid., –WM (40) 282 (4.11.40); FO 371/ 49144–Z10741/255/17.

79. FO 371/49144–Z10741/255/17, Dupuy to Simpson.

80. FO 371/28234–Z727/16/17, Dupuy's report to King.

81. FO 371/49144–Z10741/255/17; Bourbon, *Accords Franco-Anglais*, p. 9.

82. Schmitt, p. 101.

83. Ibid., pp. 103–5.

84. FO 371/28234–Z727/16/17.

85. Ibid.

86. FO 371/28234–Z21/16/17.

87. Paxton, *Vichy France*, p. 85.

88. Schmitt, p. 103.

89. Ibid.; *Procès Pétain*, testimony of Chevalier.

90. CAB 66/14–WP (40) 486 (19.12.40).

91. FO 371/28234–Z16/16/17.

92. Ibid., –Z21/16/17.

93. CAB 79/8–COS (40) 437 (24.12.40); FO 371/28234–Z21/16/17.

94. FO 371/28234–Z21/16/17; FO 371/49144–Z10741/255/17; *FRUS*, vol. II (1940) p. 434.

95. PREM 3/186A/5, p. 157.

96. CAB 65/10–WM (40) 310 (27.12.40).

97. FO 371/28346–Z359/92/17, Eden's minute of 8 January 1941.

98. Cadogan, p. 351.

99. On these leaks, see PREM 3/126/1; PREM 3/126/2; FO 371/28234–Z16/16/17; FO 371/28235–Z8908/9057/10169/16/17.

100. FO 371/28234–Z21/16/17, Eden's minute to Churchill of 6 January 1941.

101. PREM 3/186B, p. 49, Eden's personal minute to Churchill (No. PM/41/165), 28 November 1941.

102. FO 371/28234–Z1975/16/17. See also Cadogan's comment of 22 March 1941, in FO 371/28378–Z2094/132/17.

103. PREM 3/186A/3; CAB 65/14–WM (40) 212 [CA] (25.7.40); Churchill, *Finest Hour*, p. 450.

104. FO 371/24302–C10647/9/17.

105. CAB 65/16–WM (40) 285 [CA] (8.11.40).

106 Spears, *Fall of France*, p. 272, quoting Mandel.

107. It was the aide-mémoire containing this statement, added by Strang in longhand, which Rougier later tried to pass off as the first page of a secret treaty. Rougier took the carbon copy to Algiers and, after tampering with it, produced a photostat copy in *Mission secrète*. A photocopy of the Foreign Office original (FO 371/24301–C11442/11442/17) is reproduced in Thomas, Appendix 1.

108. All these messages are reproduced in Weygand, pp. 472–3.

109. FO 371/28243–Z86/22/17; ibid., –Z229/22/17.

110. Ibid., –Z780/22/17; FO 371/28372–Z380/132/17.

111. W. S. Churchill, *The Second World War*, vol. III, *The Grand Alliance* (1950) pp. 7–10.

112. PREM 3/186A/5, p. 110; Weygand, p. 477 and Appendix XIII.

113. Rougier, *Mission secrète*, p. 111; Weygand, p. 470.

114. FO 371/28372–Z528/132/17, Hollis to Strang, 30 January 1941.

115. See JP (41) 115, an Annexe to CAB 79/9–COS (41) 54 (14.2.41).

116. Churchill's personal minute (No. M149/1) of 12 February 1941, in PREM 3/186A/5, p. 96, and his note to the COS in ibid., p. 95B.

117. FO 371/28375–Z1245/132/17, Morton to Mack, 17 February 1941.

118. FO 371/24346–C13072/7328/17; FO 371/24335–C12865/7328/17.

119. See, for example, Halifax's minute of 25 July 1940, in PREM 3/186A/3, pp. 205–6.

120. General G. Catroux, *Dans la bataille de la Méditerranée* (1949) pp. 18–22. PREM 3/85B, on Catroux, remains closed. See also Bell, pp. 195–6.

121. FO 371/28346–Z446/92/17, Halifax to Hoare, No. 1051, 12 November 1940; see also the minutes by Strang on the same day in FO 371/24344–C12109/7328/17, and by Barclay and Mack on 17 and 20 December in FO 371/24346–C13242/7328/17.

122. Churchill's personal minute (No. M279) of 8 November 1940, in PREM 3/178/5, pp. 334–5, and Morton's minute to Spears in FO 371/28373–Z826/132/17.

123. Churchill's minute of 16 February 1941, in FO 371/28347–Z1252/92/17.

5   BRITAIN AND AMERICA'S 'VICHY GAMBLE'

1. CAB 66/14–WP (41) 25 (6.2.41).
2. E. L. Woodward, *British Foreign Policy in the Second World War* – official history, vol.
II (1971) p. 61.
3. CAB 66/15–WP (41) 48 (3.3.41).
4. FO 371/28348–Z3348/92/17, Cadogan's minute of 22 April 1941.
5. Hytier, p. 268.
6. Colonel G. Groussard, *Service secret 1940–1945* (1954) pp. 146–9. For Groussard's
contacts with the Free French, see ibid., pp. 200–10, and Colonel Passy, *Souvenirs*, vol. II,
Deuxième Bureau à Londres (1947) pp. 192–9. See also Schmitt, pp. 129–32.
7. FO 371/28351–Z6626/35/17, Morton's letter to Speaight of 14 August 1941.
8. Groussard, pp. 165–76. I have found no mention of the alleged meeting with
Churchill in the British records.
9. PREM 3/186A/7, pp. 304–5, Eden's personal minute to Churchill (No. PM/41/
54), 26 June 1941; CAB 79/12–COS (41) 241 (9.7.41).
10. PREM 3/186A/7, p. 305; Groussard, p. 213.
11. Groussard, pp. 223–32, 484.
12. See, for example, Churchill's telegrams of 5 May, 14 May and 11 December 1941,
in PREM 3/469, pp. 345–9, 332–3, 17. Also Churchill, *Finest Hour*, p. 450.
13. Langer's suggestion that American recognition traditionally carried no moral
overtones need not be taken too seriously: W. L. Langer, *Our Vichy Gamble* (1965, first
publ. 1947) p. 76.
14. Hull, vol. I, p. 804.
15. FO 371/28376–Z1373/132/17, minute by Mack of 27 February 1941.
16. Hull, vol. I, p. 804. Hull was so acutely sensitive to the criticism to which he was
subjected over American policy towards Vichy that he commissioned William L. Langer
to write a lengthy justification (see above, note 13). This should be read as an officially
inspired *apologia* rather than as a work of historical scholarship.
17. *FRUS*, vol. II (1940) pp. 427–8.
18. Langer, *passim*, and Hull, vols I and II, *passim*.
19. De Gaulle, *L'Appel*, p. 181.
20. Murphy, p. 103.
21. Leahy, p. 57. He went so far as to suggest to Hull in March 1941 that if de Gaulle
could be eliminated, Pétain would swing more towards the British camp: *FRUS*, vol. II
(1941) pp. 129–31.
22. CAB 65/7–WM (40) 181 (25.6.40); CAB 65/8–WM (40) 202 (13.7.40); Cadogan,
p. 313.
23. CAB 65/8–WM (40) 223 (9.8.40).
24. See Alexander's letter to Dalton on 3 January 1941, quoted by Bell, pp. 265–6.
25. Dalton, diary for 13 March 1941; Cadogan, pp. 294, 315, 383–4.
26. CAB 66/15–WP (41) 48 (3.3.41).
27. CAB 67/8–WP (G) (40) 208 (7.8.40); CAB 65/8–WM (40) 223 (9.8.40).
28. See Halifax's letter to Churchill of 28 August 1940, in PREM 4/21/1, p. 115, and
Cadogan, p. 326.
29. CAB 66/12–WP (40) 392 (27.9.40); FO 371/24303–C12183/9/17.
30. Bell, p. 260; Templewood, p. 87; see also Cadogan's and Strang's minutes of 3
January 1941, in FO 371/28372–Z296/132/17.
31. CAB 65/9–WM (40) 273 (18.10.40). To the Admiralty's protest that it had no
ships, Dalton was tempted to reply 'if no ships, then why the Admirals?'; Dalton, diary for
18 October 1940.
32. CAB 65/9–WM (40) 267 (7.10.40).
33. See Dalton's letter to Alexander on 10 November 1940 in PREM 4/95/8 and

W. N. Medlicott, *The Economic Blockade* – official history, vol. 1 (1959) p. 559.
34. CAB 66/13–WP (40) 446, enclosing CFR (40) 83 (9.11.40).
35. CAB 65/10–WM (40) 290 (18.11.40).
36. FO 371/24304–C13094/9/17, Stirling to Mack, 4 December 1940.
37. Medlicott, vol. 1, pp. 549–57.
38. CAB 65/10–WP (40) 471 and WM (40) 301 (6.12.40). Public opinion was regularly sampled by interception of mail and was found to be strongly pro-blockade.
39. PREM 3/74/6, pp. 111–13.
40. *FRUS*, vol. 11 (1941) pp. 93–6; Hull, vol. 11, p. 949.
41. See Churchill's telegram to Roosevelt in PREM 3/74/6, pp. 104–5; *FRUS*, vol. 11 (1941), pp. 89–90; Dalton, diary for 2 January 1941.
42. Hull, vol. 1, p. 853.
43. CAB 80/21–COS (40) 876 (28.10.40).
44. Eccles's letter to Makins, 15 October 1940, in FO 371/24302–C11429/9/17. He made the same point in a memorandum to the State Department on 20 April, 1941: *FRUS*, vol. 11 (1941) pp. 279–80. See also Murphy, p. 117.
45. CAB 80/18–COS (40) 744 and COS (40) 704 (JP) (12.9.40).
46. Medlicott, vol. 1, pp. 545, 567.
47. FO 371/28372–Z296/132/17; *FRUS*, vol. 11 (1941) pp. 245–7.
48. *FRUS*, vol. 11 (1941) pp. 271–4; FO 371/28314–Z2158/54/17.
49. Weygand, pp. 483–4.
50. *FRUS*, vol. 11 (1941) pp. 211–12; Murphy, p. 100.
51. Medlicott, vol. 1, pp. 568–9; FO 371/28372–Z398/132/17.
52. Foreign Office to Washington (No. 654), 3 February 1941, FO 371/28372–Z493/132/17.
53. *FRUS*, vol. 11 (1941) pp. 255–61; Hull, vol. 11, pp. 950–1; FO 371/28373–Z763/132/17.
54. Leahy, p. 30.
55. CAB 65/17–WM (41) 4 (9.1.41); Medlicott, vol. 1, pp. 561–2; CAB 66/15–WP (41) 67 (26.3.41).
56. FO 371/28312–Z447/54/17; Medlicott, vol. 1, p. 564.
57. Gascoigne's letter to Makins, FO 371/28373–Z604/132/17.
58. FO 371/28372–Z493/132/17; FO 371/28475–Z1375/1374/17.
59. FO 371/28372–Z763/132/17; Hull, vol. 11, p. 951.
60. FO 371/28471–Z1189/1189/17; *FRUS*, vol. 11 (1941) pp. 229–31; Weygand, p. 486; Langer, pp. 399–400.
61. Churchill to Halifax, 9 March 1941, in PREM 4/27/9.
62. CAB 65/18–WM (41) 23 (4.3.41); Cadogan, pp. 360–1.
63. CAB 66/15–WP (41) 48 (3.3.41); PREM 3/74/6, p. 90; FO 371/28312–Z1632/54/17; Hull, vol. 11, p. 954.
64. FO 371/28318–Z1976/54/17.
65. PREM 3/74/6, p. 84; PREM 4/27/9, p. 750.
66. Dalton, diary for 11 March 1941; see also Strang's minute of 8 March 1941, in FO 371/28475–Z1649/1374/17.
67. Paxton, *Vichy France*, pp. 116.
68. See, for example, Mack's comments of 14 October 1940, in FO 371/24302–C10647/9/17.
69. CAB 65/18–WM (41) 28 (13.3.41); Cadogan, pp. 363–4. Halifax found Churchill's volte-face 'rather astonishing'. Halifax, diary for 12 March 1941.
70. FO 371/28313–Z1704/54/17; Prime Minister's personal minute (No. M288/1) of 14 March 1941, in PREM 3/76/6.
71. PREM 3/74/6, pp. 49–50; CAB 65/18–WM (41) 30 (20.3.41).
72. Hull, vol. 11, p. 954.

73. FO 371/28313–Z1932/54/17; CAB 65/18–WM (41) 30 (20.3.41).
74. FO 371/28313–Z1978/54/17.
75. Medlicott, vol. II, p. 348.
76. Ibid., vol. I, pp. 581–2.
77. FO 371/28314–Z2241/54/17; PREM 3/74/6, pp. 21–2.
78. Former Naval Person (Churchill) to Roosevelt (No. 1747) 29 March 1941, in PREM 3/74/6, p. 19.
79. CAB 65/22–WM (41) 35 [CA] (3.4.41).
80. *FRUS*, vol. II (1941) pp. 140–2; PREM 3/179/2, pp. 91–3, 59–62; Cadogan, diary for 2–6 April 1941, pp. 368–70.
81. See the views of Kenneth Downs, International News Service correspondent in Vichy, in CAB 66/15–WP (41) 76 (3.4.41).
82. FO 371/28476–Z3249/3685/17.
83. *FRUS*, vol. II (1941) p. 158.
84. FO 371/28315–Z3555/54/17; Medlicott, vol. II, pp. 349–52.
85. FO 371/28315–Z3470/54/17.
86. CAB 65/18–WM (41) 47 (5.4.41).
87. Paxton, *Vichy France*, pp. 114–15.
88. R. Melka, 'Darlan between Britain and Germany, 1940–1941', *J. of Contemp. Hist.*, VIII 2 (1973) 68–9; G. Warner, *Iraq and Syria* (1974) pp. 101–4.
89. Paxton, *Vichy France*, pp. 109–31; *DGFP*, ser. D, vol. XII, pp. 755–74, 781–2.
90. Weygand, p. 422; R. Aron, *The Vichy Regime 1940–1944*, trans. H. Hare (1958) p. 316; Melka, pp. 68–70.
91. P. Pétain, *Paroles aux Français: messages et écrits, 1939–1941* (1941) p. 117.
92. See J. Carcopino, *Souvenirs de sept ans, 1937–1944* (1953) pp. 547–9; Aron, pp. 323–34.
93. O. Abetz, *Histoire d'une politique Franco-Allemande, 1930–1950* (1953) pp. 205–6, Melka, pp. 71–2; Paxton, *Vichy France*, p. 121.
94. Leahy, p. 45.
95. CAB 65/18–WM (41) 44 (28.4.41); FO 371/28348–Z3420/92/17; Woodward, vol. II, pp. 67–8.
96. *FRUS*, vol. II (1941) pp. 167–70; Hull, vol. II, p. 958.
97. *FRUS*, vol. II (1941) pp. 170–1; Hytier, pp. 260, 275.
98. Langer, p. 160.
99. FO 371/28470–Z3999/1374/17; Leahy, p. 45.
100. *FRUS*, vol. II (1941) pp. 349–51; Hull, vol. II, p. 961; FO 371/28477–Z4596/1374/17.
101. Foreign Office to Washington (No. 2685), 19 May 1941: FO 371/28476–Z4005/1374/17.
102. FO 371/28477–Z4596/1374/17; *FRUS*, vol. II (1941) pp. 373–4.
103. Churchill's minute of 5 June 1941: FO 371/28477–Z4657/1374/17.
104. FO 371/28478–Z5115/1374/17.
105. A. L. Funk, 'Negotiating the "Deal with Darlan"', *J. of Contemp. Hist.*, VIII 2 (1973) 87.
106. Weygand, p. 448; Hytier, p. 294.
107. Hull, vol. II, p. 1039.
108. Medlicott, vol. II, p. 360.
109. CAB 66/17–WP (40) 237 (10.10 41); FO 371/28479–Z8670/1374/17.
110. FO 371/28315–Z6209/54/17.
111. CAB 66/17–WP (40) 175 (19.7.41).
112. Ibid., –WP (41) 176 (28.7.41); CAB 65/19–WM (41) 75 (28.7.41).
113. FO 371/28479–Z7007/7134/1374/17; CAB 79/13–COS (41) 288 (15.8.41), enclosing JP (41) 666.

114. FO 371/28479–Z7840/1374/17. On the *Lorraine* episode, see PREM 3/187, *passim*.
115. For the first theory, see Aron, pp. 333–6; for the second, Hytier, pp. 299–308; and for the third, Funk, 'Deal with Darlan', pp. 86–7.
116. *FRUS*, vol. II (1941) pp. 464–6; Hull, vol. II, p. 1043.
117. Leahy, p. 77.
118. Ibid., pp. 59, 468.
119. *FRUS*, vol. II (1941) pp. 464–6; PREM 3/186A/7, pp. 279–88.
120. *FRUS*, vol. II (1941) pp. 468–9.
121. Hull, vol. II, p. 1044.
122. *FRUS*, vol. II (1941) pp. 466–8; Murphy, pp. 125–6.
123. FO 371/28480–Z9892/1374/17; Paxton, *Vichy France*, pp. 127–8.
124. Hull, vol. II, p. 1044.
125. CAB 65/24–WM (41) 110 (20.11.41).
126. FO 371/28480–Z9892/1374/17.
127. PREM 3/186A/7–JIC (41) 443 (0) (21.11.41).
128. PREM 3/187, p. 71, Churchill's personal minute (No. M1074/1) of 30 November 1941. See also Churchill's comment in PREM 3/186A/7, p. 280.
129. CAB 65/20–WM (41) 122 (1.12.41).
130. FO 371/28480–Z9892/1374/17.
131. Ibid. See also the text of the extraordinary statement made by Leahy on his return to the USA in 1942, in FO 371/31982–Z4977/175/17.
132. Hull, vol. II, p. 1045.
133. Leahy, p. 61.
134. Hytier, p. 321.
135. Langer, p. 202.

6 BRITAIN AND VICHY IN 1942

1. Churchill, *Grand Alliance*, p. 603.
2. FO 371/48176–Z1036/12/17.
3. FO 371/28375–Z1180/132/17.
4. Churchill, *Finest Hour*, p. 450.
5. Eden, p. 347.
6. FO 371/28331–Z67/67/17, minute by Mack, 16 January 1941.
7. CAB 66/25–WP (42) 233 (1.6.42); ibid., WP (42) 247 (9.6.42); CAB 66/29–WP (42) 426 (29.9.42).
8. CAB 66/24–WP (42) 285 (8.7.42).
9. Eden, p. 346.
10. FO 371/28247–Z6786/22/17, Parr to Eden, 26 July 1941.
11. De Gaulle, *L'Appel*, p. 199.
12. D. Morton, 'The Free French Movement', in A. and V. Toynbee (eds), *Hitler's Europe* (1954) p. 455.
13. CAB 65/19–WM (41) 88 (1.9.41).
14. CAB 66/8–WP (41) 221 (16.9.41); CAB 65/19–WM (41) 93 (15.9.41); PREM 3/120/2, *passim*; de Gaulle, *L'Appel*, p. 201.
15. See de Gaulle's remarkable letter to Eden in March 1942, in CAB 66/22–WP (42) 117.
16. FO 371/31964–Z967/115/17.
17. Langer, pp. 212–17.
18. FO 371/28355–Z5757/93/17, Morton to Ismay, 18 June 1941.
19. CAB 80/30–COS (41) 572 (18.9.41); CAB 79/14–COS (41) 328 (19.9.41); PREM 3/377, p. 244.

20. PREM 3/377, pp. 235–7, Morton to Prime Minister, 10 December 1941.
21. Ibid., p. 230; Hull, vol. II, p. 1129; FO 371/28356–Z10592/93/17.
22. Morton, p. 464; R. Sherwood, *The White House Papers of Harry L. Hopkins*, vol. I (1948) p. 457; de Gaulle, *L'Appel*, pp. 184–6.
23. Sherwood, vol. I, p. 458; D. Thomson, *Two Frenchmen: Pierre Laval and Charles de Gaulle* (1951) p. 186.
24. Sherwood, vol. I, p. 458.
25. Ibid., p. 459.
26. Churchill, *Grand Alliance*, p. 590.
27. Sherwood, vol. I, pp. 461–2.
28. Churchill, *Grand Alliance*, p. 591.
29. PREM 3/377, pp. 192–6.
30. Ibid., pp. 120–6, 96.
31. Ibid., pp. 93–5.
32. Ibid., p. 3.
33. A Gallup poll in July revealed that, of the 56 per cent who knew what the Free French movement was, 73.9 per cent favoured American recognition of a Free French government (as against 12.8 per cent who favoured recognising Vichy) and 80.4 per cent thought that Free France should be admitted as a member of the United Nations: FO 371/31966–Z6508/115/17.
34. Ibid., Z6839/115/17.
35. FO 371/31965–Z3922/115/17.
36. Ibid.
37. Ibid.
38. FO 371/31905–Z6679/23/17; FO 371/31966–Z6707/115/17.
39. FO 371/31965–Z3922/115/17.
40. *FRUS*, vol. II (1942) pp. 517–20.
41. FO 371/31965–Z5383/115/17; FO 371/31966–Z5662/115/17; Woodward, vol. II, pp. 338–40; Hull, vol. II, pp. 1163–4.
42. FO 371/31966–Z6039/115/17.
43. CAB 65/24–WM (41) 116 [CA], Former Naval Person to President Roosevelt (No. T382).
44. CAB 65/20–WM (41) 127 (12.12.41).
45. Churchill, *Grand Alliance*, p. 575.
46. Ibid., pp. 577–8.
47. FO 371/28531–Z10907/10733/10854/17 and Z10816/98/G.
48. FO 371/31981–Z1066/175/17; Leahy, p. 67; R. Paxton, *Parades and Politics at Vichy* (1966) p. 317.
49. FO 371/31909–Z76/25/17, minute by Cavendish–Bentinck, 27 December 1942.
50. Paxton, *Vichy France*, pp. 387–90; Hytier, pp. 316–19; Woodward, vol. II, pp. 281–2.
51. Churchill, *Grand Alliance*, p. 589; FO 371/31909–Z76/25/17.
52. *FRUS*, vol. II (1942) pp. 123–6; FO 371/31981–Z1066/175/17; Woodward, vol. II, p. 284.
53. *FRUS*, vol. II (1942) pp. 123–6.
54. FO 371/31981–Z1066/175/17.
55. Ibid.
56. Ibid., –Z1235/175/17; Medlicott, vol. II, p. 367.
57. FO 371/31891–Z1332/175/17; Woodward, vol. II, pp. 284–5.
58. CAB 65/25–WM (42) 21 (16.2.42).
59. Ibid., –WM (42) 32 (9.3.42).
60. Churchill proposed to send this as a telegram to Halifax, but Eden dissuaded him: FO 371/31981–Z1067/175/17, Prime Minister's minute (No. M21/2) of 31 January 1942.

61. PREM 3/186B, p. 78, Prime Minister's personal minute (No. M562/1) of 19 May 1941.

62. Ibid., p. 73.

63. Ibid., p. 61.

64. Ibid., pp. 48–9; FO 371/28480–Z9789/1374/17, Prime Minister's personal minute (No. M1074/1) of 30 November 1941.

65. CAB 65/20–WM (41) 122 (1.12.41).

66. CAB 65/26–WM (42) 50 (20.4.42).

67. Paxton, *Vichy France*, pp. 131–2.

68. Ibid., p. 133; Hytier, p. 332; Darlan, p. 295.

69. CAB 66/24–WP (42) 174 (21.4.42); FO 371/31940–Z4514/81/17.

70. FO 371/31981–Z3617/175/17.

71. Ibid., Z3159/175/17.

72. CAB 65/26–WM (42) 50 (20.4.42).

73. CAB 66/23–WP (42) 169 (20.4.42); Hull, vol. II, p. 1157.

74. FO 371/31981–Z3731/3456/175/17; CAB 65/26–WM (42) 52 (24.4.42). Ironically, Canada did not after all sever relations with Vichy, but recalled Dupuy for consultation instead. In July 1942 he paid yet another visit to Vichy.

75. CAB 66/25–WP (42) 233 (1.6.42).

76. Ibid., WP (42) 239 (5.6.42); PREM 3/186A/7, pp. 247–8.

77. PREM 3/186A/7, pp. 244–6.

78. CAB 66/25–WP (42) 247 (9.6.42); Woodward, vol. II, pp. 299–304.

79. CAB 66/29–WP (42) 426 (23.9.42); Morton, p. 471.

80. PREM 3/186A/7, pp. 240–1, Prime Minister's personal minute (No. M248/2) of 14 June 1942.

81. CAB 66/26–WP (42) 285 (8.7.42); PREM 3/186A/7, pp. 235–9.

82. See, for example, CAB 66/28–WP (42) 398 (4.9.42).

7 OPERATION 'TORCH'

1. W. S. Churchill, *The Second World War*, vol. IV, *The Hinge of Fate* (1951) p. 392.

2. See Roosevelt's message to Churchill of 3 September 1942, in ibid., p. 482, and Halifax's telegram (No. 4658) of 10 September 1942, in FO 371/32134–Z8346/8325/17. On the complex evolution of TORCH, see Churchill, *Hinge of Fate*, pp. 390–407, 471–92; H. Butcher, *My Three Years with Eisenhower* (1946); M. Clark, *Calculated Risk* (1951); D. Eisenhower, *Crusade in Europe* (1948); M. Howard, *Grand Strategy* – official history, vol. IV (1969); A. Funk, *The Politics of Torch* (1974); K. Sainsbury, *The North African Landings 1942* (1976).

3. CAB 79/22–COS (42) 216, enclosing JP (42) 693.

4. Eisenhower, pp. 83–4, 88; Funk, *Torch*, pp. 95–6.

5. For Murphy's riposte, see Murphy, pp. 222–3.

6. Ibid., pp. 118–21; Leahy, p. 57; Hytier, p. 274; K. Pendar, *Adventure in Diplomacy* (1945); Funk, *Torch*, pp. 18–19 and 40.

7. Hull, vol. II, pp. 951–2; FO 371/28479–Z7171/8336/8515/1374/17; FO 371/28478–Z6002/1374/17.

8. Churchill, *Hinge of Fate*, pp. 476–7, 482. See also FO 371/32134–Z8353/8325/17 and FO 371/31913–Z6215/25/17.

9. FO 371/28478–Z6002/1374/17; FO 371/28479–Z7891/8329/8336/8515/7171/1374/17; CAB 66/19–WP (41) 237 (10.10.41).

10. CAB 66/25–WP (42) 235 (2.5.42). See also FO 371/31911–Z6215/25/17.

11. CAB 66/29–WP (42) 450 (7.10.42).

12. CAB 79/57–COS (42) 107 (o)·(31.8.42).

13. CAB 65/31–WM (42) 88 (8.7.42).

14. Howard, pp. 131–2; Churchill, *Hinge of Fate*, p. 492.

15. CAB 66/27–WP (42) 349 (8.8.42); CAB 65/31–WM (42) 114 [CA] (20.8.42); Woodward, vol. II, pp. 342–5.

16. Churchill, *Hinge of Fate*, pp. 542–3; FO 371/32134–Z8350/8325/17.

17. Cadogan, p. 489.

18. Churchill, *Hinge of Fate*, pp. 573–6.

19. Funk, 'Deal with Darlan', pp. 81–2 and *Torch*, *passim*.

20. Churchill's letter to Harry Hopkins (which was not sent) dated 4 September 1942, in *Hinge of Fate*, p. 485; CAB 65/31–WM (42) 127 [CA], enclosing Prime Minister's personal minute (No. D154/2) of 21 September 1942.

21. Clark, p. 55; Butcher, pp. 71–2.

22. Eisenhower, p. 106; Funk, *Torch*, pp. 113–14; Murphy, p. 152.

23. FO 371/32133–Z8333/8325/17.

24. FO 371/28581–Z10846/7962/17.

25. FO 371/32134–Z8352/8325/17. See also FO 371/32135, *passim*.

26. Funk, *Torch*, pp. 21–5; FRUS, vol. II (1941) p. 189.

27. *FRUS*, vol. II (1941) pp. 440–1.

28. 'C' was Sir Stuart Menzies, Head of the British Secret Service.

29. PREM 3/186A/7, p. 226.

30. Ibid., p. 224.

31. CAB 79/16–COS (41) 430 (22.12.41).

32. Funk, 'Deal with Darlan', p. 87.

33. See, for example, *FRUS*, vol. II (1942) pp. 249, 283–4, 298, 301.

34. Murphy, p. 148; Funk, 'Deal with Darlan', p. 92.

35. On the political complexion of the Group, see R. Smith, *OSS: The Secret History of America's First Central Intelligence Agency* (1972) p. 40, comparing them to the Ku Klux Klan, and Pendar, p. 33. Pen portraits are given by General C. Mast, *Histoire d'une rébellion* (1969) pp. 45–6. A sympathetic judgement can be found in Funk, *Torch*, pp. 13–15, 20–1. For the account of the Group's 'leader', see J. Lemaigre–Dubreuil, *Vicissitudes d'une victoire* (1946), written under his wartime pseudonym, Crusoé. Also worth reading is General A. Van Hecke, *Les Chantiers de la jeunesse au secours de la France* (1971).

36. Murphy, p. 134 'Don't worry about Cordell', Roosevelt told him. 'I will take care of him; I'll let him know our plans a day or so before the landings.' See also FO 371/32134–Z8346/8325/17.

37. *FRUS*, vol. II (1942) pp. 379–81; Butcher, pp. 105–10; Funk, *Torch*, pp. 102–3.

38. Darlan, pp. 157–8; Funk, *Torch*, pp. 126–8.

39. Marshall to Eisenhower (No. R–2015) 16 October 1942; paraphrase of a message from Lt.–Col. McGowan (Murphy), in PREM 3/442/8, pp. 347–50.

40. Ibid. A slightly different text is given in *FRUS*, vol. II (1942) pp. 392–4. Murphy's own account dates his return to North Africa as 16 October and glosses over the Chrétien meeting: Murphy, pp. 151–2.

41. Marshall to Eisenhower (No. R–2014) 16 October 1942, in PREM 3/442/8, pp. 351–4; *FRUS*, vol. II (1942) pp. 394–6. Murphy also approached Major Dorange, Juin's aide, at this time: Funk, *Torch*, pp. 129–32.

42. No. R–2032, 17 October 1942, in PREM 3/442/8, p. 355.

43. Ibid., p. 357.

44. Eden, p. 345. Professor Funk records that 'diligent searching by archivists in charge of the Premier records' failed to turn up the British minutes of this meeting: Funk, *Torch*, p. 290. In fact, these are to be found, not in the PREM series, but as an enclosure to CAB 79/87–COS (42) 151 (o) (17.10.42). No mention of the meeting is made in Churchill's or Brooke's accounts.

45. Funk, 'Deal with Darlan', p. 96, quoting Eisenhower's papers, vol. I, pp. 625–6.

46. Eisenhower, *Crusade*, p. 105; Butcher, p. 178; Murphy, p. 152.

47. Murphy, too, concluded from the telegram which Leahy sent to him about the Downing Street meeting that he was authorised 'to initiate any arrangments with Darlan which in my judgement might assist the military arrangements'. Murphy, p. 152. Leahy's message is in *FRUS*, vol. II (1942) p. 397.

48. Funk, 'Deal with Darlan', p. 117, and *Torch*, p. 142.

49. Mast, pp. 91–126; Murphy, p. 153; Clark, pp. 67–89; Butcher, pp. 152–6; Clark's telegram to Eisenhower in PREM 3/442/8, pp. 342–5. See also Funk, *Torch*, pp. 149–64.

50. Funk, *Torch*, pp. 178, 295.

51. Ibid., pp. 181–202; Clark, p. 51.

52. Murphy, p. 155; Funk, *Torch*, pp. 106–7.

53. Funk, *Torch*, pp. 136–8; Mast, p. 122; Murphy, p. 156.

54. FO 371/32133–Z8332/8325/17; Funk, *Torch*, pp. 103–8.

55. Woodward, vol. II, pp. 357–8.

56. On the supply programme in 1942 see FO 371/31934 and 31935 *passim*, and Hull, vol. II, pp. 1161–2.

57. FO 371/32133–Z8332/8325/17.

58. Woodward, vol. II, pp. 352–3; FO 371/32134–Z8359/8363/17.

59. FO 371/32082–Z3668/3571/17, Hankey's minute of 3 May 1942.

60. FO 371/32134–Z8351/8325/17.

61. Ibid., minute by Cadogan.

62. FO 371/32135–Z8387/8408/8325/17; Churchill, *Hinge of Fate*, pp. 545–6; Woodward, vol. II, p. 358; FO 371/32133–Z8337/8325/17.

63. Cunningham, p. 478; Sherwood, vol. II, p. 644.

64. *FRUS*, vol. II (1942) p. 425. Churchill incorrectly states that Juin was privy to the conspiracy: *Hinge of Fate*, p. 548. Presumably he confused him with Mast.

65. Murphy, p. 167.

66. Eisenhower, p. 77.

67. Mast, pp. 283–5; Funk, *Torch*, p. 237; 'Crusoé', pp. 59–62; Van Hecke, pp. 220–32; Murphy, pp. 172–3, 175.

68. Clark, p. 116.

69. Murphy, p. 175; FO 371/32138–Z8767/8325/17.

70. Funk, *Torch*, p. 241.

71. Text in *FRUS*, vol. II (1942) pp. 453–7.

72. Cadogan, p. 494.

73. FO 371/32144–Z9603/8325/17. Closures of files are extremely frequent during this period, and include FO 371/32144–Z9222/115/17, which immediately follows Strang's letter.

74. Sherwood, vol. II, p. 645; Funk, *Torch*, p. 194; Warner, *Pierre Laval*, p. 319; Churchill, *Hinge of Fate*, p. 548; P. Tomkins, *The Murder of Admiral Darlan* (1965) pp. 57–66.

75. Murphy, p. 165; Eisenhower, p. 104. But see also Cunningham, p. 513, Clark, p. 109, and Sainsbury, *North African Landings*, pp. 143–5.

76. FO 371/32144–Z9600/8325/17, Mack's letter to Strang of 20 November 1942. See also the minutes by Speaight and Strang on 15 December 1942, in FO 371/32146–Z10119/8325/17; Aron, pp. 400–18; Leahy, p. 397.

77. FO 371/32137–Z8515/8325/17; *FRUS*, vol. II (1942) pp. 430–2.

78. Schmitt, pp. 172–85; P. Dhers, *Regards nouveaux sur les années quarante* (1958) pp. 141–51; Warner, *Pierre Laval*, pp. 331–2; Paxton, *Parades and Politics*, pp. 362–3; Funk, *Torch*, p. 239.

79. Schmitt, pp. 175–6; Funk, 'Deal with Darlan', p. 114. Dhers, p. 159, gives the text of Noguès's telegram.

80. Amiral Auphan, *Histoire de mes 'trahisons' ou la marine au service des Français* (1946) p. 293, quoted by Schmitt, p. 176.

81. Funk, *Torch*, pp. 247–8; Schmitt, pp. 176–8.

82. Churchill's speech to the Commons on 10 December 1942, in *Hinge of Fate*, p. 575.

83. Bullitt, p. 574. See also Thomson, p. 189.

84. Langer, p. 378. See also CAB 66/33–WP (42) 75 (13.1.43).

85. CAB 65/28–WM (42) 166 (9.12.42); CAB 65/32–WM (42) 172 (23.12.42); FO 371/32138–Z8853/8325/17; PREM 3/442/9, pp. 433–4.

86. FO 371/32144–Z9869/8325/17; FO 371/32149–Z10733/8325/17.

87. Lippmann made a speech to the Franco-American club in New York on 28 October 1942, urging recognition of the Free French National Committee as the Provisional Government of France. See the *Washington Post* for 29 October 1942, and FO 371/31966–Z8912/115/17. A selection from the American press is given in FO 371/32155–Z8983/8524/17, and an extract from a feature article by Lippmann in *Today and Tomorrow* for 19 January 1943 is given by Funk, *Torch*, p. 256.

88. FO 371/32144–Z9708/8325/17.

89. CAB 65/28–WM (42) 161 (27.11.42); FO 371/32143–Z9515/8325/17.

90. FO 371/32139–Z9013/8325/17. For the work of the Economic and Reconstruction Department, see Lord Gladwyn, *Memoirs* (1972) pp. 109–46.

91. Churchill, *Hinge of Fate*, p. 598; Sherwood, vol. II, p. 647. For the Foreign Office's anxieties about the Russian reaction, see FO 371/32141–Z9384/8325/17, FO 371/32143–Z9477/9478/8325/17, and Woodward, vol. II, pp. 385–8.

92. FO 371/32139–Z9013/8325/17.

93. For the reaction of the Norwegian government, see FO 371/34144–Z9875/8325/17; for that of the Czech, Polish and Dutch governments, FO 371/32146–Z10093/10138/8325/17, and CAB 66/32–WP (42) 576 (11.12.42).

94. M. Foot, *SOE in France* – official history (1968) p. 221. See also FO 371/31951–Z9048/90/17 and FO 371/32138–Z8758/8766/8325/17.

95. CAB 66/30–WP (42) 518 (9.11.42); Cadogan, p. 489; Woodward, vol. II, p. 357; Churchill, *Hinge of Fate*, pp. 542–3.

96. FO 371/32137–Z8613/8325/17. This was inaccurately reported to the Cabinet the next day as a willingness 'to come to an agreement with any French authority fighting on the side of the United Nations'. CAB 66/30–WP (42) 518 (9.11.42).

97. FO 371/32139–Z8885/8325/17.

98. FO 371/32140–Z9108/8325/17.

99. FO 371/32139–Z90499/8325/17; Woodward, vol. II, p. 392.

100. FO 371/32145–Z9953/8325/17. See also Léon Marchal's views as reported to Stirling on 27 November, in FO 371/32144–Z9621/8325/17.

101. FO 371/31966–Z9222/115/17.

102. PREM 3/442/9, pp. 446–7.

103. Churchill, *Hinge of Fate*, p. 576.

104. See Strang's minute on Mack's letter of 17 November 1942, in FO 371/32144–Z9714/8325/17.

105. FO 371/32145–Z9900/8325/17.

106. Woodward, vol. II, p. 363.

107. Morton to Strang, 10 November 1942: FO 371/32138–Z8756/8352/17.

108. Ibid., Z8757/8325/17, minute by Stirling.

109. PREM 3/442/9, p. 473; CAB 65/28–WM (42) 152 (12.11.42). Churchill, *Hinge of Fate*, p. 566.

110. PREM 3/442/9, pp. 471–2.

111. Woodward, vol. II, p. 364.

112. PREM 3/442/9, p. 470; FO 371/32138–Z8757/8325/17.

113. Cadogan, diary for 14 November 1942, pp. 492–3.

114. 'Giraud doesn't seem to wield any thunderbolts.' Minute by Cadogan, 14 November 1942, in FO 371/32139-Z8894/8325/17.

115. Eisenhower to Combined Chiefs of Staff (No. 527) 14 November 1942, in FO 371/32138-Z8884/8325/17; PREM 3/442/9, pp. 441-6; Eisenhower, *Crusade* p. 109; Funk, *Torch*, pp. 249-51.

116. PREM 3/442/9, pp. 438-9; FO 371/32138-Z8884/8325/17. Cunningham later wrote that the deal was 'the only possible course, and absolutely right'. Cunningham, p. 502.

117. CAB 65/28-WM (42) 153 (16.11.42).

118. PREM 3/442/9, pp. 442-3; Churchill, *Hinge of Fate*, p. 568.

119. FO 371/32138-Z8852/8325/17.

120. Full text of the statement is in PREM 3/442/9, p. 413 and FO 371/32139-Z9031/9051/8325/17. An abridged version is in Churchill, *Hinge of Fate*, pp. 568-9.

121. H. Nicolson, *Diaries and Letters*, vol. II, *1939-1945* (1967) p. 262.

122. CAB 66/31-WP (42) 537 (21.11.42); Churchill, *Hinge of Fate*, p. 570.

123. FO 371/32138-Z8884/8325/17.

124. CAB 66/31-WP (42) 565 (7.12.42). See also Cunningham's message in PREM 3/442/9, pp. 404-5.

125. FO 371/32141-Z9354/8325/17; Churchill, *Hinge of Fate*, p. 571; Clark, pp. 126-7.

126. Bullitt's letter to Roosevelt of 29 November 1942, in Sherwood, vol. II, p. 574.

127. FO 371/32141-Z9197/8325/17. Cadogan expressed the same sentiment in his diary on 12 November (p. 392).

128. FO 371/32138-Z8853/8325/17; Woodward, vol. II, p. 369. 'He will have to be eliminated sooner or later, and our present policy should be shaped to that end.' Strang's minute of 28 November 1942, in FO 371/32143-Z9456/8325/17.

129. Cadogan's minute of 21 November 1942, in FO 371/32141-Z9300/8325/17. See also ibid., -Z9354/8325/17: 'Darlan is bowling on a very tricky wicket against a 3rd eleven.'

130. Cadogan, diary for 21 and 22 November 1942, p. 496.

131. FO 371/32140-Z9080/8325/17.

132. Eden, p. 351.

133. CAB 65/28-WM (42) 156 (21.11.42); CAB 66/31-WP (42) 538 (21.11.42).

134. See Eisenhower's telegram in CAB 66/31-WP (42) 536 (21.11.42); Eden, p. 351; PREM 3/442/10, *passim*.

135. FO 371/32144-Z9714/8325/17.

136. Ibid., Z9671/9766/8325/17.

137. FO 371/32145-Z9897/8325/17; Eden, pp. 353-4.

138. FO 371/32144-Z9714/8325/17; Eden, pp. 354-5.

139. Murphy, p. 157; Hull, vol. II, p. 1198; PREM 3/442/9, pp. 455-7.

140. Leahy, p. 163.

141. FO 371/32145-Z10628/8325/17; Eden, pp. 356-7.

142. Peake to Foreign Office, 25 December 1942: FO 371/32149-Z10628/8325/17.

143. FO 371/32145-Z9886/8325/17.

144. Eden, p. 357.

145. Full text in C. Eade (ed.), *The War Speeches of Winston S. Churchill* (1965) vol. II (1965) pp. 376-89. On its reception in the House, see Nicolson, p. 266, and O. Lyttelton, *The Memoirs of Lord Chandos* (1962) p. 185.

146. CAB 66/32-WP (42) 571 (8.12.42); FO 371/32146-Z10116/10117/8325/17.

147. Minutes by Strang and Cadogan of 15 December 1942, in FO 371/32148-Z10472/8325/17; and by Eden in ibid.,-Z10549/8325/17.

148. FO 371/32149-Z10686/8325/17; Hull, vol. II, p. 1205. For Roosevelt's opinion, see FO 371/31966-Z9762/115/17.

149. FO 371/32150-Z10773/8325/17.

150. They are presumably recorded in FO 371/32149–Z10613/8325/17, which remains closed until 2013.
151. Cadogan, p. 500.
152. FO 371/32149–Z10685/8325/17.
153. Churchill, *Hinge of Fate*, p. 578.
154. Clark, p. 130. Oddly, in view of this, it was widely believed in North Africa that he had been murdered by the Axis, not by the Allies. See FO 371/32150–Z10773/8325/17.
155. FO 371/32145–Z9900/8325/17.
156. Tomkins's book contains no references and fails to inspire confidence in its conclusions. Osgood is balanced but, of course, inconclusive. See also J. Soustelle, *Envers et contre tout*, vol. II, *D'Alger à Paris* (1950) p. 77, and M. Aboulker, *Alger et ses complots* (1945) pp. 239–40.
157. CAB 66/31–WP (43) 79 (22.2.43).
158. FO 371/32144–Z9659/8325/17; Peake to Foreign Office, 25 December 1942, FO 371/32149–Z10628/8325/17.
159. Murphy, p. 180; Churchill, *Their Finest Hour*, pp. 203–4; CAB 65/28–WM (42) 169 (15.12.42).
160. Cadogan, p. 493.
161. CAB 69/4–DO (42) 20 (29.12.42). On the following day, Cadogan authorised Cunningham to deny these allegations: Cadogan, p. 501.

8 AFTERMATH

1. 'Germans are occupying the rest of France – and Corsica. I don't think we mind either much.' Cadogan, p. 491.
2. Eden, p. 347. See also Churchill's minute (No. M601/2) of 13 December 1942, in PREM 3/184/4. On the sinking of the Fleet, see A. Kammerer, *La Passion de la flotte française* (1951) and P. Varillon, *Le Sabordage de la flotte* (1954).
3. Churchill, *Hinge of Fate*, p. 560.
4. For a brief discussion of the question, see FO 371/36070–Z1732/1732/17. The British had accepted Vichy as France's *de facto* government until November 1942. Formal recognition was never withdrawn, however, because of the added impetus it would have given to Gaullist claims to be the French government. Hoare was forbidden to have official contact in Madrid. FO 371/35996–Z1587/39/17.
5. Cadogan, p. 519.
6. Minute by Cadogan, 9 May 1944, in FO 371/41839–Z3306/12/17.
7. As de Gaulle said to Eden, 'there were only two alternatives, Fighting France and Vichy. General Giraud, who tried to balance between the two, held no position at all.' CAB 65/37–WM (43) 9 (18.1.43). See also CAB 66/37–WP (43) 211 (18.5.43).
8. See the report on Lebrun by Prof. Stewart of the Foreign Research and Press Service in FO 371/32147–Z10338/8325/17.
9. On British deliberations about the possible restoration of the French monarchy, see in particular the minute by Mr Hohler of 7 June 1941, in FO 371/28331–Z4683/67/17, and the suggestion by Prof. Stewart that Pétain might hand over his powers to the Comte de Paris and Weygand in ibid., Z2863/3005/3013/3478/4183/67/17. Dupuy and Mittelman also favoured the Comte's cause: FO 371/31986–Z210/210/17. Eden's comment is in FO 371/36024–Z408/57/17. On French Royalism, see Osgood, pp. 173–9.
10. Mack's comment is in FO 371/36037–Z12653/77/17. See also Eden, p. 431, and Cadogan, p. 519.
11. CAB 65/35–WM (43) 99 (14.7.43); Eden, p. 372.
12. See FO 371/32081 and FO 371/36036 *passim*, and Eden's comments in FO 371/36037–Z12432/77/17. The respective positions of the two governments were clearly stated

at meetings between Welles and Strang in March 1943: FO 371/36036–Z4055/4457/77/17. See also Eden, pp. 372, 393–5.

13. See, for example, de Gaulle's conversation with Harold Macmillan in October 1943, FO 371/36036–Z11164/77/17 and Colonel Passy's similar warnings on 4 August 1943, in ibid., –Z8814/77/17. For Foreign Office fears of de Gaulle's ambitions, see, for example, CAB 65/37–WM (43) 9 [CA] (18.1.43).

14. See, for example, F. Israel (ed), *The War Diaries of Breckenridge Long* (1966) p. 294.

15. See Eden's report of his visit to Washington in CAB 66/35–WP (43) 130 (30.3.43) and also CAB 65/38–WM (43) 53 (13.4.43). For indications of Roosevelt's thinking on these matters, see also his statements to Lord Swinton in CAB 66/34–WP (43) 95 (5.3.43), his remarks at the Teheran conference in CAB 65/40–WM (43) 169 [CA] (13.12.43), and his comments to Oliver Lyttelton, reported in Halifax's diary for 20 November 1942. Many observers commented on the President's attitude, notably Eden, pp. 372–4, Eisenhower *Crusade*, pp. 136–7, and Murphy, pp. 185, 211–12. The Foreign Office compiled a list of his statements on these matters and set them against the categorical assurances of Atherton and Murphy that the French Empire would be fully restored. These can be found in FO 371/36036–Z1762/77/17.

16. For Roosevelt's and Hull's dislike of de Gaulle, see Eden, pp. 402, 448, and Cooper, p. 316.

17. Eden, p. 372.

18. FO 371/32175–Z9607/9482/17.

19. Minute by Rumbold, 4 April 1943, in FO 371/36036–Z4105/77/17. Strang, Mack and Speaight all indicated their agreement to this view. See also Nicolson, p. 330.

20. In May 1943 Churchill even went so far as to suggest that de Gaulle should be eliminated as a political force. For this, and Eden's response, see CAB 65/38–WM (43) 75 [CA] (23.5.43), and Cadogan, pp. 533–9.

21. See in particular Eden's memo to Churchill of July 1943, quoted extensively in Eden, pp. 397–8.

22. Minute by Cadogan, 9 May 1944: FO 371/41879–Z3306/12/17.

23. FO 371/49139–Z328/255/17. An article appeared in the *Nation* on 27 January 1945, entitled 'Murphy Will Out', accusing him of working with Lemaigre–Dubreuil and Rigault towards the creation of a Pétainist corporate state in post-war France. The two men were already implicated with Noguès in the smuggling of the gold of the Bank of Morocco to Lisbon. See ibid., –Z2883/255/17.

24. Warner, *Pierre Laval*, p. 393; F. Piétri, *Mes Années d'Espagne* (1954) p. 244.

25. Warner, *Pierre Laval*, pp. 393–5; Piétri, p. 249; Paxton, *Vichy France*, pp. 327–9.

26. Speaight's minute of 9 January 1944: FO 371/41922–Z275/275/17. See also FO 371/36077–Z12606/47/17. The file immediately preceding Speaight's remark is closed.

27. On Leahy's influence, see, for example, Nicolson, p. 416, reporting the views of Hamilton Fish Armstrong, editor of *Foreign Affairs*; Eden, pp. 447, 496; Cadogan, diary for 23 October 1944, p. 675.

28. FO 371/41922–Z1146/275/17: minute by Harvey, 9 February 1944.

29. Ibid., minute by Cadogan, 9 February 1944.

30. Hull, vol. II. p. 1428. The text is in FO 371/41922–Z2449/275/17. The American government had already made a similar statement to the French Committee of National Liberation in January; see FO 371/41876–Z615/12/17.

31. FO 371/41879–Z3306/12/17: minute by Cadogan, 9 May 1944.

32. Cadogan, diary for 7 June 1944, p. 636. Cooper, pp. 332–3.

33. On Eisenhower's attitude, see Mack's minute of 30 January 1944, in FO 371/41876–Z1038/12/17, and Eden, pp. 447, 457. On the attempt by the former Vichy

minister, who is not named, see Peake's letter to Harvey of 22 September 1944, in FO 371/42096–Z633/633/17.

34. CAB 66/51–WP (44) 329 (15.6.44).
35. Quoted by Hytier, p. 267.
36. FO 371/31964–Z967/115/17.

Index